Media and Society

The R&L Series in Mass Communication
Eileen Meehan, Louisiana State University, Series Editor

Rowman & Littlefield is pleased to announce a series of texts for mass communication courses. Edited by Eileen Meehan, Louisiana State University, and advised by an editorial board representing a cross section of universities and specialties, the series consists of "compact core" textbooks, around 200–250 pages each, providing clear and concise overviews of key areas of mass communication study. These accessible and engaging texts feature illustrations, pedagogical tools, and practical guidelines to show students how to apply concepts outside the classroom.

Future topics in the series may include media and politics, law, ethics, international communication, online communication, mass communication theory, research methods, economics, gender and media, comparative media systems, new communications technology, history, media effects, policy and regulation, management, advertising, public relations, popular culture, film, visual communication, and media literacy.

Titles in the Series

Media and Society: A Critical Perspective
Arthur Asa Berger

MEDIA AND SOCIETY

A Critical Perspective

Second Edition

ARTHUR ASA BERGER

with illustrations by the author

ROWMAN & LITTLEFIELD PUBLISHERS, INC.
Lanham • Boulder • New York • Toronto • Plymouth, UK

ROWMAN & LITTLEFIELD PUBLISHERS, INC.

Published in the United States of America
by Rowman & Littlefield Publishers, Inc.
A wholly owned subsidiary of The Rowman & Littlefield Publishing
Group, Inc.
4501 Forbes Boulevard, Suite 200, Lanham, Maryland 20706
www.rowmanlittlefield.com

Estover Road, Plymouth PL6 7PY, United Kingdom

British Library Cataloguing in Publication Information Available

Library of Congress Cataloging-in-Publication Data

Berger, Arthur Asa, 1933–
  Media and society : a critical perspective / Arthur Asa Berger.—
2nd ed.
    p.   cm.— (The R & L series in mass communication)
  Includes bibliographical references and index.
  ISBN-13: 978-0-7425-5384-2 (cloth : alk. paper)
  ISBN-10: 0-7425-5384-1 (cloth : alk. paper)
  ISBN-13: 978-0-7425-5385-9 (pbk. : alk. paper)
  ISBN-10: 0-7425-5385-X (pbk. : alk. paper)
    1. Mass media—Social aspects.   I. Title.   II. Series.
HM1206.B47   2007
                                                          2006015967

Printed in the United States of America

♾ ™ The paper used in this publication meets the minimum requirements of
American National Standard for Information Sciences—Permanence of Paper
for Printed Library Materials, ANSI/NISO Z39.48-1992.

CONTENTS

Acknowledgments   ix

Introduction: You and the Media—A Consideration   1
     Focal Points in the Study of the Mass Media   2
     CSI: Crime Scene Investigation and the Focal Points   3
     Two Anecdotes on Choice   5

1   Media in Our Thoughts and Lives: A Psycho-Social
     Perspective on Individuals, Society, and the Media   9
     Johnny Q. Public's Media Usage   9
     A Group Portrait of My Readers   10
     Statistics on Media Use   11
     Media Effects and Your Life   14
     Television Viewing and Vicious Cycles   14
     The Media in Society   16
     A Case Study: Where Did I Get That Idea?   17
     Society, the Individual, and the Communication
         Process   21

2   Media Usage in the United States   25
     The Media We Use   26
     A Primer on Communication   28
     Traditional Ways of Classifying the Media   30
     McLuhan's Hot and Cool Media   31
     The Media Help Shape the Texts They Carry   35

3 The Social Dimension of Media Aesthetics   37
    Saussure on Signs   38
    Peirce on Icons, Indexes, and Symbols   40
    Lying with Signs   41
    Editing Techniques and Semiotics   43
    The Nature of Narratives: Vladimir Propp   46
    A Proppian Analysis of a James Bond Film   49
    The Nature of Narratives: Claude Lévi-Strauss   51
    The Importance of Narratives   52
    Postmodernism and Media Aesthetics   54
    Blade Runner, Rashomon, and *Survivor:* Three
        Postmodern Texts   56

4 Audiences 1: Categories   59
    Audiences Are Specialized   59
    Problems Advertisers Face   60
    Shares and Ratings   61
    New Developments in Obtaining Ratings   63
    Demographics and Audiences   66
    Psychographics and Audiences   70
    The VALS Typology   71
    Political Cultures and Lifestyles as Audiences   74
    Active Audiences: Decoding Mass-Mediated Texts   77
    Active Audiences: Uses and Gratifications   79
    Uses and Gratifications, and Genres   82

5 Audiences 2: Effects   85
    Is Mass Culture Making Us All Morons?   85
    Johnny Q. Public and Emily Greatgal Make Dinner   87
    The Concept of Media Effects Needs Qualification   88
    Criticisms of the Mass Media and Their Texts   89
    Anti-Media Rage   101
    Defenders of the Mass Media and Popular Culture   103
    Other Defenses of the Mass Media and the Texts
        They Carry   104
    The Postmodern Solution   107

6 The Social Impact of New Media Technologies   111
    The Impact of Cell Phones   111
    The Digital World   113

The Computer and Culture   115
Virtual Communities   120
Video Games: A Bio-Psycho-Social Perspective   123
Criticisms of Video Games   125
Positive Aspects of Video Game Playing   126
The Technological Imperative   128

7   The Social Significance of Mass-Mediated Texts   131
Theories of Art: What Texts Do   132
The Texts the Media Carry Have Power   134
Convention and Invention in Texts   135
The Power of Commercials   137
Narratives in the Media   139
Aristotle on Narratives   140
Texts and Other Texts: Intertextuality   141
The Question of the Ur-Text   144
News on Television   145
9/11 and the Social Impact of Media Images   146
By Words Alone?   148

8   Media and Violence   151
How Is Media Violence Defined?   152
A Longitudinal Study of Television Viewing and
    Violence   154
Kinds of Violence   156
Violence in Texts: Quality versus Quantity   157
Violence in News Broadcasts   158
Children and Media Violence   161
"Kill 'em"   164

9   Media Artists   167
Publishing a Scholarly Book: A Case Study   168
The Book Business   171
Script Writing and Aberrant Decoding   173
Media Ethics and Journalists   175
Ethics and Advertising   178

10 The Mass Culture / Mass Society Hypothesis   187
The Mass Culture Hypothesis: Myth or Reality?   187
Round Up the Usual Indictments, or, the Language
    of Criticism in the Fifties   188

Where Are the Mass Men and Mass Women the
Critics of the Fifties Warned Us About?   189
Does Popular Culture Destroy Our Ability to Enjoy
Elite Culture?   191
Are We Becoming Homogenized? Are the Mass
Media Uniform?   192
Mass Culture and the Melting Pot   194
Mass Culture and American Society: The Myth of the
Monolith   197

11 Media in Society   203
Media Consolidation   203
On Cultural Imperialism: The "Coca-Colonization"
Hypothesis   206
A Note on Ideology and the Media   208
The Problem of Pornography   209
A U.S. Supreme Court Decision on Virtual Child
Pornography   211
The Spiral of Silence: Public Opinion and Political
Ideology   212
Government Regulation and Deregulation of
Broadcasting   215
Ethnic Media: A Complicating Factor   218

Glossary   221

Selected Bibliography   235

Index   249

About the Author   257

ACKNOWLEDGMENTS

I'm delighted to be offering a second edition of *Media and Society* to my readers. I was asked to write this new edition because the first edition of this book had enough readers to warrant an updating and expansion of the book. It's always a great pleasure for an author to find out that people have actually read one of his books. You always hope your book will find an audience, but you can't be sure that it will.

In the years since the book was published, I decided to deal with a number of new aspects of the media, and I had some ideas about how some topics in the first edition of the book might be expanded. For example, I've dealt here in more detail with postmodernism and its relation to modernism, and with postmodern texts such as *Blade Runner*, *Rashomon*, and *Survivor*. I've also added discussions of theories of art and the functions of works of art, and you'll find in this edition new drawings and images. I've had the benefit of a number of useful suggestions from professors who have used *Media and Society*, for which I am grateful. And I want to thank Eileen Meehan, the editor of the series, and Brenda Hadenfeldt, my editor for this book, for their continued support and encouragement. I also want to thank April Leo, my production editor, and John Shanabrook, my copyeditor, for their assistance. Things move so rapidly in the media that it is impossible to keep up with them, but by focusing on concepts that can be used to understand the media, I hope I have provided you the reader with a number of ideas and theories that will enable you to make sense of the media yourself.

I hope you like this book, and that you'll learn something interesting about the role the media play in society and also—which is of particular importance—in your life. If you are a typical student, you spend a great deal of time with the media, and you use a great deal of media. The question is, How do the media use you? You might be interested to discover how the media might be affecting you, your friends, and the members of your family, and to investigate the role the media play in society in general.

Introduction

YOU AND THE MEDIA— A CONSIDERATION

One night in 2006 a young college student—let's call her Emily Greatgal—turns on her television set to watch a rerun of *CSI: Crime Scene Investigation*. This action, which is similar to what millions of us do every day when we "watch television," involves the following **focal points**:

1. A **text**. In this case, the text is the show *CSI: Crime Scene Investigation*. I will adapt the convention used in academic discourse and will call television programs, films, print advertisements, commercials, and the like, *texts*.
2. An **audience**. Here the audience is Emily Greatgal.
3. The many different kinds of **artists** such as actors, actresses, producers, directors, camerapersons, and script writers who are responsible for the text.
4. The larger entity of which the audience is a part. Here, that entity is **America**.
5. The **medium** (television in this case) that "carries" the program.

Let's assume that Emily Greatgal is a citizen of the United States of America—that is, she's an American. (I will generally use the term

1

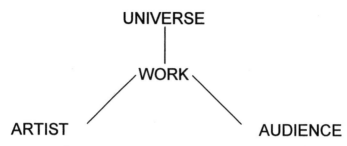

Figure I.1   M. H. Abrams's Diagram.

American in this book to stand for *the United States* so I don't have to keep writing *the United States* all the time. And when I write *society* I will be discussing American society, unless otherwise noted.) Audiences are part of a larger entity, namely society, because not everyone in a given society watches the same program on television at any given time during the day or night (and not everyone watching a television program in America is an American citizen).

This discussion of focal points builds upon a framework originated by a literary scholar, M. H. Abrams. In his book *The Mirror and the Lamp: Romantic Theory and the Critical Tradition*, Abrams suggests there are four relationships to be considered when analyzing literary works (see figure I.1).

In my own work on focal points, what I have done is add the media (or mediums) to the mix and change *universe* to *society*. Abrams was writing about literary works, so the medium (print) was not an important consideration for him. In my analysis, however, there are many different media and they play varying roles in the creation and dissemination of texts.

FOCAL POINTS IN THE STUDY
OF THE MASS MEDIA

What we have then are focal points that can be used in dealing with the media in a given society. For the sake of alliteration, which may help you remember these focal points, I will use words that begin with an *A* for four of them. We have then,

art work	(texts in various genres)
audience	(of varying sizes)
artists	(of all kinds)
America	(the United States of)
medium	(such as television, film, video, or print)

All of these are, or can be, connected to each other. For example, there are interrelationships that exist between a text carried on television, the audience for whom the text is created, the artists who are involved in creating and performing the text, the society in which the audience lives, and the medium (television) in which the text is carried. Depending on our interests, we can focus on one or more of these focal points in studying the media.

Since this book deals with the social aspects of the mass media, it will focus on mediums, audiences, and society—but it will also have a good deal to say about mass-mediated texts and media artists. We must always keep in mind that the media carry texts, and we must not neglect aspects of these texts due to our fascination with social, political, economic, or cultural matters related to the media. We also must remember that the media affect the texts they carry. And in some cases audiences are global, which means society expands from, say, America, to other countries and in some cases—such as in the broadcast of the Super Bowl—to much of the world.

CSI: CRIME SCENE INVESTIGATION AND THE FOCAL POINTS

Let's take an episode of the show *CSI: Crime Scene Investigation* and plug it into the focal points chart. This may help you see more clearly what I'm talking about.

art work	*CSI: Crime Scene Investigation* (an episode of)
audience	the general public
artists	writers, production staff, directors, and actors
America	(and other countries)
medium	television

Writers (and artists of all kinds) always must think about their audiences. For example, my most immediate audience for this book is
college students taking courses dealing with the media in the United
States, but I hope the book might be used in other countries as well.
When I wrote this book I had a specific audience in mind—
including people like you, my reader—which I assumed was otherwise made up of undergraduates taking college or university courses
on the media, popular culture, or **communication**. If I had had a
different audience I was trying to reach—for example, PhD candidates in communication—I would have written this book in a much
different manner. So the potential audience affects the way books are
written and, by extension, the way all texts carried by the mass media
are created.

You can see from this example that there are many different
topics to consider when dealing with the media and society. There
is also a logical problem involved with writing about the media and
society: Where does the author best deal with a particular topic,
since some topics can be put in any number of different places? For
example, does the author write about **media ethics** in a chapter
on media, in a chapter on society, or in a chapter on media artists
and creators?

In this book, I put my discussion of media ethics in the chapter
on artists and creators, since they are the people who most directly
face ethical problems in creating their texts (see chapter 9). Is it ethical to make a print advertisement for cigarettes? Is it ethical to
make a television commercial that slanders a political figure? Is it
ethical to write a television script or make a movie or video game
full of gratuitous violence? These are the problems that artists and
creators face, even though there may be other people and other factors involved in the process of creating and disseminating texts—
such as the people who work for the networks that carry violent
shows. But in short, I have tried to place the topics where I thought
they best fit.

I hope that after reading this book you will have a better understanding of the role that the media and the texts they carry have
played (and continue to play) in your life, in the lives of your friends
and the members of your family, and in the society in which you find

yourself. Although you may make individual choices of what media to consume (and what other products and services to consume), your decisions are affected by demographic factors such as your age, socio-economic class, gender, educational level, and zip code. You may not realize it but you fit into certain marketing categories, and thus your behavior is, in a certain sense, predictable. For example, if you are eighteen to thirty-four years old, live in an upscale area, are college-educated, and white, you are a typical member of the audience of *CSI: Crime Scene Investigation*, according to the Nielsen ratings. (There is some question, I might add, about how reliable the Nielsen ratings are.)

TWO ANECDOTES ON CHOICE

This matter of the predictability of our behavior is quite interesting, and it extends to activities other than choosing films to see or television programs to watch. In the summer of 2002 my wife and I took a cruise from San Francisco to Alaska and back. During the cruise we were given a tour of the ship's galley. The maître d', who was leading the tour, told us that the cruise line was able to predict, with remarkable accuracy, what people would choose to eat at every meal. Long experience had taught them what to expect.

Thus at a given dinner, while there may have been five main courses, the ship's cooks knew that 80 percent of the diners would

Jonathan Edwards

order a certain main course, such as lobster, 10 percent would order a different main course, and so on. This anecdote serves as an analogy for our media usage. We can choose anything we like (given what is available, that is) but we tend to like certain programs, depending upon our demographic and psychographic profiles and other variables.

The Puritan preacher Jonathan Edwards raised this matter of choice and action many years ago. He was trying to figure out how human beings could be free if God was all-powerful. His solution was to suggest there were two realms to be considered: the realm of choice, where God was all-powerful, and the realm of action, in which people could do whatever they wanted. The problem with this notion is that if God determines what choices we will make and then allows us to choose whatever we want, in reality we only have the illusion of freedom, since our choices have already been determined.

I should note here that age is a very important factor in the question of choice and predictability. In 1984 I was a visiting professor at the Annenberg School for Communication at the University of Southern California. I had a class of two hundred students taking a course in popular culture, and I brought a number of visitors from the media world to speak to my students. One visitor was a vice president of an easy-listening, light-rock station. When I introduced him and mentioned the station where he worked, my students all laughed.

"That's all right," he said. "You're laughing now, but when you're forty years old you'll be listening to my station. And I've got statistics to prove it." So the music we like when we are twenty may not be the music we like when we are thirty or forty, and the same applies to all the media.

Scenes with alcohol, tobacco, and/or illicit drugs are present in seven out of ten prime-time network dramatic programs. Scenes of drinking alcoholic beverages are seen an average of every twenty minutes. . . . More major characters in prime-time television drink alcoholic beverages than anything else. . . . Female smokers now outnumber male smokers among major characters in prime-time television. . . . In a sample of the 40 highest-grossing movie titles for the years 1994 through 1995, 39 (97.5 percent) contain portrayals of alcohol, smoking and/or illicit drugs. Those who view the most popular music video channel see alcohol use an average of every fourteen minutes, tobacco use every twenty-five minutes, and illicit drugs every forty minutes. . . . The use of addictive substances is shown as generally risk-free. More than nine out of ten drinkers, more than eight out of ten smokers, and six out of ten illicit drug users experience positive health effects or no health effects. . . . Addictive substances appear much more frequently in movies and music videos than on prime-time television. Only one of the forty movies surveyed does not have scenes involving alcohol, tobacco, and/or illegal drugs. . . . Two titles do not include any portrayal of alcohol, and six titles do not have any smoking. Illicit drug scenes are present in over one-third of the movies, more than twice their presence on prime-time television. . . . A child who grows up watching only three hours of prime-time television a day on one channel will have watched 32,000 characters who demonstrate tobacco as a part of their lives. Over 2,500 tobacco smokers will have been playing central roles in the stories being told. Yet the story of the negative health affects and addiction is not one of them. The child will have to view 2,200 smokers on television before seeing one who experiences negative health effect. (2001: 69–70, 73, 75)

—George Gerbner, "Drugs in Television, Movies, and Music Videos," in Y. R. Kamalipour and K. R. Rampal, *Media, Sex, Violence, and Drugs in the Global Village*

1

MEDIA IN OUR THOUGHTS
AND LIVES

A Psycho-Social Perspective on Individuals, Society, and the Media

Although I've never met you, my reader, there are certain things I *think* I know about you. There is one important qualification I must make, however, and that is I must assume that you are a typical American college student taking a course that deals, one way or another, with media and society. Before I tell you what I might know about you, let me begin by telling a story involving Johnny Q. Public, who I imagine is someone probably very much like you.

JOHNNY Q. PUBLIC'S MEDIA USAGE

The hero of this story is Johnny Q. Public who has an apartment in Normal City, USA, about a thirty-minute drive from Central State University, where he is a junior, majoring in media studies. At 7:30 A.M. his clock radio turns on. It is a news show that has information on traffic and a weather report every ten minutes. He takes a shower, brushes his teeth, and then reads the news online while he has breakfast. Then he jumps in his car to drive to Central State University just in time (or maybe a few minutes late) for his 9:00 class. He listens to the radio while he is driving. He's finished with classes by 2:00 P.M.

and goes to his part-time job in a gym where he is a trainer. He works until 5:00 P.M. At the gym, pop music is played over the loudspeakers. Johnny drives back to his apartment, listening to the radio again, and gets home by 5:30. He turns on the TV and microwaves dinner. He watches television while he eats. He does an hour of homework while he listens to music on his iPod. Then he calls his girlfriend, Emily Greatgal, and they agree on which movie to see Friday night. Johnny then watches television for three or four hours. After watching Jon Stewart, Johnny checks his e-mail. Next he plays a video game for half an hour. Finally, he washes up, makes sure his clock-radio alarm is set for the right time, and goes to bed late at night. He has spent close to the nine hours per day average that Americans spend with media of one kind or another. When he wakes up the next morning, he wonders, "Why am I so tired?"

During the course of a normal day, Johnny has listened to the radio for a couple of hours, watched television for three or four hours, listened to music at work and at home for an hour or so, spent some time on the Internet, played a video game, and spent fifteen or twenty minutes reading a newspaper online. Johnny's media usage is probably a bit less than most people's because he attends college and has a part-time job, but he's pretty close to the average.

A GROUP PORTRAIT OF MY READERS

Given the fact that you are reading this book, I can make the following assumptions about you. There is a good possibility that

1. You are between seventeen and twenty-five years old.
2. You are studying at a college or university.
3. You grew up watching three or four hours of television a day, on average.
4. You have been subjected to hundreds of thousands of print advertisements and television and radio commercials over the past ten or fifteen years.
5. You believe that while you are aware of these commercials, they do not influence your decision making in important ways.

6. You believe that while you "consume" eight or nine hours of media each day, your media diet doesn't have a significant impact on your life.
7. You also listen to the radio an hour or two each day and probably have some kind of gizmo such as an iPod that plays the kind of music you like when you're not at home.
8. You use a computer to do such things as write letters, term papers, and other reports; take notes; keep journals or blogs; pay your cell-phone bill; check movie listings; and send e-mail to friends. While you work at the computer, you might also be listening to music or to the radio. That is, you often *multitask*—use several different media at the same time.
9. You own a cell phone and use it regularly throughout the day.
10. You believe in *individualism*, whatever that means to you, though you may not know where the term comes from.

Of course, I could be all wrong. You could be a precocious fourteen-year-old or a seventy-five-year-old retired person, and you don't watch television or listen to the radio, and you hate popular music. Instead, you spend your days reading poetry and listening to chamber music and opera. You might have checked this book out from the library; or an older brother or sister had it, and you noticed it and picked it up because you're interested in media—because you suspect that some media may, in some way, be having an effect on your life.

It could be that you don't even know who Jessica Simpson is.

But I doubt it.

STATISTICS ON MEDIA USE

These assumptions I made are based on data that researchers have accumulated about media usage in the United States. A study released on March 9, 2005, by the Kaiser Family Foundation gives some interesting statistics on media usage in the lives of eight- to eighteen-year-old Americans. It was based on a survey, a nationally representative sample, of 2,032 young people eight to eighteen years of age. The survey found, in dealing with recreational (nonschool) use of TV, videos, music, video games, movies, computers, and print, that

> the total amount of media content young people are exposed to each day has increased by more than an hour over the past five years (from 7:29 to 8:33), with most of the increase coming from video games (up from 0:26 to 0:49) and computers (up from 0:27 to 1:02, excluding school-work). However, because the media use diaries indicate that the amount of time young people spend "media multi-tasking" has increased from 16% to 26% of media time, the actual number of hours devoted to media use has remained steady, at just under 6½ hours a day (going from 6:19 to 6:21), or 44½ hours a week. (http://kff.org/entmedia/entmedia030905nr.cfm)

This means the typical eight- to eighteen-year-old American is spending more than a full-time work week every week with media.

Figure 1.1   In a typical day, 54 percent of American eight- to eighteen-year-olds use a computer; 47 percent go online.

These statistics suggest that young people in America spend about 2,300 hours with media each year. More than 1,100 of these hours come from watching television, but while American young people are watching television, they may be doing other things involving media use, such as reading a book or chatting with a friend on the telephone. Contrast that amount of time spent with media with a typical course in a university that is around 45 hours for a semester, and you see how important a place media, of all kinds, has in most young people's lives. Children eight to eighteen have the following in their bedrooms: a television set (68 percent of children), a CD player (75 percent), and a video game player (45 percent). The bedrooms of American children have become media emporia, so to speak.

Data from Student Monitor, a market research firm, indicates that there are more than 15 million students in two- and four-year colleges and graduate schools in the United States, and these students have a purchasing power of some 270 billion dollars. According to a report by Teenage Research Unlimited, mentioned in the January 13, 2003, issue of the *New York Times*, the average sixteen-year-old

---

Websites on Children and the Media

Some websites devoted to children and the media are:

Children Now
www.childrennow.org

Children's Advertising Review Unit
www.caru.org

Don't Buy It: Get Media Smart
http://pbskids.org/dontbuyit

The Henry J. Kaiser Family Foundation
www.kff.org

Media Literacy Online Project
http://interact.uoregon.edu/MediaLit/mlr/home/index.html

now spends $104 a week. So teenagers and college students have a lot of money, and advertising agencies and marketers are out to do what they can to channel this money into spending for the "right" things—that is, the goods that they are promoting or selling, such as clothes, fast food, diet foods, CDs, and movies.

MEDIA EFFECTS AND YOUR LIFE

If I were to ask you, "What effect has the media had on your life?" you might offer the following answer: "I am *aware* of the media, but I'm not *affected* by it!" I say this because several years ago I was interviewed by a reporter from a newspaper in New York City about the fact that teenagers in a survey had reported that they were "aware" of advertising but not "influenced" by it to any significant decree. The reporter thought that these teenagers were deluding themselves and wanted to know what I thought about the matter.

So the question arises: What influence (or in the language of social science, what *effect*) has your incredible exposure to the media had on your life and on the lives of all kinds of other people like you who, collectively, form American society, or who are members of any other society? That is the question this book will try to answer, and it will do so by looking at the role the media play in American society and at the impact American society has upon the media. It is a complicated matter, but I will try to get to the heart of it in the pages that follow. To begin, let me suggest one way that the media, and television in particular, might affect some people.

TELEVISION VIEWING AND
VICIOUS CYCLES

In his book *A Psychiatric Study of Myths and Fairy Tales*, psychiatrist Julius E. Heuscher suggests that young children who are exposed to material on television programs that is too adult for them—given their age levels and their developmental levels—become very disturbed. As he explains:

The child who is being presented with an over-abundance of adult-life conflicts and desires and who thereby is being pushed toward grownup ideas, tends to become afraid of growing up and is therefore stunted in his maturation process. (1967: 325)

I am talking about stories with nasty arguments between men and women, stories full of violence, and stories about broken families, divorces, and infidelity, for example.

This isn't a problem with books, because very young children are not able to read the material in books that will disturb them. But children can see the stories on television and follow what happened. As a result of their exposure to this material, some of them become upset and anxious, and this anxiety affects them as they grow older. They fear growing up and becoming adults. They become distrustful of others, especially members of the opposite sex, and avoid intimate relationships with them and with others because they are afraid that they will be rejected or will become involved in bad relationships—just like the people in the television shows they watched when they were youngsters. This leads to a fear of marriage, to nonrelational sexual behavior, and to an inability to have intimate relationships of all kinds.

As a result of this kind of behavior, these adults are unhappy, which leads to various kinds of escapism, often in the form of compulsive shopping, but especially in viewing television programs, which they watch to obtain relief. Thus they become locked in a vicious cycle. Because they have difficulty forming relationships with others, they are lonely. To assuage this loneliness they end up watching a great deal of television, and thus they develop a kind of dependence on television—the same medium that led to their sorry state of affairs. Ironically, they become dependent for relief on the medium that actually helped cause their unhappiness and anxiety. Television provides that relief, but at the same time it reinforces their childhood fears—fears that cause their self-destructive behavior.

This kind of thing can also result from watching movies, but as a rule, children don't watch movies as much as they watch television, and movie watching is often controlled by parents, while television watching often isn't. Is it possible, I ask, that you or someone you

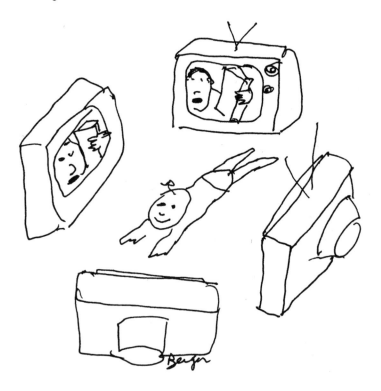

know has been caught up in a vicious cycle like this? It's an interesting question to consider.

THE MEDIA IN SOCIETY

The media (*media* is the plural form of the term **medium**) are, we must remember, part of society. The media are one of the many different institutions that exist within a society—*institutions* being the term used by sociologists to stand for enduring entities and organizations that play an important role in maintaining society. Some of the more important institutions in modern societies are those involving education, the family, religion, politics, and of particular importance to us, those that represent the **mass** media. The media entertain us, socialize us, inform us, educate us, sell things to us (and sell us, as audiences, to advertisers), and indoctrinate us—among other things. The media help shape our identities, our attitudes toward racial and ethnic minorities, and our attitudes about sexuality.

There are, I should point out, a number of different and conflicting views about how to characterize the media and understand the role they play in society and in our lives. Some scholars see the media as essentially transporting texts, while others focus on the way the media access material people have stored in their brains and use it to generate certain responses, which is called the **responsive chord theory**. Some scholars study the broadcast media by focusing upon the **genres** they carry (commercials, cop shows, action-adventure shows, game shows, talk shows, and so-called reality shows, among other types of shows). Other scholars are concerned with **media aesthetics** and the way light, color, camera work, and editing create certain effects. I deal with a number of these matters in various parts of this book.

The **mass communications** media seem to have taken an increasingly dominant role in society in recent years; now the media seem to affect all other institutions. Our political and governmental institutions have the legal power to help determine how **broadcasting** media operate, since the airwaves are public property, but all too often it seems now that the broadcasting media, thanks to the power of political advertising, are the "tail" wagging a government "dog."

A CASE STUDY: WHERE DID I GET THAT IDEA?

In the United States, where we believe in the American Dream of the self-made man or woman, and where we believe in individualism, many of us also believe that we alone determine our destiny, that we have, so to speak, the whole world in our hands. The term *individualism* was first used by Alexis de Tocqueville, a Frenchman who traveled in the United States in 1831 and wrote a fascinating book, *Democracy in America*, about American character and culture based on what he had observed. He suggested that we Americans are egalitarians, and that this egalitarianism has shaped all our other values and institutions. Thus, Tocqueville derives our individualism from our egalitarianism:

> I have shown how it is that, in ages of equality, every man seeks for his opinions within himself: I am now to show how it is that, in the same ages, all his feelings are turned towards himself alone. *Individualism* is a novel expression, to which a novel idea has given birth. Our fathers were only acquainted with *égoisme* (selfishness). Selfishness is a passionate and exaggerated love of self, which leads a man to connect everything with himself and to prefer himself to everything in the world. Individualism is a mature and calm feeling, which disposes each member of the community to sever himself from the mass of his fellows, and to draw apart with his family and his friends; so that after he has thus formed a little circle of his own, he willingly leaves society at large to itself. Selfishness originates in blind instinct: individualism proceeds from erroneous judgment more than from depraved feelings; it originates as much in deficiencies of mind as in perversity of heart. (1956: 193)

Of course Tocqueville, who didn't think much of our individualism, wrote before we developed our mass media. We still are individualists in America, though not in quite the same way that we were in the 1830s when Tocqueville visited the country; we are now immersed in media and not all of us (especially when we grow older, get married, and have children) want to leave society to itself.

So the notion of individualism is something that we learn from American society. We are not born knowing about individualism or the "self-made man or woman." We have to be taught these things. Some political figures who believe in a radical or extreme form of individualism argue that there's no such thing as society, that *society* is just an abstraction, a term for a collection of individuals. (That point was made by Margaret Thatcher when she was British prime minister.)

Thus ironically, people who learn about individualism from society sometimes find themselves arguing that society doesn't exist. This, in essence, is the point that sociologist Karl Mannheim makes in his book *Ideology and Utopia* when he says, "Strictly speaking, it is incorrect to say that the single individual thinks" (1936: 3).

A French sociologist, Emile Durkheim, offers a solution to this matter of the complicated relationship that exists between individuals and society. He writes, in his classic work *The Elementary Forms of the Religious Life* (first translated into English and published in 1915):

> Society is a reality *sui generis*; it has its own peculiar characteristics, which are not found elsewhere and which are not met with again in the same form in all the rest of the universe. The representations which express it have wholly different contents from purely individual ones and we may rest assured in advance that the first add something to the second.
>
> . . . Collective representations are the result of an immense cooperation, which stretches out not only into space but into time as well; to make them, a multitude of minds have associated, united and combined their ideas and sentiments; for them, long generations have accumulated their experience and their knowledge. A special intellectual activity is therefore concentrated in them which is infinitely richer and complexer than that of the individual. From that one can understand how the reason has been able to go beyond the limits of empirical knowledge. It does not owe this to any vague, mysterious virtue but simply to the fact that according to the well-known formula, man is double. (1967: 29)

These are important points. The intellectual activity of society is much more rich and more complex than an individual's intellectual

activity. And this is because, Durkheim explains, we have a history that enriches our thought. He continues with his analysis of the relation between the individual and society in the following manner:

> There are two beings in him: an individual being which has its foundation in the organism and the circle of whose activities is therefore strictly limited, and a social being which represents the highest reality in the intellectual and moral order that we can know by observation—I mean society. This duality of our nature has as its consequence in the practical order, the irreducibility of a moral ideal to a utilitarian motive, and in the order of thought, the irreducibility of reason to individual experience. In so far as he belongs to society, the individual transcends himself, both when he thinks and when he acts. (1967: 29)

We are all, in a certain sense then, "double." *On the one hand, we are in society, and on the other hand, society is in us.* We have physical bodies and personalities that are our own—that is, we are individuals—but we also are social animals, and much of what we think is based on this fact. We are taught in schools and we are socialized by our parents and peers and priests and pop stars (that is, the media), so there is a strong social dimension to our lives, even if we believe that somehow we are self-made.

Marx explained that our consciousness is social. As he puts it in *Selected Writings in Sociology and Social Philosophy,*

> Morality, religion, metaphysics and other ideologies, and their corresponding forms of consciousness, no longer retain therefore their appearance of an autonomous existence. They have no history, no development; it is men, who in developing their material production and their material intercourse, change, along with this their real existence, their thinking and the products of their thinking. Life is not determined by consciousness, but consciousness by life. (1964: 75)

What Marx is arguing here is that life—that is, our social existence—shapes our consciousness, which means that since the media play so large a role in our lives, the media help shape our consciousness.

In his book *Marxism and Literature*, British media and communication theorist Raymond Williams uses the term **hegemony** to describe the process by which the ruling class shapes the consciousness of the masses. He distinguishes between rule, which is political and ultimately based on force, and **hegemonial ideological domination**, which is broader than class-based ideology and which pervades a society, so people are unable to locate what it is that shapes their thoughts and ideas. As he explains:

> Hegemony is then not only the articulate upper level of "ideology," nor are its forms of control only those ordinarily seen as "manipulation" or "indoctrination." It is a whole body of practices and expectations, over the whole of our living: our senses, our assignments of energy, our shaping perceptions of ourselves and our world. It is a lived system of meaning and values—constitutive and constituting—which as they are experienced as practices appear as reciprocally confirming. It thus constitutes a sense of reality for most people in the society, a sense of absolute because experienced reality beyond which it is very difficult for most members of the society to move, in most areas of their lives. (1977: 110)

Hegemonial ideological domination can be characterized, then, as that "which goes without saying." We are dominated but cannot recognize that such is the case because the domination is ubiquitous and seems to be nothing more than common sense. The function of this domination is to help maintain the status quo and solidify the role of the ruling class in society.

SOCIETY, THE INDIVIDUAL, AND THE COMMUNICATION PROCESS

In his book *Ferdinand de Saussure*, Jonathan Culler makes an important point about the relationship that exists between individuals and society:

> For human beings, society is the primary reality, not just the sum of individual activities, nor the contingent manifestations of Mind; and

Figure 1.2   Individuals frequently forget that they are part of a larger entity, society, which makes it possible for them to pursue their personal interests.

if one wishes to study human behavior, one must grant that there is a social reality. . . . In short, sociology, linguistics, and psychoanalytic psychology are possible only when one takes the meanings which are attached to and which differentiate objects and actions in society as a primary reality, as facts to be explained. And since meanings are a social product, explanation must be carried out in social terms. It is as if Saussure, Freud, and Durkheim had asked, "What makes individual experience possible? What enables men and women to operate with meaningful objects and actions? What enables them to communicate and act meaningfully?" And the answer they postulated was social institutions which, though formed by human activities, are the conditions of experience. To understand individual experience one must study the social norms which make it possible . . . Saussure, Freud, and Durkheim thus reverse the perspective which makes society the result of individual behavior and insist that behavior is made possible by collective social systems individuals have assimilated, consciously or unconsciously. (1986: 86–87)

Culler raises an important point. If signs are to be meaningful, there must be a society that, one way or another, teaches people how those signs are to be interpreted. The meanings of signs are not natural but determined by society. Individual behavior, Culler argues, is the result of there being something we call society, and individuals are not the creators of society.

Perhaps what extreme individualists like Margaret Thatcher are really arguing is that society may exist but that it is irrelevant. Many people probably agree with her. They can say this, but if we take into account the nine hours a day most of us spend immersed in the mass media, which require all kinds of social, economic, political, and media institutions to create and disseminate their texts, the argument sounds a bit hollow. It is important that we keep this insight in mind—that we are all, as Durkheim puts it, dual creatures, and that we are in society and society is in us—as we investigate the mass media and its role in society, because the same thing applies to it: the mass media are in society and society is, in many different and important ways, in the mass media.

The average American spends 9.2 hours each day using consumer media. More households report having video game equipment (62%), than having a subscription to a daily newspaper (50%). Of those U.S. homes with children, 70% own video game systems. Per day, children spend 59 minutes reading a book; 52 minutes using a home computer; and 45 minutes playing video games. 18% of teenagers 13–17 read "often," 50% read "sometimes," and 32% never read. American children who have home video games play with them about 90 minutes a day. Teenagers spend an average of 2.5 weekday hours on a home computer . . . 66% of U.S. children have a television set in their bedrooms. Children spend about 28 hours per week watching television. Over the course of a year, this is twice as much time as they spend in school. . . . Teenage boys spend nearly twice as much time watching MTV as reading for pleasure.

—Popular Culture and the American Child
site on World Wide Web

McLuhan became frustrated trying to teach first-year students in required courses how to read English poetry, and began using the technique of analyzing the front page of newspapers, comic strips, ads, and the like as poems. . . . This new approach to the study of popular culture and popular art forms led to his first move towards new media and communication and eventually resulted in his first book, *The Mechanical Bride*, which some consider to be one of the founding documents of early cultural studies. While the *Bride* was not initially a success, it introduced one aspect of McLuhan's basic method— using poetic methods of analysis in a quasi-poetic style to analyze popular cultural phenomena—in short, assuming such cultural productions to be another type of poem. (2001: 4–5)

—Donald Theall, *The Virtual Marshall McLuhan*

2

MEDIA USAGE IN
THE UNITED STATES

The statistics I have offered above give us a pretty good idea of media usage in the United States. Surveys reveal that 32 percent of American teenagers never read and that only 50 percent "sometimes" read—a matter that is quite disturbing, since it is reading that is all-important in developing the critical thinking skills that are connected both to individual social mobility and to participating intelligently in the political process. Those who don't read become captives of the kinds of activities that require relatively little intellectual effort: listening to the radio, watching television, listening to CDs, watching films, and playing video games.

Let me break down the figures to give a better notion of how much time American kids spend with media in a typical day. According to a 2005 Kaiser media usage study (http://kff.org/entmedia/entmedia030905nr.cfm; see chapter 1), young people (ages 8 to 18) spend

3:04 hours a day watching TV
1:44 hours a day listening to music
1:02 hours a day using a computer
0:49 hours a day playing video games
0:43 hours a day reading
0:32 hours a day watching videos, DVDs

0:25 hours a day watching movies in a theater
0:14 hours a day watching prerecorded TV

The study also provides information on new media use in this age group, relative to what devices young people own and what they do with them:

66 percent use instant messaging
64 percent have downloaded music from the Internet
48 percent have streamed a radio station through the Internet
39 percent have a cell phone
35 percent have created a personal Web site or Web page
34 percent have a DVR such as a TiVo in their homes
18 percent have an MP3 player
13 percent have a handheld device that connects to the Internet

What these statistics suggest is that we now live in a media-saturated environment and that young people are immersed in media to an extent that can only be described as remarkable. One reason they are exposed to so much media is that about a quarter of the time, they are using two or more media at the same time. We can see that we and they spend a lot of time, each day, using consumer media. The question we must ask is, What effect, if any, does this use of consumer media have upon us as individuals and upon our families, friends, and American society?

THE MEDIA WE USE

Let me list here the media we use in a typical day. I am using the term *media* in the way it is traditionally used, that is, *as something that carries some kind of communication*. **Communication** involves sending messages from one or more senders to one or more receivers who can understand (or to use a communication theory term, *decode*) the message that has been sent. The media not only *carry* texts, they also *affect* these texts in different ways. The most common media are then, in no particular order:

Figure 2.1   We live in a media-saturated environment.

our voices (as in conversations)
computers
our bodies (as in body language)
newspapers
telephones of all kinds
magazines
television
books
radio
billboards
recordings (CD, MP3, DVD, etc.)
photographs
films
video games

This list could be broken down in a number of different ways. For example, we could classify media according to whether they are essentially linguistic (using language) or photographic (using such things as images, facial expressions, gestures, and body language).

Communication theorists tell us that in a typical conversation, 70 percent or 80 percent of the information is generated by our facial expressions, body language, and other forms of **nonverbal communication**. But in some media, such as television programs and films for example, we find both verbal and nonverbal communication techniques being used to generate messages, so the distinction between verbal and nonverbal, while interesting, can be improved upon. I will say more about different ways of classifying the media shortly, after a primer on communication.

A PRIMER ON COMMUNICATION

The mass media are, technically speaking, the mass media of communication. We can distinguish between different levels of communication and see where mass communication and the mass media belong:

intrapersonal	internal dialogue (talking to oneself)
interpersonal	talking to one person or a few people
small group	communicating with a small group of people
mass communication	using the media to communicate with many people

There are many different models and theories of communication. Let me offer two classic and influential ones, which will give you a pretty good idea of how scholars see the communication process working. The first is that of Roman Jakobson, a linguist, who said there are six elements in any speech act (see figure 2.2).

Let me explain each of these items in more detail.

1. the *sender*   sends (creates)
2. the *message*   is the content of the communication (the text)
3. the *receiver*   is the object of the message (the audience)
4. the *code*   is the way the message is packaged (for example, in English)
5. the *contact*   is the medium used (such as conversation or TV)
6. the *context*   is that which helps us understand the message better (society)

The *sender* can be one person, as in a conversation, or a group of people, such as those who write scripts and the others who perform them (as in a film or television show); the *message* can be words that contain information, or a combination of words and sounds and images; the *receiver* can be one individual or a million who may be seeing a film or watching a television show; the *code* is the way the message is presented—in language alone or by using a combination of words, images, and sound, as in films or television programs; the *contact* is the medium used to send the message; and the *context* is the situation in which the message is sent, which helps determine its meaning. For example, the request "Pass the hypodermic needle" will mean something different depending on whether the context is a dark alley or a hospital.

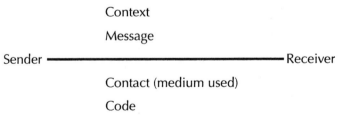

Figure 2.2   Roman Jakobson's Six Elements of Communication.
Source: McQuail and Windahl 1993.

Jakobson's model of communication offers us an insight into the people involved in communication and the way they communicate. It is one of the most famous and most useful models. Let me mention one other model (traditionally, a **model** is defined as an abstract representation of what occurs in the real world), also very famous, which was offered by a political scientist, Harold Lasswell, in 1948. Lasswell asks:

Who?
Says what?
In which channel?
To whom?
With what effect?

Actually, this model is very similar to Jakobson's, as table 2.1 shows.

Jakobson's model doesn't deal with effects the way Lasswell's model does, but there are, we can see, a number of similarities. Interestingly enough, Lasswell's **theory** has been criticized for bringing in the matter of effects, since **communications** scholars are divided on the matter of whether the mass media have long-lasting and important effects.

TRADITIONAL WAYS OF CLASSIFYING THE MEDIA

Now that we have an understanding of the process of communication, we can discuss the question of how to classify the media. A commonly used classification breaks the mass media down into electronic, print, and photographic media. This gives us the information shown in table 2.2.

Table 2.1   Lasswell and Jakobson Models Compared

Lasswell Model	Jakobson Model
who	sender
says	code
what	message
in which channel	contact (medium)
to whom	receiver
with what effect	—————

Table 2.2 Ways of Classifying the Media

Electronic Media	Print Media	Photographic Media
telephone	books	photographs
television	magazines	films
radio	newspapers	videos
recordings	billboards	

Some media theorists link electronic media and photographic media into a hybrid they call "photo-electronic media." If we use that concept, columns 1 and 3 would be merged together. As a rule, we spend a great deal more time with electronic media and photographic media than we do with print media. The average person in the United States watches around four hours of television a day, which means television is the dominant medium in America (and in many other countries as well), followed by radio, and listening to music on iPods and other new technology devices that can store many hours of songs. Americans don't, as the statistics on media use show, spend much time with print media, relatively speaking.

McLUHAN'S HOT AND COOL MEDIA

The late Canadian media theorist Marshall McLuhan used a different approach and classified media according to whether they were "hot" or "cool." He argued this in a famous aphorism: "The medium is the message." That is, the medium is more important than the textual content that the medium carries. While the medium has an impor-

tant impact on the content it carries, McLuhan's notion that the medium is basic in the communication process because it alters our sense-ratios and modes of perception is not generally accepted. His theories about hot and cool media, however, are worth considering in some detail.

According to McLuhan, *hot* media have high definition, by which he means that they are full of data, which leads to low audience participation. *Cool* media, on the other hand, have low definition, because they have little data, and high audience participation.

As McLuhan writes in *Understanding Media*:

> There is a basic principle that distinguishes a hot medium like radio from a cool one like the telephone, or a hot medium like the movie from a cool one like TV. A hot medium is one that extends one single sense in "high definition." High definition is the state of being well filled with data. A photograph is visually "high definition." A cartoon is "low definition," simply because very little visual information is provided. Telephone is a cool medium, or one of low definition, because the ear is given a meager amount of information. And speech is a cool medium of low definition, because so little is given and so much has to be filled in by the listener. On the other hand, hot media do not leave so much to be filled in or completed by the audience. Naturally, therefore, a hot medium like the radio has very different effects on the user from a cool medium like the telephone. (1965: 22–23)

McLuhan's discussion of the work that audiences must do to make sense of cool media anticipates some of the thinking of scholars who talk about reader response theory and the role an active audience plays in decoding texts in all media, topics that will be discussed later in this book.

Table 2.3 offers examples of hot media and cool media in paired oppositions.

We as an audience have to be more active in **decoding** the texts carried by cool media. They invite our participation more than hot media do, because hot media supply a great deal of information and there's less for us to do. For example, radio conveys more information than a phone call, and a photograph has much more information in it than a cartoon.

Table 2.3   McLuhan's Hot Media and Cool Media

Hot Media	Cool Media
radio	telephone
movie	television show
photograph	cartoon
printed word	speech
book	dialogue
lecture	seminar

McLuhan also speculated on the difference between print media and electronic media. There are, he suggests, certain logical implications that are connected to each kind of media. Print suggests linearity (we read lines of type, typically), logic, rationality, connectedness, and individuality. Electronic media, on the other hand, are associated with what might be described as "all-at-once-ness" and emotion. Table 2.4 is a comparison of McLuhan's notions about these two kinds of media.

These oppositions come from McLuhan's writings—in particular, from his book *Understanding Media.* They reflect the intellectual, social, and political implications that stem from what McLuhan argued are the essential nature of the two different kinds of media.

Figure 2.3   According to McLuhan, a cell phone is a "cool" medium and a book is a "hot" medium. "Hot" media provide the user with more information.

Table 2.4   Print (Books) and Electronic Media (Radio) Compared

Print	*Electronic Media*
the eye	the ear
interconnectedness	simultaneity
logical thinking	emotional responses
rationality	mythic spheres
books	radio
individualism	community
detachment	involvement
separation	connection
data classification	pattern recognition

It is possible to see how McLuhan derives linear thinking and individuality from books. When we read a book, we read letters that form words that form sentences that are printed, generally speaking, in horizontal lines of type. And books are read by individuals, who move through them at their own pace. So we can see how individualism and separation and detachment might be connected to the book. Electronic media are much different—they are often consumed by groups. They can be heard by individuals but also by groups, and thus they tend to bring people together instead of separating them, the way books do. The realm of sound involves, McLuhan suggests, pattern recognition rather than data classification, and this brings us together into communities and thus closer to the realm of ritual and the mythic than print does. So a change in the popularity of a medium leads to other important changes in society, changes that ultimately have an impact on individuals, since we are all social beings.

McLuhan's ideas were very popular for a number of years, and he became a media celebrity. Then his theories came under attack by many communications scholars, and he faded from sight. Recently, however, McLuhan's ideas have been making a comeback, in part because media scholars see a connection between his theories of hot and cool media, for example, and the new digital technologies. His theories might help explain the current passion people have for using cell phones, for example.

THE MEDIA HELP SHAPE THE
TEXTS THEY CARRY

What many communications scholars don't deal with in their theories is the fact that we don't watch television per se. I mean that we don't *watch* a television . . . except when the screen goes blank and we stare at a blank screen, like dummies, waiting for the program we were watching to resume. The media always carry texts of one kind or another: news shows, sitcoms, sports programs, commercials, and so on. And because of the power of the media through the use of editing and other manipulations to profoundly influence the sounds we hear and images we watch, the media do more than just transport texts. This notion that the media just transport texts is often known as the transportation theory of the media. It suggests that the media are relatively inert, a belief that is not generally accepted today.

Most media theorists believe that the media have an important role in shaping the texts they carry. In movies, for example, the shots a director uses—zooming in, quick cutting, fading out, and so on— all shape our perception of what is happening in the film we are watching. Or think of the difference between watching a football game in a stadium and watching the same game on television, where the director can show a given play from three or four different camera angles, where he can zoom in on a player, and where there are shots from blimps hovering above the stadium while the game is being played. This matter of the power of a medium to shape the texts it carries will be dealt with in some detail in my chapter on media aesthetics, which follows.

Everyday media experiences are not usually at the level of a major aesthetic experience, but for many persons *the most moving* cultural experience will be through popular media rather than classical art. A powerful emotion experience can be triggered by an otherwise trivial song floating out an alley and awakening rich associations. The important quality in the aesthetic experience, whether it is an emotional, earthshaking, life-changing encounter or a quiet, simple, weightless sense of deep appreciation is your subjective response. Seeing a captivating movie, hearing the right popular song at the right time, interacting electronically at maximum capability, getting caught up in a popular novel's sweeping narrative—these are sources of aesthetic experience shorn of artistic pretentiousness. By inspiring such moments, media culture can take on exceptional power, meaning, and importance. (1996: 13)

—Michael R. Real,
Exploring Media Culture: A Guide

During the Iran-Contra hearings that made Oliver North a national celebrity, Democrats learned what it meant to "lose control of the pictures." Steven Spielberg, the Hollywood director, was visiting Washington during the televised hearings. As he watched the hearings with some Democratic congressmen, he offered them a lesson in camera angles. "Watch this," Spielberg said, as he turned down the sound then directed the congressmen's attention to North's image on the screen. "The camera on North is shooting up, from about four inches below his eyes. This is the way they shot Gary Cooper in the western, *High Noon*, to make him look like a hero." When the camera panned to the committee members questioning North, Spielberg pointed out, the lighting was dim. Seen at a distance, they looked sinister. "It doesn't matter what Oliver North says. He has already won the battle, because he looks like the hero and everyone else looks like the villain." This realization shocked the congressmen. (1993: 13)

—Kiku Adatto, *Picture Perfect: The Art and
Artifice of Public Image Making*

3

THE SOCIAL DIMENSION OF
MEDIA AESTHETICS

In order to understand how **mass-mediated violence** or any other kind of mass-mediated programming works on its audiences the way it does, we must understand something about **media aesthetics**. Aesthetics is generally defined as a branch of philosophy involved in the study of beauty; but *media aesthetics*, as I will use the term, involves analyzing how creative artists use the technical capacities of the various media to achieve the effects they want. The term *aesthetics* has to do with sense perceptions, and so our concern is with how film and television and other media shape these perceptions. Media aesthetics deals, then, with how artistic effects are achieved, and these effects, I believe, play an important role in making a text meaningful to audiences. As the quotation above from Kiku Adatto shows, things that we seldom think about or are aware of—like camera angles—can be very important.

I will be focusing our attention mostly on television, but there is an aesthetic dimension to all media. Even in live theater, where performers have only their voices, facial expressions, and body language to use, we find directors using lighting, sound, costuming, action, and settings to create effects.

It is important that we recognize that how a text is edited to clarify and intensify its message often has a social, economic, and political significance. For our purposes here, how a story is told is as

37

revealing as what is told. For example, the way a political commercial is edited plays an important role in getting the commercial's message across. Style in fashion, we recognize, has social and often political content; we can say the same about the aesthetic aspects of mass-mediated texts. Let's begin this study of media aesthetics with a brief discussion of semiotics, the science of signs.

SAUSSURE ON SIGNS

How do we find meaning in things? How do we know how to interpret a particular facial expression or hairstyle? These questions are actually quite difficult, but there is a discipline devoted to finding answers to such questions. It is called **semiotics**, the science of signs. The term *semiotics* comes from the Greek work for sign, *semeion*. A **sign** can be defined as anything that can be used to stand for something else. For example, a frown generally signifies or stands for the fact that one is unpleased; and the term *tree* stands for a large, leafy plant.

One of the founding fathers of semiotics, the Swiss linguist Ferdinand de Saussure, said that signs were composed of two compo-

nents: a *signifier* (a sound or object) and a *signified* (a **concept** or idea). He wrote in his book *Course on General Linguistics*:

> I propose to retain the word sign [*signe*] to designate the whole and to replace concept and sound-image respectively by *signified* [*signifié*] and *signifier* [*signifiant*]; the last two terms have the advantage of indicating the opposition that separates them from each other and from the whole of which they are parts. (1966: 67)

The relationship between the signifier and signified is arbitrary, based on convention. For example, there is nothing natural or logical in the relation between the word *tree* and the large, leafy plant that we call a tree. The large, leafy plant could easily have been called something else. Words, then, are signs that stand for things—but there are many other kinds of signs.

In the same book, Saussure wrote:

> Language is a system of signs that express ideas, and is therefore comparable to a system of writing, the alphabet of deaf-mutes, symbolic rites, polite formulas, military signals, etc. But it is the most important of these systems.
>
> *A science that studies the life of signs within society* is conceivable; it would be a part of social psychology and consequently of general psychology. I shall call it *semiology* (from Greek *semeion* "sign"). Semiology would show what constitutes signs, what laws govern them. (1966: 16)

This may be considered one of the charter statements of semiotics. Saussure called his science *semiology*, but that term has been replaced by the term *semiotics* in recent years.

Saussure made another point that is very important. Concepts have meaning because of the web of relationships in which they are found; they don't have meaning by themselves. He wrote, "Concepts are purely differential and defined not by their positive content but negatively by their relations with the other terms of the system" (1966: 117). He added that "the most precise characteristics" of these concepts "is in being what the others are not." This means that it isn't content per se that determines meaning but *relationships* among the elements in a system. We make sense of concepts, then, by seeing them as the opposite of something else. Rich is the opposite of poor, and weak is the opposite of strong.

For Saussure, nothing has meaning by itself, and the meaning of everything has to be learned. What this means is that we all have to learn media aesthetics, informally and on our own, as we watch films and television programs and play video games, if we are to understand everything that is going on in them.

PEIRCE ON ICONS, INDEXES, AND SYMBOLS

The other founding father of semiotics, who gave the science its current name, was the American philosopher Charles Sanders Peirce (pronounced "purse"). He had a different theory than Saussure's, though both men were interested in signs. Peirce said there were three kinds of signs: *icons*, which communicate by resemblance; *indexes*, which communicate by cause and effect; and *symbols*, which have to be learned. Table 3.1 shows these three kinds of signs.

We can see that there is a difference between Saussure's ideas about signs and Peirce's. For Peirce, only symbols are conventional and have to be learned. He once said, "The universe is perfused with signs, it is not composed exclusively of signs" (quoted in Sebeok 1977: v), which suggests that for Peirce, semiotics is the key to finding meaning in anything.

We can combine Saussure and Peirce, and suggest that we find meaning in the world by seeing everything as either a signifier of something else (the signified—that is, a concept or idea) or as generating meaning by being iconic, indexical, or symbolic. We swim, like

Table 3.1   Peirce's Three Kinds of Signs

Kind	Icon	Index	Symbol
Signified by	resemblance	cause/effect	convention
Example	photographs	fire/smoke	flags
Process	can see	can figure out	must be taught

fish, in a sea of signs, and everything is a sign of something else. An **image**, for our purposes, can then be defined as a visual sign or as a collection of visual signs. In many cases, of course, we have signs within signs. For example, the White Perfume advertisement shown here has two figures in it (the two bottles of perfume) and also words, so there are many smaller signs within the larger collection of signs that we can describe as the image. The expressions on the faces of the models, the clothes they are wearing, their ages, their body language, the jewels in the woman's navel, the design of the ad, its lighting, and its color also function as signs.

LYING WITH SIGNS

One problem with signs is that they can be used to lie. As Umberto Eco, the distinguished semiotician and novelist, writes in *A Theory of Semiotics*:

> Semiotics is concerned with everything that can be *taken* as a sign. A
> sign is everything which can be taken as significantly substituting for

Figure 3.1   This perfume advertisement is filled with signs, from the expressions of the models to the design of the ad.

something else. This something else does not necessarily have to exist or to actually be somewhere at the moment in which a sign stands for it. Thus *semiotics is in principle the discipline studying everything which can be used in order to lie.* If something cannot be used to tell a lie, conversely it cannot be used to tell the truth; it cannot in fact be used "to tell" at all. (1976: 7)

Bald men who wear wigs, brunettes who dye their hair blonde, and malingerers who pretend to be ill are examples of people lying, in varying degrees of seriousness, with signs. Eco's point is that if a sign can be used to tell the truth, it can also be used to lie.

As I write this book, I pause for a moment and look out the window of my study. I see very tall plants (trees) and large objects (houses) with rectangular shapes in them (windows). When we are born, we know almost nothing. One of the things we do, as we grow up, is learn a language or perhaps a number of languages. And what are languages? They are, simply put, compositions of words (which are kinds of signs) that tell us what things are and of rules (grammar) that tell us how to use these words. As we grow up we also unconsciously learn various **codes**, which can be defined as systems of signs and symbols that have meaning—though one that is often not apparent. In espionage, codes are secret rules for unlocking the meaning of coded messages; we can think of cultural codes as being very similar in nature to the codes spies use.

From a semiotic perspective, stage actors and actresses, if you think about it, lie with signs. They pretend to be certain characters who have certain emotions, which they express by such things as what they say, how they say it, their facial expressions, their body language, and the clothes they wear. We don't consider this kind of lying or dissimulation to be serious; in fact, we seek it out. We know that it's going on, but we are caught up in a temporary and willing suspension of disbelief, and so we become emotionally involved with what these performers are doing. But when we move from the theater, from live performance, to mediated texts such as those found in videos, video games, television shows, and films, things become much more complicated. In the case of video games, for example, we are not merely spectators but actually become involved, interactively, in the story, and our actions can affect its outcome.

EDITING TECHNIQUES AND SEMIOTICS

When we consider texts in visual media such as film and television, we are dealing with works in which editing, different kinds of camera shots, lighting, music, and sound effects play an important role, and one that is perhaps, in some cases, a more important one than the dialogue spoken by the performers. It is useful to apply Saussure's distinction between signifier (sound, object) and signified (concept, idea) to different kinds of camera shots, camera movements, and editing techniques. Different camera shots and editing techniques function as signs, or as cues to viewers—cues that tell them what to think and feel—and these cues are based on the aesthetic codes viewers learn while watching television and films. Editing, for our purposes, will be considered the sequencing of different kinds of camera shots to create a sense of continuity in a text and to generate certain desired effects. These camera shots are used with other variables of presentation such as sound, music, color, and lighting.

Camera Shot (signifier)	Definition of Shot	Meaning (signified)
establishing shot	large overview	location
close-up	head and shoulders	intimacy
extreme close-up	part of face	inspection
medium shot	head and torso	personal relations
full shot	complete body of person	social ambiance
long shot	setting and people	context, scope
extreme long shot	person in wider context	orientation
z-axis	vertical action from screen	involvement

As we grow up and become used to watching television, we learn the meanings of the various camera shots. We may not be able to articulate these meanings, but we get a sense of what the shots mean. If we move to camera work, we find other meanings of interest.

Figure 3.2   This print advertisement uses an extreme close-up photograph to attract attention.

Camera Movement	Definition of Movement	Meaning
pans down	camera looks down on	power and authority
pans up	camera looks up to	weakness, smallness
dollies in	camera moves in	interest, observation
dollies out	camera moves out	scope, context
zoom in	lens moves in on	detail, focus
zoom out	lens moves out from	scope, context
arc	semicircular movement	investigation
truck left/right	horizontal movement	different perspective

Now I will deal with some of the more important transitional editing techniques that are conventionally used. These techniques enable editors to move from one image to another. The cut is the most commonly used editing technique, but there are others that are available.

Editing Technique	Definition of Technique	Meaning
fade in	black to image	beginning
fade out	image to black	ending

cut	switch from one image	simultaneity
wipe	screen image replaced by other	imposed ending
dissolve	image dissolves into next	weak ending

We can see, then, that there are many possibilities that directors and editors can use in shooting a text, and I haven't covered all of the different things that can be done in postproduction to a text. In some commercials, there is an incredible amount of quick cutting—some commercials can have as many as sixty different images in a thirty-second time span. So editing is an important element of the mass-mediated arts.

We can think of the use of different kinds of shots and editing techniques as "instructions" to viewers to think certain things or have certain emotions. The order of images in a film conveys meaning to viewers in the same way that the order of words in a book does, and these meanings often have a social as well as a psychological dimension to them.

Editing involves the way media makers use different kinds of shots and different kinds of camera work to create the effects they want. As viewers watch a television program, for example, their ideas and emotions are affected by the words the characters utter and their actions, but also by the different shots and combinations of shots and by the lighting, the sound, the music, and the colors used, among other things. Let's briefly discuss some of the techniques, mentioned above, that directors and production artists can use to intensify the meanings of texts.

Color

Colors have culturally important meanings to people, and these meanings differ from country to country. We know, for example, that black means a certain thing in the United States and something different in other countries. Villains in American cowboy films were conventionally dressed in black and heroes were dressed in white. Hospitals now paint their walls peach and similar colors rather than white because they've found that these colors relax people.

Lighting

Lighting is an important cue for us about what is happening in a dramatic text. If the lighting is dark, we are in the realm of mystery and, in some cases, horror. Bright lighting, on the other hand, means something quite different and is associated with less dramatic entertainment genres, such as situation comedies.

Music

Music is used to help viewers of films and television programs connect, emotionally, with what is being shown on the screen. Music offers cues to audiences to help them understand better what they are seeing and anticipate what might be coming. It establishes the emotional mood that the filmmakers want to generate and is also related to the pace or rhythm of the images being shown.

Sound Effects

Sound plays a role in giving audiences a better idea of what is going on in a text and in helping intensify their experience. We live in a world of sound, and it is only natural that films, television programs, video games, and all audiovisual texts use the sounds that we are accustomed to so as to make their texts seem more realistic. As we grow up we learn what certain sounds mean. Not surprisingly then, sounds are a way of conveying information to audiences about how they should feel or what they might expect when they are watching a text.

THE NATURE OF NARRATIVES: VLADIMIR PROPP

A large percentage of the texts people watch on television and see at the movies are **narratives**, that is, stories. Stories have two axes: a linear or *syntagmatic* one, which involves one action following another sequentially in time (like words in a sentence or links in a chain); and a horizontal or *paradigmatic* one, in which actions and characters take on meaning in the way concepts do: by differentiation, that is, by being the opposite of something else.

Linear Axis	Horizontal Axis
Propp	Lévi-Strauss
syntagmatic	paradigmatic
sequence	relations
meaning from place in story	meaning from sets of oppositions

There have been many different attempts to understand how texts generate meaning as their plots develop sequentially. One of the most influential theories was developed by a Russian folklorist, Vladimir Propp. He said that the most important thing to deal with in narratives is the actions of the characters, which he called "functions." He listed thirty-one functions that he found in Russian fairy tales, and we can find the same functions (with minor modifications and updates) in contemporary narratives from fairy tales to James Bond films.

His thirty-one functions are below. (Note: Propp also found in fairy tales an *initial situation* in which the members of a family or a hero is introduced, for example, but the initial situation is not considered a function.) These functions frequently are paired, and there is a logical nature, based on how the mind works, to the way they are used in narrative texts. Propp believed that the sequence of events in narrative was invariable, but we don't need to accept Propp's idea about the invariability of sequences of events to benefit from his analysis of narrative texts.

Function	Action
1. Absentation	One of the members of the family absents self.
2. Interdiction	Interdiction addressed to hero. (Can be reversed.)
3. Violation	Interdiction is violated.
4. Reconnaissance	Villain makes attempt to get information.

5. Delivery	Villain gets information about his victim.
6. Trickery	The villain tries to deceive his victim.
7. Complicity	Victim is deceived.
8. Villainy	Villain causes harm to family member.
8a. Lack	Member of family lacks something, desires something.
9. Mediation	Misfortune made known. Hero dispatched.
10. Counteraction	Hero agrees to counteraction.
11. Departure	Hero leaves home.
12. First Donor Function	Hero tested, receives magical agent or helper.
13. Hero's Reaction	Hero reacts to agent or donor.
14. Receipt of Agent	Hero acquires use of magical agent.
15. Spatial Change	Hero led to object of search.
16. Struggle	Hero and villain engage in direct combat.
17. Branding	Hero is branded.
18. Victory	Villain is defeated.
19. Liquidation	Initial misfortune or lack is liquidated.
20. Return	Hero returns.
21. Pursuit, Chase	Hero is pursued.
22. Rescue	Hero rescued from pursuit.
23. Unrecognized Arrival	Hero, unrecognized, arrives home or elsewhere.
24. Unfounded Claims	False hero presents unfounded claims.
25. Difficult Task	Difficult task is proposed to hero.
26. Solution	The task is resolved.
27. Recognition	The hero is recognized.
28. Exposure	The false hero or villain is exposed.

29. Transfiguration	The hero is given a new appearance.
30. Punishment	The villain is punished.
31. Wedding	The hero is married, ascends the throne.

Propp also believed that there are only two kinds of heroes: *victim* heroes (who suffer from some action), and *seeker* heroes (who are sent on missions to accomplish something). In stories with victim heroes (and heroines), the focus is on how they are victimized and how they end their victimization. In stories with seeker heroes and heroines, the focus is on the way they help others who have suffered from some kind of villainy or are in danger. (To avoid the awkwardness of writing *heroes* and *heroines* all the time, I will use the term *heroes* to stand for male and females henceforth.) Seeker heroes often have helpers who aid them in various ways. These helpers often have special powers, or they give the heroes some kind of magic agent that enables them to prevail over villains.

A PROPPIAN ANALYSIS OF A JAMES BOND FILM

Propp argued that all heroes are either seeker heroes or victim heroes. Quite obviously, many of the heroes in contemporary narratives are involved with rectifying some victimization that they or some member of their family may have undergone, or are sent on missions to accomplish some goal. In some cases we have a combination—such as the James Bond novels and films where Bond is sent on missions to accomplish some goal. In some Bond novels, for example *Dr. No*, agents belonging to the British Secret Service (Bond's "family") have been killed, so James Bond functions both as a victim hero from a victimized family (or organization) and a seeker hero.

In *Dr. No*, Bond is sent by spy master M to Jamaica. Before he leaves, Bond is given certain weapons by a character known as Q. While in Jamaica, Bond undertakes a hazardous mission to explore a small island controlled by Dr. No. He is captured by the villain, Dr.

No (an example here of personal victimization), and must undergo the ordeal of escaping from his confinement—during which time his life is continually threatened—so he can kill Dr. No (who has a mad plan to conquer the world) and then end up in bed (the moral equivalent of marrying the princess) with the character Honeychile Rider, a beautiful woman Bond befriended earlier in the book. Rider is introduced in a chapter of the book titled "The Elegant Venus."

Some Proppian functions found in *Dr. No*:

8. Villainy	Villain causes harm to family member.
9. Mediation	Misfortune made known, hero is dispatched.
14. Receipt of agent	Hero acquires use of magical agent (from Q).
15. Spatial change	Hero led to object of search.
16. Struggle	Hero and villain join in direct combat.
17. Branding	Hero is branded (captured, imprisoned).
30. Punishment	Villain is punished (Dr. No is killed).
31. Wedding	Hero is married (goes to bed with Honeychile Rider).

The Bond novels and films then, can be seen as updated versions of fairy tales, and we can find many Proppian functions in them, though in modernized versions and not in the rigid order Propp thought all narratives had to obey. We could also perform the same analysis on other narrative texts, and the reader might find it interesting to use Propp's list of functions to analyze his or her favorite contemporary film or television show.

This particular Bond novel had negative portrayals of people of color, in particular black people and Asians, leading to many critics describing the book as racist. In recent years we have become increasingly aware of the role the media play in giving people of color, women, ethnic minorities, gays, and other groups negative

stereotypes, which have destructive effects upon them. The use of negative stereotyping continues to be a problem with the media. Writers use stereotypes because stereotypes enable them to "explain," quickly and easily, why characters act the way they do.

THE NATURE OF NARRATIVES: CLAUDE LÉVI-STRAUSS

Propps's method of looking at the order of actions or events in a narrative is known as *syntagmatic analysis*. A *syntagm* is a chain, so Propp's analysis looks at the chain of functions he believed all stories must have. Syntagmatic analysis tells us what happens in a text; but to understand the deeper or hidden meaning of the events in a text, we must apply a different theory, based on the work of the French anthropologist Claude Lévi-Strauss.

Lévi-Strauss's theory is known as *paradigmatic analysis*, and is based on Saussure's notion that concepts don't mean anything in themselves. I quoted Saussure earlier to the effect that "concepts are purely differential." Saussure has also said that "in language there are only differences" (1966: 120). We can extend this notion of concepts to include heroes and villains and their actions in narrative texts.

Lévi-Strauss is known as a *structuralist*, that is, he was interested in how the elements in something—a myth or a story—relate to one another. Literary critic Jonathan Culler has explained in his book *Structuralist Poetics* that structuralists take "the binary opposition as a fundamental operation of the human mind basic to the production of meaning" (1975: 15). We make sense of things in general, then, by fitting them into sets of polar oppositions that our mind supplies to us. And we make sense of texts by seeing every action and every character in terms of the binary oppositions that exist in all texts—oppositions whose meaning we all know. Our minds decode these texts, providing us with oppositions that enable us to make sense of what is going on in the texts at all times.

It is possible to see some of Propp's functions in terms of oppositions between heroes and villains, the two main characters in narratives. What follows in table 3.2 are very general oppositions. These aren't always evident in every text, of course.

Table 3.2   Oppositions in Propp's Functions

HERO	VILLAIN
young (son)	old (father)
handsome	ugly (often grotesque and monstrous)
love	lust
heroine (rescued by hero)	enchantress (bewitches hero)
seeming villainess	false heroine
imagination, invention	technology, manpower
seeks something	hinders hero
suffers from villain's acts	punishes hero
is dispatched	engages in reconnaissance
gets helpers (magic powers)	has henchmen
undergoes ordeals	creates ordeals
defeats villains	loses to hero

You can see from table 3.2 that many important oppositions can be found in narratives; and this list is only suggestive. As we read a book or watch a movie or television program, we are continually setting up oppositions in our mind's eye between the characters, events, and objects that we see and their imagined or real opposites—that is how we find meaning in texts, and by extension, everyday life. It's quite easy, for example, to apply these oppositions to *Star Wars* films, James Bond films, and most films, as a matter of fact.

While many of the villains in such films are evil individuals, criminals, or monsters of one sort or another, they have a social significance beyond the role they play in a particular text. The triumph of the hero over these characters confirms our sense that there is justice in the world, and that good must inevitably triumph over evil, thereby reinforcing our belief in goodness and the value of democratic institutions. Thus, when James Bond defeats the monstrous Dr. No, Bond's victory is both personal and political. There are, of course, many texts that are overtly political, such as television shows about the White House (*The West Wing*) and the Supreme Court, and, when elections come around, the numerous political commercials that are broadcast on radio and television.

THE IMPORTANCE OF NARRATIVES

Narratives are important in more ways than we might imagine. As Laurel Richardson writes:

Narrative is the primary way through which humans organize their experiences into temporally meaningful episodes. . . . Narrative is both a mode of reasoning *and* a mode of representation. People can "apprehend" the world narratively and people can "tell" about the world narratively. According to Jerome Bruner . . . narrative reasoning is one of the two basic and universal human cognition modes. The other mode is the logico-scientific. . . . The logico-scientific mode looks for universal truth conditions, whereas the narrative mode looks for particular connections between events. Explanation in the narrative mode is contextually embedded, whereas the logico-scientific explanation is extracted from spatial and temporal events. Both modes are "rational" ways of making meaning. ("Narrative and Sociology," *Journal of Contemporary Ethnology* 19 [1990]: 118)

So narratives are more than entertainments. They are a means by which we seek to make sense of the world, both for ourselves and for others. This suggests that the conversations we have, the stories we read, the television shows we watch, the films we see, the songs we listen to, the comics we read, the video games we play, the jokes people tell us, and every other narrative that we experience play an important role in our consciousness and the development of our identity. Our "story" (by which I mean our identity) is, in a sense, a story we build out of all the other stories we know and to which we have been exposed.

One thing that this investigation of narratives reveals is that members of audiences are much more active than we might imagine. They have to interpret the meaning of every shot and sequence of shots they see; they have to make sense of the lighting, the music, and the sound. They also have to find meaning in what the characters in a text look like, what they say, what they do, and so on. In short, there's a great deal that an audience and we must do every time we read a passage in a book or see a film or television program or video. Of course, we have a lot of practice and experience doing this kind of work.

POSTMODERNISM AND MEDIA AESTHETICS

There is a great deal of controversy about what **postmodernism** is and isn't, and what its influence has been on society and culture in the United States and elsewhere. Scholars suggest that the movement known as **modernism** lost favor around 1960 and was replaced by postmodernism: a philosophical system that argues that the old philosophical beliefs that used to guide people—such as faith in progress and reason—no longer are valid. Some theorists have argued that postmodernism is really another name for the advanced form of capitalism found in the United States and elsewhere. Here are some contrasts between postmodernism and modernism to help you see the difference between the two more clearly:

Modernism	**Postmodernism**
master narratives accepted	incredulity toward master narratives
belief in progress	skepticism about progress
can know reality	can't know reality

acceptance of hierarchy, elitism	rejection of hierarchy, egalitarianism
separation of reality and simulations	simulations and mediated experiences basic
unified style	many styles at same time, eclecticism
serious	playful
elite arts vs. popular arts	elite arts and popular arts unified

Sociologist Norman Denzin describes the postmodern sensibility, as reflected in the cinema and television, in his book *Images of Postmodern Society: Social Theory and Contemporary Cinema*, as follows:

> The ingredients of the postmodern self are given in three key cultural identities, those derived from the performances that define gender, social class, race and ethnicity. . . . These cultural identities are filtered through the personal troubles and the emotional experiences that flow from the individual's interactions with everyday life. These existential troubles look back to the dominant cultural themes of the postmodern era, including the cult of Eros, and its idealized conceptions of love and intimacy. The raw economic, racial, and sexual edges of contemporary life produce anxiety, alienation, a radical isolation from others, madness, violence, and insanity. Large cultural groupings (young women, the elderly, racial and ethnic minorities, gays and lesbians) are unable either to live out their ideological versions of the American dream or to experience personal happiness. They are victims of anhedonia, they are unable to experience pleasure. . . . They bear witness to an economy, a political ideology, and a popular culture which can never deliver the promised goods to their households. (1991: viii)

Among the films Denzin deals with in his study of postmodern film are *Blue Velvet*; *Wall Street*; *Crimes and Misdemeanors*; and *Sex, Lies, and Videotape*. Other writers have included such films as *Blade Runner* and *The Terminator*, to this list. Such postmodern films, videos, and television programs reflect with great power many of the problems that different groups of people—ethnic minorities, women, gays, and lesbians—face in society, and the alienation they feel. These works also play a role in giving young people identities and belief systems. From the postmodernist perspective, identities are flexible: you change your identity when you feel like it. The notion that identity involves something constant and nonchanging is a modernist one; nowadays, we try on and cast off our identities as often as we wish.

BLADE RUNNER, RASHOMON, AND *SURVIVOR:* THREE POSTMODERN TEXTS

The film *Blade Runner* raises the problem of what it means to be human. In the film there are characters known as *replicants* that look exactly like humans, but are really androids. One of these replicants, it seems, has been programmed to think that she is a human. The hero of the film, a human, falls in love with her. *Blade Runner* asks us to define, in a sense, where being human begins and ends. The setting of the film, in a seamy, futurist Los Angeles, is also very postmodern.

Another postmodern film is the Japanese masterpiece by Akira Kurosawa, *Rashomon.* In *Rashomon*, a bandit overcomes a Samurai in a grove and ties him up. Then he fetches the Samurai's wife, who has been waiting near the grove, brings her back to the grove, and rapes her in front of her husband. The events are seen by a woodcutter who stumbles onto the drama taking place in the grove and observes it from a distance. Later, the Samurai is found dead. At a trial scene, each person involved in the event gives a different version of what went on. The bandit says he killed the Samurai after a tremendous battle; the wife says that in a trance, caused by her husband's hateful stare, she killed him; the Samurai, speaking through a medium, says that broken hearted, he committed suicide; and the woodcutter says that the battle between the bandit and the Samurai was pathetic because each was scared to death of the other. The problem the film raises involves the matter of what we can know of reality. Can we ever know what happened in that grove?

Reality television shows such as *Survivor* can also be seen as postmodern in nature. One of the dominant motifs of postmodernism is the use of *pastiche*, which is the blending of different styles and, in this case, genres. Consider the different genres found in *Survivor.*

- a girlie, beach-bunny show, with women in bikinis and various stages of undress running around
- a soap opera, with various intrigues by the participants who are trying to win a million dollars
- an action-adventure show, with various tasks required of the team members
- a game or contest show, with numerous contests that teams have to win

These shows are highly edited, so although they are not scripted, the editing process functions as a kind of script to generate drama and excitement.

The postmodern sensibility can also be seen in television commercials that don't seem to mean anything and don't seem to convey a message (this applies to any number of perfume commercials), and in novels that don't come to a logical ending, such as Thomas Pynchon's *The Crying of Lot 49*. It has been suggested that, as a result of exposure to postmodern works, contemporary youth now have a postmodern sensibility that puts them at odds with the older generation, which has a modernist perspective on things. What is called "generational conflict" is based not only on age but on the difference between a modernist and a postmodernist sensibility—one that is reflected in many of the films and television programs of the last forty years. (I will discuss other aspects of postmodernism, as it involves the relationship between elite and popular culture, in chapter 10.)

What media aesthetics attempts to do is determine, with some precision, how texts work and the way individuals decode or make sense of these texts, hour after hour, day after day, without a second thought. It also is concerned with how aesthetic factors help shape texts and consciousness. This is important if we wish to understand the social and cultural significance of the images and the characters and their activities in narratives and other mass-mediated texts.

The place of the audience in the social structure makes a difference. Those who are well off are likely to be affected by a message about increases in taxation differently from those who are badly off.

An important factor has to do with **what the audience believes already**. Someone believing in self-sufficiency and independence will respond to an advertisement encouraging people to start up small businesses in a different way from somebody who believes in job protection and a job for life. **The greater the match between the views and knowledge of the audience and what is said in the communication, the more the communication will be believed**. (1990: 169)

—Graeme Burton, *More Than Meets the Eye:*
An Introduction to Media Studies

The critic may have access to a demographic profile of the audience, which includes the sociocultural categories that the audience members belong to: sexual identity, sexual orientation, religion, ethnicity, race, profession, educational level, income level, age, and political affiliation, to mention a few. The demographic profile will suggest a psychographic profile. . . . There are always individual differences and variations from the norm, but most public messages are designed to make sense to the largest possible audience, and they do. Even though Americans, for instance, may identify with very different cultural groups, they are exposed to many of the same messages via school, parents, and media, and therefore develop many of the same codes for making sense of messages. (1998: 20)

—Jodi R. Cohen, *Communication Criticism:*
Developing Your Critical Powers

4

AUDIENCES 1: CATEGORIES

I ndividuals may not be aware of it, but media and marketing organizations have developed elaborate ways of classifying people into
different categories, which is of interest to advertising agencies, who
are trying to reach people to sell them goods and services. Each of us
may think of ourselves as unique individuals, but for marketers, our
distinctive identities are of no concern—we're all, as far as they are
concerned, members of some group or category based on **demographics** (our age, gender, race, religion, ethnicity), **psychographics** (values and beliefs), or something else.

AUDIENCES ARE SPECIALIZED

Audiences for many mass-media texts are now global—think, for
example, of the global audiences for American **popular** music,
American films, the Olympics, and the Super Bowl. In this chapter I
will focus upon audiences in the United States, though what I write
has applications to global audiences. We must remember, first of all,
that audiences are part of a larger entity, namely the society (or societies with access to global media) in which they are found.

In the United States we have a number of different and specialized audiences for the various genres of radio shows: news, talk,
sports, and music such as country western, classical, hard rock, light

rock, rap, jazz, blues, easy listening. . . . I could go on and on. There are probably a dozen or more niche audiences for specific kinds of music on the radio. That is why radio can be considered a **narrow-casting** medium, appealing, as a rule, to limited and very specific audiences, as contrasted with **broadcasting**, which aims for much larger audiences.

In many cases, people in what we can describe as microaudiences are members of various **subcultures** that exist within the broader category of American **culture**. There are, for example, many different genres of video games, and video game players can be classified depending on which kind of console they use or whether they play on personal computers. And audiences are much more active than we might imagine, both in terms of the texts they select and the way they interpret these texts.

PROBLEMS ADVERTISERS FACE

Radio stations, television stations, and radio and television networks are interested in knowing how many people are listening to and watching their shows, and what these audiences are like, because radio and television commercials are sold on the basis of the size and characteristics of the audiences of specific shows. If you're selling a luxury car, it doesn't pay to advertise on a program mainly watched by viewers who cannot afford these cars. So advertisers have to pay careful attention to the programs on which they advertise.

The development of new technologies such as TiVo, a popular brand of digital video recorder that enables people to record television programs and delete commercials, is causing all kinds of problems for advertisers. Some are dealing with this problem by increasing the use of *product placement* in shows, that is, paying to have their products used in films and television programs, which is a kind of "stealth" approach to advertising. But product placement alone cannot solve the problems new technologies pose to the advertising industry and the companies for which advertising agencies work. Just showing a bottle of soda pop isn't the same thing as broadcasting a commercial about it.

Figure 4.1 Video game audiences can be subcategorized by what kind of system or systems they use.

There is also the problem of clutter, in which viewers of television programs are assaulted by so many commercials that they forget what they have seen and get the commercials all mixed up in their heads. As advertisers become more and more desperate to attract the attention of audiences, and try to do so by finding new and more fantastic images, they become involved in an ultimately self-defeating war for viewers. In addition, viewers quickly learn that the promises advertisers make are often spurious, and so audiences have become increasingly skeptical and increasingly more difficult to reach.

SHARES AND RATINGS

Media researchers distinguish between *ratings* and *shares* when dealing with audiences. The difference between the two is explained in Barry L. Sherman's *Telecommunications Management: Broadcasting/Cable and the New Technologies*. Sherman writes:

> *Rating* refers to the percentage of people or households in an area tuned to a specific station, program, or network. For example, if, in a Nielsen sample of 1,000 homes, 250 households were tuned to the ABC network, the rating for ABC during that time period would be (250 div 1,000), or 25%. For ease of reporting, the percentage sign is dropped in the ratings book. *Share* refers to the number of people or households tuned to a particular station, program, or network correlated with sets in use. Continuing the above example, if only 750 of the sampled households were actually watching television in the time period covered, ABC's share would be (250 div 750) = 33%. Since there are always more sets in a market than there are sets in use, the share figure is always higher than the rating. (1995: 389)

These figures are important because radio and television networks are "selling" their audiences to advertisers, so a show with very high ratings and a high share (and the right kind of listeners or viewers) can charge much more for commercials than one with low ratings and a low share, or with the wrong kind of listeners or viewers. For example, a network broadcasting the Super Bowl charges millions of dollars for each thirty-second commercial because it knows it will have a huge audience. Advertising works on a cost-per-thousand (CPM) basis, so a television show that is seen by hundreds of millions of people may actually cost less on a CPM basis than a show that doesn't charge very much, relatively speaking, but has a very small audience.

There is also the question of how reliable the various ratings systems are. Nielsen, for example, asks people to keep a "Peoplemeter," and then uses the data obtained from this device for its national ratings. Sherman describes the process:

> The national Nielsens are produced through the use of the Nielsen Peoplemeter, a device resembling a cable box with a remote control.
>
> Over 4,000 homes in the United States comprise a sample which, theoretically at least, represents TV viewing in America's more than 94 million TV homes. The peoplemeter is attached to each set in the participating household. Viewers push buttons assigned to them to track their viewing activity. The data are transmitted to the Nielsen Company and processed overnight so that ratings information can be used by programmers and advertisers by the beginning of business the following day. (1995: 383)

A sample size of 4,000 homes can get fairly accurate information about a television-viewing population of 260 million people if the sample is truly *representative*, and if the people using the Nielsen Peoplemeter are diligent.

There are questions about how representative the Nielsen sample is and how accurately the people using the Peoplemeters report their television viewing. The only way to be absolutely certain about television usage in America would be for all station changes to be recorded automatically in each household and for a camera to record how many people are in front of a given television set when it is on. Obviously, this is quite impossible. So we have to make do with statistical sampling, which while not perfect, yields quite accurate information if done correctly.

NEW DEVELOPMENTS IN OBTAINING RATINGS

An article by Jon Gertner in the April 10, 2005, *New York Times Magazine*, "Our Ratings, Ourselves," discusses new developments in obtaining more accurate ratings. As noted in this article, the Nielsen corporation has teamed up with a Maryland company called Arbitron to test a device called the PPM (Portable People Meter), which keeps track of the television and radio programs that individuals wearing the device are exposed to during the day. Arbitron is testing the device in Houston, Texas. The PPM works by registering an inaudible digital code encoded in the audio tracks of most of the radio and television stations broadcasting in metropolitan Houston. The encoding covers over-the air television, cable television, and satellite television, but not satellite radio.

The PPM is passive in that people wearing the device don't have to record what they've listened to on the radio or watched on television, the way they do in active research testing and the way in which Nielsen currently obtains information on ratings. It's been evident for some time that although Nielsen obtains information from a representative sampling of Americans, asking people to record what they've seen or listened to is not terribly accurate. This is not a prob-

Did You See That Sign?

Nielsen Outdoor, a unit of Nielsen Media Research, is trying to find out whether it can do a better job of measuring the effectiveness of outdoor advertising. It gave 850 people in the greater Chicago area something it calls an "Npod," a small electronic device that looks like a cell phone and is equipped with a global positioning system. The people with the "Npods" were tracked for nine days in the summer of 2004 to see how often they passed by outdoor advertising. Nielsen discovered that a typical resident of the Chicago area, age eighteen or older, was exposed to forty signs a day, and adults who lived in Chicago proper were exposed to sixty-six signs per day.

Although Nielsen's experiment determined, with a creditable degree of accuracy, how many times a person was near a sign, it couldn't show whether or not people actually looked at the advertising and if they did, whether or not they were influenced by it. Nevertheless, Nielsen is planning to expand this pilot program and use it globally. The outdoor medium is one of the fastest-growing media other than the Internet, and it is considerably less "cluttered" than other outlets. Even as a $5.5 billion a year industry in the United States, however, outdoor advertising accounts for only about 2 percent of the estimated $276 billion spent on advertising in the United States in 2005.

What the Npod represents is an attempt by advertisers in all media to do a better job of finding out whether the money they spend on advertising is effective. It has been said by various pundits that "half of the money spent on advertising is wasted, but we don't know which half!" Nielsen hopes to change the odds in favor of advertisers. And they are not alone. A number of other companies and many advertising agencies are involved in trying to determine when advertising is effective. But even if only half of advertising is effective, corporations are not spending $276 billion dollars a year without having reason to believe that their expenditures are justified.

Sources: Stuart Elliott, "Did You See that Sign? Advertisers Will Have Their Answer at Last," *New York Times*, December 7, 2005, www.nytimes.com; Nielsen Outdoor, www.nielsenoutdoor.com/npod.html; "Outdoor Seeks Ratings Equality," *Adweek,* December 6, 2005, www.adweek.com/aw/national/article_display.jsp?vnu_content_id=1001615230.

lem with digital cable. As Gertner points out, the digital cable companies can obtain detailed information about what the people who use their services are watching whenever they are watching cable television. Since some 25 million Americans currently subscribe to cable services (and the figure is expected to double in five years), the digital cable companies have an enormous amount of information about their viewers' preferences. Federal laws, and problems caused by people using analog set-top boxes, have prevented digital cable companies from utilizing this information, but now, Gertner says, third-party companies are trying to figure out how to protect viewer privacy yet at the same time use the information they obtain on viewer preferences.

All of this effort to secure more accurate ratings is being made so that television networks and television stations and radio stations can provide their advertisers with detailed information about how many people, and what kind of people, are watching broadcast or television cable programs or listening to radio stations. Ultimately, the ratings companies hope to be able to provide advertising agencies with information about how specific advertising campaigns are working. Advertising executives commonly say that they know that advertising works, but they don't know how it works. It is hoped, Gertner writes, that this new, detailed information about preferences in media will help companies and advertising agencies learn how certain advertisements and commercials work their magic.

We cannot separate the media organizations that rely on Nielsen ratings, such as radio networks and television and cable networks, from the marketing organizations that are so intimately connected with them. Advertising agencies have to choose certain programs on which to broadcast the commercials they produce, for example. Broadcast media organizations and marketing organizations are, it is fair to say, different sides of the same coin.

In the discussion that follows, I will consider some of the different ways of breaking down the American market so as to reflect segments of audiences in America. I will also use other *typologies* (classification systems) to distinguish between different ways of classifying audiences in America. Let's start with demographics, which can be defined, broadly speaking, as the study of social, economic, and other characteristics of human populations.

DEMOGRAPHICS AND AUDIENCES

Marketers divide audiences into a number of different demographic categories based on distinguishing characteristics such as age, education, income, race, gender, ethnicity, marital status, and residence. Let me list some titles of books on marketing to different demographic groups. These titles appeared in a catalog I was sent a number of years ago, *Marketing Power: The Marketer's Reference Library.*

Wise Up to Teens
Everybody Eats: Supermarket Consumers in the 1990s
Kids as Customers
Marketing To and Through Kids
Mature Americans: Myths and Markets
Hispanic Market Handbook
Mindstyle of the Affluent
Marketing to Women
Target the U.S. Asian Market

These groups are all *target audiences* that marketers try to reach since members of these audiences presumably have special characteristics and purchasing patterns.

Here are the blurbs for two of the books just listed. The first is for *Wise Up to Teens: Insights into Marketing and Advertising to Teenagers* (1995), by Peter Zollo:

> Here at last is the expert analysis that will help you capture your share of the nearly $100 billion that teenagers spend. This book explains where teenagers get their money, how and why they spend it, and what they think about themselves and the world around them. It presents five rules that will make your advertising more appealing to teens. Learn about brands teens think are cool, words to use in advertising to teens, which media and promotions teens prefer, and how much influence teens have over what their parents buy. This is a fascinating look into the world of teens—a market whose income is almost all discretionary.

Zollo's book deals with an important demographic group for broadcasters and film studios: teenagers. A large percentage of the movies

Figure 4.2   Teenagers are a major market segment for the movie industry and advertisers.

that are made now have this segment of the American public (and teens in other countries as well) in mind.

The second book, *Target the U.S. Asian Market* (1993) by Angi Ma Wong, is described in similar terms:

> This book explains how to effectively reach the most affluent, well-educated, and fastest-growing consumer group in the nation—one that numbers 7.3 million, with an impressive $225 billion in purchasing power. These consumers are a fascinating blend of centuries-old traditions and contemporary American culture. This marketing guide shows you where to get information: the impact of education and culture on the decision-making process; how to avoid potentially offensive intercultural mistakes; how number, colors, names, and *feng shui* affect your business; basic etiquette and much more.

We see, then, that for marketers, the United States is a collection of different demographic groups, each of which can be seen as an audience, each of which has particular characteristics, and each of which can be reached, so that their decision making about purchasing products and services will be the way advertisers want this decision making to be—that is to say, in favor of the products and services the advertisers are selling.

As I suggested earlier, we all think of ourselves as discrete individuals, and in one sense, in terms of our personal identity—our genetic makeup, our personalities, the way we look and think—we are. For marketers, however, we don't exist as individuals but as people who can be classified as members of various market segments and groups that theoretically can be reached by those who know (or who have worked hard to figure out) how to "press the buttons" that motivate members of these groups. In this respect, you might consider why it is that you buy certain brands of clothes, watch certain television shows, go to certain films, use certain shampoos, and eat certain foods, which is a way of identifying the extent to which you have been, as advertisers would put it, "branded."

In addition to defining audiences by demographic factors like age, race, and religion, some marketers look at audiences in other ways, such as in terms of the magazines they read. According to one research company, Yankelovich and Partners, and based on a survey it conducted, the magazines people read are a more valuable indication of consumer behavior than demographic factors. People, the authors of this study argue, choose magazines primarily by their editorial content, and this editorial content is generally a reflection of the values, beliefs, and interests of the magazines' readers. The Yankelovich survey argues that people's behavior as consumers is coherent and logical, and their choice of magazines is an index, so to speak, to other choices they make as consumers.

It is useful for us to remember that the radio stations we choose to listen to and the television programs we choose to watch are also a form of consumer consumption, though we may not think of it as such. And as the Yankelovich survey suggests, there is a connection between the media we consume and our other kinds of consumption—namely, that of goods and services advertised in the media.

Marketers also look at groups in terms of their zip codes (that is, their specific locations in cities and states) and the **lifestyles** that researchers have associated with these zip codes. One marketing research company, Claritas, has broken American society down into more than sixty different groups, based primarily on their zip codes (see table 4.1). Claritas argues that "birds of a feather flock together," and suggests that people who live in areas identified by certain zip codes have many similarities in terms of their tastes in products.

For example, one segment of the people who live on the Upper East Side of New York City (the 10021 zip code) falls into Claritas's Money and Brains lifestyle group. This group has a median income

Table 4.1   One Market Research Company's Lifestyle Groupings

1. Upper Crust	34. White Picket Fences
2. Blue Blood Estates	35. Boomtown Singles
3. Movers and Shakers	36. Blue-Chip Blues
4. Young Digerati	37. Mayberry-ville
5. Country Squires	38. Simple Pleasures
6. Winner's Circle	39. Domestic Duos
7. Money and Brains	40. Close-In Couples
8. Executive Suites	41. Sunset City Blues
9. Big Fish, Small Pond	42. Red, White, and Blues
10. Second City Elite	43. Heartlanders
11. God's Country	44. New Beginnings
12. Brite Lites Li'l City	45. Blue Highways
13. Upward Bound	46. Old Glories
14. New Empty Nests	47. City Startups
15. Pools and Patios	48. Young and Rustic
16. Bohemian Mix	49. American Classics
17. Beltway Boomers	50. Kid Country, USA
18. Kids and Cul-de-Sacs	51. Shotguns and Pickups
19. Home Sweet Home	52. Suburban Pioneers
20. Fast-Track Families	53. Mobility Blues
21. Gray Power	54. Multi-Culti Mosaic
22. Young Influentials	55. Golden Ponds
23. Greenbelt Sports	56. Crossroads Villagers
24. Up-and-Comers	57. Old Milltowns
25. Country Casuals	58. Back Country Folks
26. The Cosmopolitans	59. Urban Elders
27. Middleburg Managers	60. Park Bench Seniors
28. Traditional Times	61. City Roots
29. American Dreams	62. Hometown Retired
30. Suburban Sprawl	63. Family Thrifts
31. Urban Achievers	64. Bedrock America
32. New Homesteaders	65. Big City Blues
33. Big Sky Families	66. Low-Rise Living

Source: Compiled from www.claritas.com

of $82,570, is highly educated, is aged forty-five and up, listens to news radio, drives expensive sports cars, reads business magazines, and supports the arts. What this means is that advertisers for companies that produce or sell sports cars, business magazines, and tickets to cultural events will look for the kinds of radio shows and television programs that people at the 10021 zip code most likely will listen to and watch. Our media, we must remember, are businesses. In order to survive they must sell access, via advertisements and commercials, to the audiences they attract.

The sixty-six consumer clusters listed in table 4.1 apply, I suggest, to media tastes as well as general consumer preferences. We can see this directly in the Money and Brains group, which has two media preferences: news radio and business magazines. A number of different groups or clusters may be found at a given zip code, I should add, so not everyone at a given zip code is like everyone else at that zip code.

PSYCHOGRAPHICS AND AUDIENCES

Marketers and media researchers also classify audiences in terms of **psychographics**—the psychological characteristics of audiences. Research organizations have come up with a number of interesting classification systems, or typologies, for various audience subgroupings based on whether members are "inner-directed" (they think for themselves) or "outer-directed" (they follow others), and categories like that. The psychographic-marketing theorists suggest that values and beliefs are more important than demographics. Consumer motivations, psychographic marketers tell us, are not always identical to **socioeconomic** status and other demographic factors.

This means that people watch television programs, for example, because these shows reflect and reinforce their values and beliefs (which they may never have articulated or brought to consciousness) and are congruent with their lifestyles. People who watch *American Idol* or *Survivor* have different values and beliefs than people who watch *The NewsHour with Jim Lehrer*. Thus, the psychographic theorists argue, the psychological profile of an audience can be more important than its age and income level. Let me offer, as an example, a well-known psychographic typology called VALS—which originally stood for Values and Lifestyles.

THE VALS TYPOLOGY

This **typology**, or classification system, was developed a number of years ago by a think tank in Menlo Park, California, SRI International, and it focuses on people's lifestyles rather than on demographic statistics about them. The VALS 1 typology is based on theories of psychological development, and it divides audiences into nine different and distinctive kinds of people. There have been changes to the VALS typology over the years, but I will focus on the original system here. Breaking the market down into nine categories of consumers is important, SRI suggests, because advertisers can then target their appeals to the specific values of each kind of consumer, or, for our purposes, each kind of audience member.

In his preface to *The Nine American Lifestyles: Who We Are and Where We're Going*, Arnold Mitchell, director of the SRI Values and Lifestyles Program, writes:

> By the term "values" we mean the entire constellation of a person's attitudes, beliefs, opinions, hopes, fears, prejudices, needs, desires and aspirations that, taken together, govern how one behaves. One's interior set of values—numerous, complex, overlapping, and contradictory though they are—finds holistic expression in a lifestyle. . . . We now have powerful evidence that the classification of an individual on the basis of a few dozen attitudes and demographics tells us a good deal about what to expect of that person in hundreds of other domains. (1983: vii)

So, if Mitchell is correct, knowing people's values enables marketers and broadcasters to know a great deal about them and their tastes and preferences in many different areas.

The description of the VALS 1 typology that follows uses material from articles by Niles Howard (*Dun's Review*, August 1981) and Laurie Itow (*San Francisco Sunday Examiner and Chronicle*, June 27, 1982). In her article, Itow explains the VALS system:

The system . . . draws on behavioral science to categorize consumers, not only by demographics such as age, sex, and the products they use, but according to their state of mind. Marie Spengler, VALS director at SRI, says the program is based on an analysis of cultural trends that can be used to develop products and target markets as well as match employees with jobs and make long-range business decisions such as where to build plants.

Categories of Consumers

VALS, Spengler says, captures "a deep, underlying sense of what motivates the consumer," using data from a thirty-question survey. Consumers are questioned about demographics, such as age and sex. But more importantly, they're also asked about their **attitudes** and **values**. This provides SRI with the data needed to create the various categories of consumers found in VALS. For our purposes in this discussion of audiences, we can think of each of these categories of consumers as a segment of the more general American audience. The nine categories of consumers in the VALS typology are as follows:

Need-Driven

These consumers are "money restricted" and have a hard time just affording their basic needs. They make up approximately 11 percent of the U.S. adult population, and are divided into two subcategories:
1. *Survivors*: old, poor, and out of the cultural mainstream
2. *Sustainers*: young, crafty, and on the edge of poverty but want to get ahead in the world

Outer-Directed

These consumers, who often live in Middle America, want others to feel positive about them. They make up close to two-thirds of the adult population in America, so if you're advertising something for mainstream Americans, the appeal should be to outer-directed types. There are three subcategories of outer-directed consumers:
3. *Belongers*: conservative and conventional in their tastes; nostalgic, sentimental, and not experimental
4. *Emulators*: upwardly mobile, status conscious, competitive, and distrustful of the establishment. They want to "make it big."

5. *Achievers*: the leaders of society who have been successful in the professional world, in business, and in government. They have status, comfort, fame, and materialistic values.

Inner-Directed

These consumers tend to purchase products to meet their inner needs rather than by thinking about the opinions of other people. The group made up around 28 percent of the adult population in 1990 and has, perhaps, grown considerably since then. There are three sub-categories of inner-directed consumers:

6. *I-Am-Me's*: young, narcissistic, exhibitionist, inventive, impulsive, and strongly individualistic

7. *Experientals*: an older version of the I-Am-Me's, and concerned with inner growth and naturalism

8. *Societally Conscious Individuals*: believers in simple living and smallness of scale, and supporters of causes like environmentalism, consumerism (not the same thing as consumption), and conservation

Integrateds

9. *Integrateds*: the last subcategory, characterized by psychological maturity, tolerance, assuredness, and a self-actualizing philosophy. These people tend to ignore advertising, and relatively few advertisements are made to appeal to them. Integrateds make up only around 2 percent of the adult American population, but they are very influential and are disproportionately found among corporate and national leaders. While integrateds may not be as susceptible to advertising as other groups, their taste in lifestyle products may be highly influential and they may function as what might be described as "taste opinion leaders."

This typology, which focuses on kinds of consumers, can also be thought of as listing microaudiences: segments of a larger audience that are different from one another based on their values and beliefs and the way these values and beliefs are expressed not only in their consumption of products and services but also, I would suggest, in their consumption of media. We can think of the programs the media carry as products to be consumed by segments of the American public (or other publics and audiences in other countries in certain cases). As you reread the above list of VALS categories, you might want to consider which one of them applies to you, your friends, your parents, and other people you know.

POLITICAL CULTURES AND LIFESTYLES AS AUDIENCES

The late Aaron Wildavsky, an extremely influential political scientist who taught at the University of California for many years, developed a way of breaking down democratic societies into four discrete **political cultures**. In an unpublished paper, "Conditions for a Pluralist Democracy or Cultural Pluralism Means More Than One Political Culture in a Country," Wildavsky explained how he derived his political culture:

What matters to people is how they should live with other people. The great questions of social life are "Who am I?" (To what kind of a group do I belong) and "What should I do?" (Are there many or few prescriptions I am expected to obey?). Groups are strong or weak according to whether they have boundaries separating them from others. Decisions are taken either for the group as a whole (strong boundaries) or for individuals or families (weak boundaries). Prescriptions are few or many indicating the individual internalizes a large or a small number of behavioral norms to which he or she is bound. By combining boundaries with prescriptions . . . the most general answers to the questions of social life can be combined to form four different political cultures. (1982: 7)

There are, then, two basic questions: *Who am I?* (Does the group I belong to have strong or weak boundaries?), and *What should I do?* (Does the group I belong to have few or many prescriptions or rules?). These two questions lead to four political cultures, based on whether a group's boundaries are strong or weak and whether its rules, or prescriptions, are few or many. The four political cultures are, Wildavsky suggested:

fatalists:	prescriptions numerous, group boundaries weak
individualists:	prescriptions few, group boundaries weak
elitists:	prescriptions numerous, groups boundaries strong
egalitarians:	prescriptions few, group boundaries strong

Fatalists think they are victims of bad luck, and are apolitical; individualists stress the importance of limited government, which they believe should do little more than protect private property, and they believe in free competition; elitists believe that stratification in society is necessary, but they also have a sense of obligation toward those below them, unlike the individualists; egalitarians emphasize that everyone (especially the downtrodden fatalists) has certain needs that must be taken care of, and they tend to oppose mainstream political thought in America.

According to Wildavsky, you need all four groups for democracy to flourish in a country, and the four groups need one another. He saw the individualists and elitists as being the dominant, or core, groups in America and the egalitarians as the loyal opposition. People in America may not recognize that they belong to one of these political cultures, or may not be able to articulate the beliefs of their given political culture, but their membership in one of these political cultures (and there can be no more than four) influences their decision making. The matter is further complicated by the fact that people sometimes move from one group to another, except for the fatalists, who are stuck down at the bottom of the totem pole and seldom have the chance to rise.

If you think about it, each of these four political cultures also represents a kind of audience for books, radio shows, television programs, films, and other media. When I taught courses on the media and **popular culture**, I used to play a learning game with my students in which we looked at these groups as audiences. One premise we used was that people seek reinforcement in the media for their basic beliefs and values and wish to avoid **cognitive dissonance**. Thus people will watch television programs that affirm and support the values they believe (and provide reinforcement) and avoid ones that attack their values and beliefs (and generate cognitive dissonance). Table 4.2, adapted from one of our game-playing sessions, offers an example of the four political cultures as audiences.

From this table, I think you can see how it might be that members of different political cultures, with different core values and beliefs, might choose to read certain books, watch certain films, and decide who to vote for in elections. These four audiences may not always articulate their beliefs to themselves or others and may not be

Table 4.2   Political Cultures and Representative Popular Texts

TEXT	ELITIST	INDIVIDUALIST	EGALITARIAN	FATALIST
Books	The Prince	Looking Out for Number One	I'm Okay, You're Okay	1984
Films	Top Gun	Color of Money	Woodstock	Rambo
TV Shows	News Hour	Survivor	American Idol	Smack Down Wrestling
Songs	God Save the Queen	I Did It My Way	We Are the World	Anarchy in the UK
Sports	Polo	Tennis	Frisbee	Roller Derby
Games	Chess	Monopoly	New Games	Russian Roulette

conscious of what motivates them, but it can be seen that there is a logic, in many cases, to the choices members of audiences make as far as consuming media is concerned. It seems rather obvious that people who watch *American Idol* or *CSI: Crime Scene Investigation* are probably quite different from those who watch *Nova* or *Nature*.

What complicates matters is that in some cases, an individual who is a member of one political culture (for example, individualists) may be thinking of moving to another one (for example, elitists) which means that person's media choices could be based on the change that person is contemplating making in political cultures rather than reinforced by the political culture to which he or she belongs.

Wildavsky made use of the theories of a British social anthropologist, Mary Douglas, with whom he collaborated on a number of projects. Douglas developed what is known as grid/group theory. She also wrote an article, "In Defence of Shopping," in which she asserted that what Wildavsky described as political cultures were what she called "lifestyles," and these four (and only four exist in any society) lifestyles shaped our preferences. As Douglas put it, "Cultural alignment is the strongest predictor of preferences in a wide variety of fields" (1997: 23)—including, I would suggest, media preferences.

ACTIVE AUDIENCES: DECODING MASS-MEDIATED TEXTS

In recent years we have begun to recognize that members of audiences are more active than we thought they were. When the **hypodermic needle theory** of the media was popular and we believed that everyone got exactly the same message from a mass-mediated text, the role of members of an audience (from one individual watching a television show to huge numbers of people watching the same show) was not considered important.

Now, however, the hypodermic theory has been abandoned and been replaced by what is known as **reader response theory**, or **reception theory**, which is the opposite of the hypodermic theory. Wolfgang Iser, one of the leading advocates of reader response theory, explains his thinking:

The text as such offers different "schematized views" through which the subject matter of the work can come to light, but the actual bringing of light is an action of *Konkretisation*. If this is so, then the literary work has two poles, which we might call the artistic and the aesthetic: the artistic refers to the text created by the author, and the aesthetic to the realization accomplished by the reader. From this polarity it follows that the literary work cannot be completely identical with the text, or with the realization of the text, but in fact must lie halfway between the two. The work is more than the text, for the text only takes life when it is realized and furthermore the realization is by no means independent of the individual disposition of the reader—though this in turn is acted upon by the different patterns of the text. (1988: 212)

Iser is talking about literary works, but we can extend the notion of a literary work to cover any text carried by the mass media. Everyone who watches a mass-mediated text interprets it on the basis of his or her temperament, education, background, and knowledge-base.

For example, when we watch a show on television, we bring to the process of watching that show our culturally shaped knowledge-base that enables us to make sense of what we are watching. This involves applying the aesthetic codes that we acquired as we grew up watching television, our knowledge of rules of behavior, our understanding of spoken language and body language, and any number of other things. That is, we are always decoding the texts we see on television.

In the case of a novel, according to Iser, that novel without its reader is inert; it takes a reader to bring a novel to life, and readers play an important part in interpreting novels and other kinds of mass-mediated texts. At the very least, in the case of films and television shows, audiences have to interpret visual phenomena, sound effects, and dialogue.

Iser's approach may seem a bit extreme, but it serves to point out the role audiences play in the scheme of things. As audiences, we are not, at the very least, passive receivers of texts. We have to learn how to "read" television programs and films and all kinds of other texts in ways analogous to the way we read books. And our place in the social structure, as British media scholar Graeme Burton points out, also affects the way we read texts. All of these complications involved in interpreting texts suggest that the question we must ask when dealing with a film or television program or any other text is not whether our interpretation is right or wrong but whether it is interesting and comprehensive—whether it reveals important matters found in the text and explains the power the text has over audiences.

In other words, our reading of texts is based on our experiences in our societies and on the "grid" that growing up in a given culture and time period imposes on our minds. This helps explain why works of art are so useful in understanding the society and culture in which they are produced—for that grid, or schema, is also, to varying degrees, in the mind of the creator of a given text. We can say that it doesn't make sense to argue whether the interpretation of a text is correct or incorrect, and that taste is not important, for tastes vary, and one might say that in a postmodern world, taste is irrelevant. You may or may not have liked *King Kong* or *Date Movie*, but that's not important. What is important is the degree to which your interpretation of those movies explains their texts and relates them to social, psychological, and cultural concerns, thus providing a stimulating analysis.

ACTIVE AUDIENCES: USES AND GRATIFICATIONS

This notion, that there is often a logic to the choices people make in selecting one or another television program, for example, leads to my next topic: the uses we make of the television shows and the films we watch and the gratifications that these television shows and films (and by extension all kinds of other texts in other media) provide. The **uses and gratifications** approach to audiences contrasts with the most commonly used approach, which focuses on the media's effects on individuals, groups of people, and society in general. There are some who argue that the study of uses and gratifications is dated, but it seems to me that it is important that we think about how people use mass-mediated texts and, conversely, how these texts use people.

Figure 4.3   Keeping informed about world events is one reason people use media such as newspapers and books.

Let me offer here a list of some of the more important uses and gratifications of the media. This list was compiled from various sources and studies. I will separate uses from gratifications, and will assume that *uses* concerns matters essentially involving the relation of individuals to society, and that *gratifications* refers primarily to psychological matters, though my separation of the two is, admittedly, somewhat arbitrary.

Uses

1. to share experiences with others in some group or community
2. to find models to imitate
3. to help gain an identity and a personal style
4. to obtain information about the world
5. to affirm and support basic values
6. to see order imposed upon the world

Gratifications

1. to see authority figures deflated or exalted
2. to experience beautiful things

3. to identify with the divine
4. to find diversions and distractions
5. to empathize with others
6. to experience strong emotions in a guilt-free and controlled situation
7. to reinforce a belief in the ultimate triumph of justice
8. to reinforce a belief in romantic love
9. to reinforce a belief in the magical, the marvelous, and the miraculous
10. to see others make mistakes (and feel satisfaction in not having made those mistakes oneself)
11. to participate in history and events of historical significance in a vicarious manner
12. to be purged of unpleasant feelings and emotions (catharsis)
13. to obtain outlets for sexual drives in a guilt-free manner
14. to explore taboo subjects with impunity and with no risk
15. to experience the ugly and the grotesque
16. to affirm moral, spiritual, and cultural values
17. to see villains in action

We must recognize that a given text might provide a number of different uses and gratifications and that different people will obtain different gratifications and make different uses of events in a given text. For example, viewers of talk shows might get information about how to deal with problems they face, might gain information about topics of interest, or might see models they wish to imitate (in terms of the guests on a show and their clothes, the way they talk, their "style," and so on).

Our knowledge of these uses and gratifications comes, in large measure, from surveys in which social scientists have asked people (who, for our purposes, can be seen as members of audiences) questions about why they watch soap operas or what they get from listening to certain kinds of music. One problem with uses and gratifications is that it is difficult for researchers to determine, in an objective manner, which uses and gratifications are generated by specific events in a given text, and it is also difficult to quantify the results of this kind of research. Nevertheless, it should be obvious that audiences are attracted to various specific mass–mediated texts because there is some payoff in the texts for them, and these payoffs are the uses these texts can be put to and the gratifications they provide. This explains why huge numbers of people watched the final episodes of *Frasier* and *Everybody Loves Raymond*, and why the media were so obsessed with popstar Michael Jackson's trial in 2005.

USES AND GRATIFICATIONS, AND GENRES

The texts we watch can also be classified according to their genres. A genre is a kind of show, such as a sitcom, a news broadcast, a talk show, and so on. I would suggest that genres provide for certain gratifications and are used in various ways by media consumers. Table 4.3 shows some of these uses and gratifications according to genre.

Texts and the genres we use to classify them have many different

Table 4.3   Media Uses and Gratifications by Genre

Uses and Gratifications	Genre
to satisfy curiosity and be informed	documentary, news show, talk show, quiz show
to be amused	situation comedy, comedy show
to identify with the deity and the divine	religious show
to reinforce belief in justice	cop show, law show
to reinforce belief in romantic love	romance novel, soap opera
to participate vicariously in history	media event, sports show
to see villains in action	cop show, action-adventure show
to obtain outlets for sexual drives in a guilt-free context	pornography, fashion show, commercials (some), soap opera
to experience the ugly	horror show
to find models to imitate	talk show, action-adventure show, award show, sports show, commercials (some)
to experience the beautiful	travel show, art show, cultural shows (symphony concert, opera, ballet, etc.)

effects on people, which is a matter of great interest to media researchers, and this will be the subject of the next chapter. And people use these texts in a number of different ways as well.

In her book *Reading the Romance*, which is based upon research on readers of romance novels, Janice Radway offers some insights into the way individuals and groups of readers can resist the power of those who control the media. As Radway explains:

> If we can learn, then, to look at the ways in which various groups appropriate and use the mass-produced art of our culture, I suspect we may well begin to understand that although the ideological power of contemporary cultural forms is enormous, indeed sometimes even frightening, that power is not yet all-pervasive, totally vigilant, or complete. Interstices still exist with the social fabric where opposition is carried on by people who are not satisfied by their place within it or by the restricted material and emotional rewards that accompany it. (1991: 222)

We can conclude then that people use the media and the media use—or attempt to use, influence, or manipulate—people, and the relationship between users or consumers of the media and producers of the media remains a complex one.

The entire study of mass communication is based on the premise that the media have significant effects, yet there is little agreement on the nature and extent of these assumed effects. This uncertainty is the more surprising since everyday experience provides countless, if minor, examples of influence. We dress for the weather as forecast, buy something because of an advertisement, go to a film mentioned in a newspaper, react in countless ways to media news, to films, to music on the radio, and so on. There are many reported cases of negative media publicity concerning, for instance, food contamination or adulteration, leading to significant changes in food consumption behaviour. Our minds are full of media-derived information and impressions. We live in a world saturated by media sounds and images, where politics, government and business operate on the assumption that we know what is going on in the wider world. Few of us cannot think of some personal instance of gaining significant information or of forming an opinion because of the media. (1994: 327)

—Denis McQuail, *Mass Communication Theory:*
An Introduction

5

AUDIENCES 2: EFFECTS

The media affect us on many levels: they give us ideas, they help shape our opinions and attitudes, they affect our emotions, they affect us physiologically, and they affect our behavior, among other things. But are these effects significant and are they long lasting? Are the media doing things to us that may be harmful? Are the media doing anything socially constructive? Let me begin this chapter on media effects with a question that is at the heart of many of the criticisms of the mass media and mass culture.

IS MASS CULTURE MAKING US ALL MORONS?

Some media theorists argue that the mass media and popular culture—sometimes combined into "mass-mediated culture"—*must* destroy the elite arts (by which I mean things like serious novels, poetry, classical music, and plays) since Gresham's law suggests that junk art always drives out good art. But this doesn't appear to have come true. Let me cite some statistics about the book publishing industry for the year 2003 taken from www.bookwire.com. I've not offered data for certain categories of books, such as those on medicine, home economics, and music.

Category	Number of Books Published (rounded off)
Arts	6,500
Biography	8,250
Business	5,300
Education	6,150
Fiction	17,000
History	10,400
Juveniles	16,200
Literature	4,700
Philosophy	7,100
Poetry, Drama	4,200
Religion	10,000
Science	9,700
Sociology, Economics	18,000
Technology	8,800
Travel	2,800

In 2003 in the United States 164,000 books were published, which comes to approximately 450 books each day. Each day, 49 different sociology and economics titles, 46 fiction titles, 28 science titles, and 19 philosophy titles were published. In 2003 the book publishing industry was a $23.7 billion industry, larger than the film industry and the video game industry combined.

A large number of these books were, no doubt, of poor quality: formulaic romances, trashy novels, and so on, but we must remember that a large percentage of books published in the so-called elite art forms—serious novels, poems, plays—are also second- or third-rate works. In the final analysis, it is the skills and abilities of the writers and artists, not the art forms they use, that counts. A great writer like Dashiell Hammett can take a low-brow genre like the hard-boiled detective novel and turn out a masterpiece like *The Maltese Falcon*.

It is reasonable to argue that popular taste is not, as a rule, elevated, and that has been the case for centuries. But this does not mean that a considerable amount of great art is not produced—for a relatively small percentage of the population, generally speaking—and it is unlikely that popular culture is driving out good art and rapidly moronizing us all . . . or even most of us.

JOHNNY Q. PUBLIC AND EMILY GREATGAL MAKE DINNER

In this vignette, we find Johnny and Emily multitasking like so many media users in America and other societies at well.

> Johnny and Emily are making dinner at her apartment before watching *CSI: Crime Scene Investigation*. They are in the kitchen, but the television set, in the living room, is turned on. Emily is opening a bag of packaged lettuce and making a salad of lettuce, tomatoes, cucumbers, and avocados. Johnny is grilling hamburgers on a George Foreman electric grill. They are both listening to the program on the television and occasionally walking into the living room to glance at it. For dinner they have the salad Emily made, grilled hamburgers on buns, and the frozen french fries that Johnny zapped in the microwave. For dessert they have cookie-dough ice cream. After dinner they go into the living room to watch *CSI*.

Johnny and Emily are like the millions of other people who do other things while they are watching television. The fact is that, generally speaking, people do not sit hour after hour with their eyes glued to the television set, but do a number of different things while their sets are on. Life goes on in front of the television set—people pet their dogs, leave and go to the bathroom, chat with one another, go to the kitchen for snacks, read newspapers and magazines, and so on. So we have to make a distinction between watching television and simply having a television set on; not everyone watches television with undivided attention.

We must keep this in mind when we read about the number of hours people watch television and the effect that television has on people. Television is part of our lives, but relatively small numbers of us give it all our attention. The "boob tube" is blaring away, but Johnny and Emily are doing a number of things at the same time. Like many people, they are just using television programs as a kind of background to their activities.

The preceding chapter dealt with different ways of classifying audiences, with some of the ways that members of audiences use the media, and with the gratifications they obtain from them. Now let's

take a different approach and consider the effects that the media *may* have on members of their audiences. Denis McQuail, in the quote at the beginning of this chapter, makes an important point: we all believe that the media have effects—or, more precisely from my point of view, that the texts carried by the media (and in part shaped by them) have effects. But we have a very hard time proving, to the satisfaction of scholarly researchers, that these mass-mediated texts have long-term and important effects.

THE CONCEPT OF MEDIA EFFECTS
NEEDS QUALIFICATION

I think it is somewhat of a simplification to talk about media effects when dealing with television since, as I have pointed out, we don't watch television per se but specific texts: programs carried by television (and other means such as cable and satellite). And the same, of course, applies to all the media. The reason we talk about media effects the way we do is because we're looking for ways of dealing with large aggregates of people and texts, and so we simplify things and talk, for example, about the amount of violence on television (generally, on an hourly basis) or the way television portrays women (in commercials, or in narratives and other genres).

This is perfectly understandable, but we should always remember that texts play an important role in providing a context for and characterizing events that take place in them—as the example of saying "Pass the hypodermic needle" in a dark alley or in a hospital demonstrates. I will focus my attention on television here since it is the medium with which we spend the most time and is the most powerful of our daily media experiences. But what I say about television can be applied to movies, music videos, video games, and other media.

Many of the texts we see on television are narratives of one sort or another—that is, they tell a story and therefore have some kind of a beginning, some kind of conflict to be worked out or problem to be solved, and some kind of a resolution. This is important because narratives have the power to move us and to affect us in profound ways, emotionally and intellectually. I alluded to this in my discussion of the vicious cycles in television (see chapter 1). We should also keep in mind the fact that genres not commonly seen as narratives—such as commercials (which are often microdramas), sports programs, talk shows, and game shows—often have powerful narrative and dramatic components to them. Even news shows can be seen as being composed of little narratives that form a larger narrative.

With all these qualifications and caveats in mind, let me offer some of the most commonly held criticisms of the mass media and the popular culture texts they carry.

CRITICISMS OF THE MASS MEDIA AND THEIR TEXTS

I offer here a number of common criticisms of our mass-mediated texts, sometimes offered as attacks on the mass media in general and at other times as attacks on television, the medium everyone loves to hate. All through history, members of various social, intellectual, and aesthetic elites have attacked the taste of the common people by making the kind of arguments I offer below.

You may find some of the attacks quite convincing, and others you might consider rather extreme. The important thing is to be aware of what many critics consider to be the numerous negative effects that come from spending the amount of time we do with the media, in general, and television in particular. I will focus my attention on television because the average viewer in the United States watches around four hours each day, though, as I mentioned earlier, the arguments I make here about television (taken from a variety of sources) can also be made about other media.

Viewers' Critical Faculties Overwhelmed

The argument here is that television overwhelms us. Due to the amount of television to which we are exposed as well as the power of this medium, we eventually and inevitably abandon our critical faculties and our capacity for clear thinking and rational decision making. If we don't completely abandon it, our capacity to think clearly is certainly greatly diminished. The constant bombardment of our sensorium by rapidly moving images and by music and sound effects eventually makes it very difficult for us to make rational decisions about anything. In this respect, the subtitle of Todd Gitlin's book on media is most interesting: *Media Unlimited: How the Torrent of Images and Sound Overwhelms Our Lives*. The metaphor that informs this title suggests that media is a wildly charging river that carries everyone along with it.

Viewers Desensitized to Violence

As a result of all the violence to which we as viewers of television are exposed, we become desensitized to violence's real nature, leading to a lack of concern about violence and, perhaps, a tendency by some of us to rely on violence in our own lives to solve problems. This desensitization to violence may also have an impact on our attitudes toward sexuality, since it can be argued that there is often a psychosexual dimension to violence.

Picture of Reality Distorted

Television doesn't show the world the way it really is, but rather offers a highly distorted picture of it. The world shown on television

Figure 5.1   How "real" are reality TV shows like *Survivor*? Do you think media can give us a false sense of reality? Why or why not?

is full of violence and sexual innuendo; we watch countless killings and murders on television, while most of us will never see anyone killed or murdered in real life. The new, so-called reality programs such as *Survivor* and *The Real World* are, in a sense, frauds—they are highly edited, and the people in them are not a cross section of the kinds of people we deal with in our everyday lives.

Many of the people we see on television are unusual. For example, the female models in TV commercials tend to be tall and exceedingly slim, and the men often are very handsome. Ethnic minorities, people with disabilities, people of color, children, the elderly, and women are all underrepresented. We don't get a representative sampling of American society on television by any means. The reality we find on television, we must remember, is always a mediated, highly edited, distorted image of reality. As Todd Gitlin points out in *Media Unlimited*, even the news is a distorted picture of life. He writes:

> The news is not in any simple way a "mirror" on the world; it is a conduit for ideas and symbols, an industrial product that promotes

packages of ideas and ideologies, and serves, consequently, as social ballast, though at times also a harbinger of social change. The news is a cognitive warp. The world is this way; the media make it appear that way. (2001: 2)

Gitlin's point is that the news media don't mirror the world; instead, they project a world as interpreted by the editors and others who control the images we are allowed to see and the words we are allowed to hear on their news shows.

Serious Creative Artists Diverted

Because television pays such incredible salaries, it seduces many serious writers, directors, and performers into working for it, diverting them from the theater and other elite art forms and depriving the audiences for this kind of art of their contributions. (This is particularly true of the film industry, which once used to hire stables of great writers to crank out film scripts.) The financial attractions of the media are so great that it is difficult for serious artists to resist them, which means that fewer serious dramatic and literary works are created.

Escapism

Television provides essentially escapist fare: silly situation comedies, violence-ridden action-adventure shows, and similar kinds of material with little redeeming social or aesthetic value. Because these shows don't deal with serious issues and are so superficial, people can consume enormous quantities of this material. Even news shows have become dominated by the need to entertain. It has been pointed out by media critics that nowadays there are relatively few television documentaries dealing with serious issues, compared to twenty or thirty years ago.

False Consciousness Created

The stories shown on television tend to suggest that the so-called American Dream is alive and well and that anyone with enough determination and willpower will, inevitably, succeed. Most of the characters in television narratives tend to be middle-class or affluent people. This implies that we live in a society that is classless because it is portrayed, for all practical purposes, as exclusively middle-class. Minorities, ethnic groups, and racial and other groups tend to be ignored, and the terrible difficulties that people in the working class face are seldom dealt with. Some critics of television argue that it can be seen as a subtle kind of brainwashing, meant to convince people to accept the status quo and to assume that nothing can be changed.

Formulaic Nature

In order to enable audiences to understand quickly what is going on in a narrative, television script writers use conventional, stereotypical characters and story lines. That is, television is very formulaic, and avoids material that might be challenging because what is original and inventive requires a certain amount of effort on the part of viewers. Because watching television and films requires so little intellectual effort, many children and adolescents find it difficult to put in the effort required to read a book.

Fragmentation

The way a typical hour of television broadcasting is broken up, with numerous commercials and station promotions, leads to a sense of life in general as fragmented and disorderly. In addition, the fact that one often sees a large number of commercials for different products, one after another, often exacerbates the problem. Finally, in the course of an evening's viewing, one can see any number of different kinds of programs: news shows, sitcoms, horror shows, and action-adventure shows, which also reinforces a sense of life as fragmentary, cluttered, and lacking coherence. Postmodern theorists argue that the pastiche, or hodgepodge (that is, a mixture of different styles and genres), is the dominant metaphor for understanding contemporary American culture, so it might be that our mass media both reflect and reinforce a postmodern sensibility.

Todd Gitlin deals with this matter of fragmentation in *Media Unlimited*. Discussing the research of Professor Berndt Ostendorf of the University of Munich, Gitlin writes about how formulaic story-telling and stereotypical characters in television shows fit together:

> To make spaces for commercial breaks, and keep viewers' attention, production companies divided programs into short units—*acts*, producers still call them, hanging on to the theatrical precedent, even if they are but a few minutes long. Viewers, disposed to be fidgety, came to expect these breaks. Now, Ostendorf writes, the plot, with its traditional unities of time, place, and action, "is chopped up into short sequential bursts, each with their own simulacrum of a microplot. . . . The goal is to create an unending series of reversals, moments of ecstasy and anticipation, which then may be usurped by the commercial." Interruption was thus built into the program. Not surprisingly, in the era of television, the term *attention span* began to be heard—and worried about. (2001: 109–10)

So television's very nature more or less requires that television shows be designed to have many interruptions for commercials, and the impact of this process has been a decrease in the attention spans of many of us.

Homogenization

The other side of the psychological fragmentation argument is that television, film, and American popular culture in general are spreading American culture all over the world (especially in Third World countries). This media imperialism **hypothesis** (sometimes known as "Coca-Colonization") leads, it is held, to a destruction of weaker native cultures and the dominance of American and Western culture, and ultimately to a kind of global homogenization in which all cultures are more or less alike: watching American films, eating McDonald's hamburgers, drinking Starbucks espressos, and abandoning their native traditions and culture. In addition, some critics argue that American popular culture also spreads a Western capitalist ideology, which is hidden in its texts and is not obvious to those who consume them. (Some scholars, I should point out, do not accept the media imperialism hypothesis.)

Hyperactivity

As a result of the rapid bombardment of images and the kind of instant gratification that television provides, there is reason to suspect that television viewing contributes to hyperactive behavior in many children. Children who watch television are used to being endlessly amused and entertained and do not develop the ability to be quiet in classrooms and to concentrate on their studies. The incredible rise in the number of children (and now adults) being diagnosed with attention deficit disorder (ADD) or attention deficit hyperactivity disorder (ADHD) may be connected to high levels of television viewing and media exposure.

Irresponsibility

The argument that the people who decide what to show on television are irresponsible and more interested in profit than in the well-being of their audiences raises an ethical concern. The airwaves are owned by the public, and in principle, television and radio should further the public's well-being. Instead, in a mad quest for ratings, television producers broadcast a great deal of junk that has wide appeal but may be harmful. For example, many beer commercials are directed toward adolescent sensibilities and are shown on programs that adolescents tend to watch. This, critics assert, has led to a serious drinking problem in many young people, large percentages of whom have been found to be binge drinkers.

Isolation

Although television creates a huge audience of viewers, almost all of the people viewing television programs at any time are isolated into little family groups. Statistics reveal that a large percentage of school-age children have their own television sets in their rooms, which means that even the family group is no longer a television-viewing audience because now children watch television shows in their own rooms. This argument ultimately suggests that television leads to increased alienation, and results in people who cut themselves off from others—even, sometimes, those in their own families.

Babies and the Media: A Fool's Wager

Many parents expose their young children, even when they are babies, to television and other media—assuming that the media will not affect them in any way. It's not unusual for harried parents to let very young children watch television, for example, and there are even some programs that have been created for babies. I was astounded when one of my students told me she regularly had her six-month-old baby watch television. My student and all those who allow young babies to watch television are not aware that television can be, and quite likely is, detrimental to their well-being. A Harvard Medical School psychologist, Susan Linn, has said, "There is no evidence that media is beneficial for babies and [we] are starting to find evidence that it may be harmful. Until we know for sure, we shouldn't risk putting them in front of the television."

Television may overstimulate babies, it may scare them, and in some cases it may even traumatize them. And young children may not realize that comic violence, which is prevalent in children's television shows, is still a form of violence. Longitudinal studies have shown that the more a child is exposed to violence, the more likely it is that he or she will act in a violent manner at some time.

There is good reason to suggest, then, that parents should prevent babies from watching television and limit their exposure to all media. Statistics show that American children consume an enormous amount of media in a typical week. If Susan Linn is correct, and there is good reason to believe she is, we shouldn't put our babies at risk—and when they are older we should limit the amount of television we allow them to watch.

Sources: Don Oldenburg, "Experts Rip 'Sesame' TV Aimed at Tiniest Tots," *Washington Post*, March 21, 2006, C01, www.washingtonpost.com; "Can You Tell Me How to Crawl to Sesame Street?" *USA Today*, April 4, 2006, 7D.

Lowest Common Denominator

One of the most commonly made attacks on television (and the mass media in general) is that it is aimed at the lowest common denominator. This means that TV waters things down, oversimplifies things, and avoids important issues in an effort to please as many people as it can. In theory, the "lower" you go, the more people you'll attract, which implies that there are forces at work to generate programs that are best described as moronic—such as the infamous celebrity boxing match between Tonya Harding and Paula Jones in March 2002. This show received very high ratings, supporting the Gresham's Law notion of some critics that bad programming drives out good programming.

Manipulation

Television, it is asserted, manipulates its viewers by using humor, sexuality, and anything else it can to attract audiences and, through commercials, to get people to purchase the products and services it advertises. In addition, because television only shows certain perspectives of news events, it manipulates public opinion. People say seeing is believing without thinking that when they watch television, someone else always determines what they see and that what they see may be taken out of context, or in scholarly jargon, *decontextualized*.

Narcotic

There is reason to believe that television functions like a narcotic, judging from the number of people who become psychologically dependent on it and who sometimes even describe themselves as "hooked" on TV. They have become, in other words, television addicts. Like many addicts, these people lack an awareness of their addiction, seeing themselves instead as people who like television but can live without it. Some viewers even develop parasocial relationships with certain characters they watch on television, and feel that they actually know these characters and the performers who play them. These viewers have a need to be with these characters on their favorite shows, which can be seen as a pathetic substitute for forming real relationships with real people.

Limited Topics

Television is obsessed with a relatively narrow range of topics—violence, sexuality, consumption, youth, celebrity, and a few others—if we judge from the vast number of topics relative to the human condition that it could deal with. Television executives argue, "We only give people what they want," neglecting the fact that audiences can only select from what is available on television, satellite, or cable on a specific night. This narrowness of focus in television leads, ultimately, to a diminished sense of possibility in viewers and a constricted notion of what it means to be a human being. Television, it could be said, doesn't give people what they want, but teaches them to want what they get.

Passivity Induced

Watching television is, generally speaking, a passive experience: one sits and watches. The only physical activity involved might be pressing a button, or eating. The television-viewing experience therefore is typically punctuated by trips to the bathroom and the refrigerator. As a result of all the television viewing that young people do, many of them are growing obese in alarming numbers. And obesity is now an epidemic in America. Thus, television watching has certain physiological as well as psychological effects on the members of audiences. And these physiological changes have social implications, because obese people tend to suffer more frequently from medical problems such as heart disease and diabetes, which leads to higher medical costs for everyone. In some cases we find an interesting contrast: passivity while watching television, and hyperactivity when not watching television.

Privatism

The argument that television leads to privatism claims that viewers of television learn to focus on their own lives and personal concerns and in general to neglect social matters and the public realm. We become distracted from serious matters—involving politics, for example, or decisions about social issues—and focus instead on our own concerns, in particular, on our desires for consumer products and services. Thus television viewing leads to materialism. Researchers have found, for example, that many young people know very little about history, in many cases, but know everything about pop-culture celebrities and also have incredible "product knowledge" (which they've learned from advertising). This privatism on the part of the general public means that small groups that are politically motivated and well-organized can sometimes exercise inordinate power over our social and political agendas. Large numbers of people do not vote in elections because they are all wrapped up in themselves, so the argument goes, and can't be bothered with anything else, even though the political decisions made by their elected officials affect their lives in profound ways.

Sentimentalism

Television dramas are often criticized for being excessively sentimental, that is, for generally having happy endings, or for calling up more emotion than is necessary in the various kinds of narratives they present. Television, it is argued, tends to neglect the tragic dimensions of human life, washing everything over with a veneer of optimism and seeing everything through rose-colored glasses.

"Sexploitation"

The roles women are given in television dramas and the way they are portrayed in television commercials and other texts exploit

---

What We Know

According to a recent survey of America's most elite universities, nearly all college seniors could identify Beavis and Butt-Head but 40% could not place the Civil War in the right half-century. A national history test of high-school seniors found a majority of them identifying Germany, Italy, or Japan as a U.S. ally in World War II. Still another survey of Americans at large found a third attributing the line "from each according to his ability, to each according to his needs" to the Constitution rather than Karl Marx.

Source: Wall Street Journal, Feb. 4, 2003, W15, www.opinionjournal.com/taste/?id = 110003070.

women's sexuality and use them to create sexual excitement and sell products. Even though feminists have spent many years attacking the roles women are given in narratives and the way television exploits female sexuality, there has been little improvement. Generally speaking, women are not portrayed in realistic ways; the focus is on their bodies and their sexuality and not on their minds, characters, or personalities.

It might be that there is so much vicarious sexuality available on television that the interest of viewers in real sexual activity becomes diminished, or that the erotic fantasies generated by television dominates their thinking, leading to negative feelings toward real-world partners.

Setting Trends

Interestingly enough, large numbers of Americans pride themselves on their individuality and uniqueness, and on "doing their own thing," yet television has an incredible power to create trends, fads, and crazes—usually involving matters like clothing styles, hair styles, and the use of new slang terms. It has been argued, perhaps carrying things to extremes, that we are a nation of sheep. Each of us has the illusion that we are different from others—even though we may look like everyone else and talk like everyone else—in our culture in general or in some subculture to which we belong. We are caught in a contradiction: we want to be ourselves, but we also aspire to be "trendy" or "hip."

Violence as a Solution

It has been suggested that many mass-mediated narratives use violence as an easy solution to dramatic problems. Much of what we know about the world is based on what is called "incidental learning," which is learning that we pick up outside the class room, and it may be that what many people learn from these mass-mediated dramas, without being conscious of what they are learning, is that violence is the best way to deal with certain difficulties. Thus, all of a sudden so it seems, we read about all kinds of "rages" that have recently been identified, such as road rage and air rage.

There is now evidence to suggest that media organizations are cutting down somewhat on the amount of violence and "sexploitation" in the texts they carry. A survey taken in 2002 shows a decrease in the amount of violence and sexuality in television—perhaps in response to all the negative publicity media organizations have received about violence and sexual exploitation in the media. But this decrease does not mean that there is not still excessive use of violence and "sexploitation" on television, in films, and in many music videos.

These are the criticisms that commonly are made about the mass media, and especially television. I offer next a discussion of some extreme attacks on the media that were made in earlier years—examples of what I call "anti-media rage."

ANTI-MEDIA RAGE

It is interesting to consider the vehemence with which the mass media have been attacked by some scholars. Is this, perhaps, in an era of road rage and other such rages, an example of anti-media rage? As an example, let me cite from the introduction by Bernard Rosenberg to a book he coedited with David Manning White, *Mass Culture: The Popular Arts in America*—an important anthology on the media published in 1957. It is generally considered one of the first books to seriously examine the mass media and popular culture—or mass-mediated culture. In the passage that follows, I've summarized Rosenberg's argument, using many of the terms Rosenberg uses in his critique of popular culture and the mass media. I have italicized Rosenberg's most negative terms.

> People in mass cultures become *dehumanized, deadened, anxiety-ridden, exploited, entrapped, lonely, debased,* and their lives are *standardized, vulgarized* and *manipulated* by mass culture, which is a threat to our autonomy, and this situation is exacerbated by things such as *sleazy fiction, trashy films, bathetic soap operas,* creating, in the general public, *unrest, lives emptied of meaning and trivialized,* as well as *alienation* (from past, work, community and possibly one's self) leading to that horrendous entity, mass man. Mass culture is *cultural pap* and *gruel* that

Are New Media Corrupting Our Children?

In a *Wired* magazine article, "The Culture War: How New Media Keeps Corrupting Our Children," Tom Standage discusses Senator Charles Schumer's comment that certain video games aimed at children "desensitize them to death and destruction." This kind of statement, Standage writes, is typical of the way older generations react to new forms of entertainment. The process, Standage writes, "goes like this: Young people embrace an activity. Adults condemn it. The kids grow up, no better or worse than their elders, and the moral panic subsides. Then the whole cycle starts over."

Standage offers examples of how various "scourges" (new technologies) were criticized when they first became popular:

Novels
"The free access which many young people have to romances, novels, and plays has poisoned the mind and corrupted the morals of many a promising youth. . . ."—*Reverend Enos Hitchcock, Memoirs of the Bloomsgrove Family, 1790*

The Telephone
"Does the telephone make men more active or more lazy? Does [it] break up home life and the old practice of visiting friends?"—*Survey conducted by the Knights of Columbus Adult Education Committee, San Francisco Bay Area, 1926*

Video Games
"The disturbing material in *Grand Theft Auto* and other games like it is stealing the innocence of our children and it's making the difficult job of being a parent even harder. . . ."—*U.S. senator Hillary Rodham Clinton, 2005* (Tom Standage, "The Culture War: How New Media Keeps Corrupting Our Children," *Wired,* www.wired.com/wired/archive/14.04/war.html)

Although Standage makes light of the impact of new media on young people and chooses some extreme examples to poke fun at, there is reason to believe that he is wrong and that contemporary critics of our new media are correct. Computers, the Internet, cell phones, iPods, and video games may not all be "scourges," but they have a powerful impact, in some cases quite destructive, upon individuals and the societies where they are found.

cretinizes our taste, *brutalizes* our senses (paving the way for totalitarianism), and destroys our taste so that all we like is kitsch. (See 1957: 3–12)

Rosenberg, quite obviously, thinks that popular culture, the mass media, and **mass culture** are highly destructive of our well-being, as individuals and collectively, and as a society. He hypothesizes that it is mass culture, made possible by modern technology, that lies at the root of our problems—not our national character or our economic system. In essence, he is suggesting that mass culture is the logical and necessary result of the development of modern technology.

DEFENDERS OF THE MASS MEDIA AND POPULAR CULTURE

Not everyone is as negative as Rosenberg, of course. His coeditor David Manning White offers a different and more positive assessment of television. He writes:

> Take, for example, the offerings of the television networks on Sunday, March 18, 1956, a Sunday which I chose at random. The televiewer would have been able to see on this day a discussion of the times and work of Toulouse-Lautrec by three prominent art critics; an inspiring interview with Dr. Paul Tillich, the noted theologian; a sensitive adaptation of Walter von Tilburg Clark's "Hook," a story of a hawk's life; a powerful documentary on mental illness with Orson Welles and Dr. William Menninger; an interview with the Secretary of Health, Welfare and Education; an interview with the Governor of Minnesota on the eve of the primary elections in his state; an hour and a half performance of *Taming of the Shrew* in color with Maurice Evans and Lilli Palmer. (1957: 18)

White points out that there is a lot of excellent programming on television, and adds that critics of mass culture "will invariably choose the mediocre and meretricious" to focus their attention on when they deal with the media and popular culture. In other words, their attention is highly selective; they neglect anything that is good and focus their attention and fury on anything that is mediocre or bad.

Let's look at an updated version of David Manning White's 1956 review. Television offerings for March 18, 2006, were affected by the fact that it was a Saturday and the annual NCAA college basketball tournament (March Madness) was in full swing. Here are some of the programs that aired March 18, 2006, in San Francisco, as listed by the *San Francisco Chronicle*.

Channel 9: Public Television
American Soundtrack: This Land Is Your Land
Benise Nights of Fire
Roy Orbison and Friends: A Black and White Night

Channel 5: CBS
College basketball
The King of Queens
Everybody Loves Raymond
CBS News Special

Channel 7: ABC
Jeopardy
Wheel of Fortune
The Sixth Sense (film)

Channel 11: NBC
Access Hollywood
Saturday Night's Main Event

Based on this listing of programs, was broadcast television offering anything of cultural significance? I would say that it was not and that these offerings were instead trying to reach an audience representing the mythical "lowest common denominator." On cable, few programs were of radically different cultural importance. This lineup would have given David Manning White little reason to argue that television and cable were bringing culture to the millions.

There are, it is fair to say, many scholars who defend television and the mass media on a number of different fronts. I will deal with some of these defenses below.

OTHER DEFENSES OF THE MASS MEDIA AND THE TEXTS THEY CARRY

Defenders of the mass media, mass-mediated culture, and popular culture (or for our purposes, the texts carried by the mass media) have a number of points to offer concerning the attacks made by critics of the media, and some arguments to make on their own behalf. I once wrote an article with the title "Why Is Popular Culture So Unpopular?" My point in the article was that popular culture is very popular with the masses of people for whom it is created; it is unpopular, however, with academics, scholars, and various elites, who argue that most popular culture is junk (which is generally true) and that its effects have generally been very harmful (which is debatable).

William McGuire, a psychologist at Yale University, has offered the following assessment of what might be called the debate over television and the mass media. His essay "Who's Afraid of the Big Bad Media?" discusses research on a variety of subjects related to media effects. He writes:

> Evidence in support of the claim that the media have sizable direct impact on the public is weak as regards each of the dozen most often-mentioned intended or unintended effects of the media. The most commonly mentioned intended effects include: (1) the influence of commercial advertising on buying behavior; (2) the impact of mass media political campaigns on voting; (3) public service announcements' efficacy in promoting beneficial behavior; (4) the role of prolonged multimedia campaigns in changing lifestyles; (5) monolithic indoctrination effects on ideology; and (6) the effects of mass-

Figure 5.2 We spend much of our lives consuming mass media, but experts disagree on how this affects us.

mediated ritual displays on maintaining social control. The most often cited unintended effects of the mass media include: (1) the impact of program violence on viewers' antisocial aggression; (2) representation of the media as a determinant of social visibility; (3) biased presentation of media as influencing the public's stereotyping of groups; (4) effects of erotic materials on objectionable sexual behavior; (5) modes of media presentation as affecting cognitive styles; and (6) the impact of introducing new media on public thought processes. (Berger 1991: 274)

McGuire argues that there is little evidence that the media have the effects they are held to have by critics. Thus, many of the criticisms found in the section above on negative media effects can be attacked as speculative, theoretical, and perhaps ideological—that is, not based on empirical evidence—or as involving short-lived and relatively limited phenomena.

Defenders of television and the mass media also suggest, as David Manning White does, that TV and the mass media have brought ballet, opera, serious drama, and other works of so-called elite culture to millions of people—works that they never would have seen otherwise. Thus it is argued, the mass media have, on balance, positive effects for their audiences. This assertion that television and the mass media have brought culture to the masses is correct, but I would counter that the amount of culture provided is minimal contrasted with the amount of third-rate material that is available.

I would suggest that now the dominant view among researchers is that most of the evidence available leads to the notion that media effects are not weak and limited, but are strong and powerful. For example, as a colleague of mine, Chaim Eyal, has written:

The limited effects notions are conceptualizations of the past. Very few, if any, theoreticians cling to those ideas. In the first place, the notion of null, or limited, effects originated from a very narrow line of research—the impact of political campaigns, studies in the late 1940s and early 1950s. Not much later it was recognized effects are not only in the realm of behavior but also in the area of cognition: awareness, knowledge, opinions, etc. With this recognition, which paralleled the development of the concept of attitudes by social psychologists, came the recognition that the mass media do have an impact—indeed different types of impact—in specific areas of people's thoughts, information processing and life in general. (personal communication, 1999)

There is reason to believe that the effects of television and the mass media are not as limited and minor as defenders of the mass media argue.

THE POSTMODERN SOLUTION

Earlier I discussed postmodernism with a focus on the way it is reflected in films (see chapter 3). I pointed out that postmodern society is characterized by a lack of adherence to overarching philosophical systems and beliefs. The phrase that Jean-François Lyotard, a French scholar, uses to characterize postmodernism in *The Postmodern Condition: A Report on Knowledge* is "incredulity toward metanarratives" (1984: xxiv). In postmodern societies, people no longer accept the old philosophical systems that once were used to justify beliefs and actions.

Eclecticism and the pastiche have become the dominant metaphors for postmodern societies. People can have multiple identities, which means they can, at different times, be members of many different audiences. As Lyotard explains,

Eclecticism is the degree zero of contemporary general culture: one listens to reggae, watches a western, eats McDonald's food for lunch and local cuisine for dinner, wears Paris perfume in Tokyo and "retro" clothes in Hong Kong; knowledge is a matter for TV games. (1984: 76)

That is, an individual can have multiple identities and consume many different kinds of culture in the course of a day or week.

One significant thing about postmodern thought is that it breaks down the barrier between elite culture and popular culture. In

essence, postmodernists argue, elite culture and popular culture aren't that different, and in many cases it is hard to tell the difference between them. Take for example an Andy Warhol painting of the comic-strip hero Dick Tracy. Is that elite culture or popular culture? For postmodernists, there is just culture, and different kinds of culture appeal to different groups, subcultures, media audiences, or interpretive communities within society. Douglas Kellner writes:

> As opposed to the seriousness of "high modernism," postmodernism exhibited a new insouciance, a new playfulness, and a new eclecticism embodied above all in Andy Warhol's "pop art" but also manifested in celebrations of Las Vegas architecture, found objects, happenings, Nam June Paik's video-installations, underground film, and the novels of Thomas Pynchon. In opposition to the well-wrought, formally sophisticated, and aesthetically demanding modernist art, postmodernist art was fragmentary and eclectic, mixing forms from "high culture" and "popular culture," subverting aesthetic boundaries and expanding the domain of art to encompass the images of advertising, the kaleidoscopic mosaics of television, the experiences of the post-holocaust nuclear age, and an always proliferating consumer capitalism. The moral seriousness of high modernism was replaced by irony, pastiche, cynicism, commercialism, and in some cases downright nihilism. ("Postmodernism as Social Theory: Some Challenges and Problems," *Theory, Culture and Society* 5, nos. 2–3 [June 1988]: 239)

Thus, it can be argued that postmodernist thought cuts the Gordian knot created by the tangled and complicated debate over elite culture and popular culture by eliminating the barrier that critics once used to separate them. If popular culture and elite culture are more or less the same, as the postmodernists argue, then the debate over the effects of popular culture and the mass media becomes irrelevant.

If I may be allowed a historical analogy: the technically advanced societies are at a point in their history similar to that of the emergence of an urban, merchant culture in the midst of feudal society in the Middle Ages. At that point practices of the exchange of commodities required individuals to act and speak in new ways, ways drastically different from the aristocratic code of honor with its face-to-face encounters based on trust for one's word and its hierarchical bonds of interdependency. Interacting with total strangers, sometimes at great distances, the merchants required written documents guaranteeing spoken promises and an "arms length distance" attitude even when face-to-face with the other, so as to afford a "space" for calculations of self-interest. A new identity was constructed, gradually and in a most circuitous path to be sure, among the merchants in which a coherent, stable sense of individuality was grounded in independent, cognitive abilities. In this way the cultural basis for the modern world was begun, one that eventually would rely upon print media to encourage and disseminate these urban forms of identity.

In the twentieth century, electronic media are supporting an equally profound transformation of cultural identity. Telephone, radio, film, television, the computer and now their integration as "multimedia" reconfigure words, sounds and images so as to cultivate new configurations of individuality. (1998: 255–56)

—Mark Poster, "Postmodern Virtualities," in
Arthur Asa Berger, *The Postmodern Presence: Readings*
on Postmodernism in American Culture and Society

6

THE SOCIAL IMPACT OF NEW MEDIA TECHNOLOGIES

We tend to think of the new media technologies that are developing so rapidly now in terms of their primary functions, which involve entertainment or communication. The impact of new technologies on these areas has been incredible. But these new media technologies also are having important social, economic, cultural, and political consequences as Mark Poster, quoted above, suggests. Most of us are aware that American culture and society are changing (and the rest of the world as well) as the new technologies start making their impact felt, but we don't, as a rule, appreciate the incredible influence these technologies are having on American culture and society.

THE IMPACT OF CELL PHONES

Large numbers of people now have cell phones, which are very convenient and useful in many different circumstances. But some cell phone users make terrible nuisances of themselves, conducting the most intimate conversations, often in a loud voice, anywhere they happen to be—in restaurants, in airport lounges, and even in toilets. Cell phones now ring in the middle of plays, at symphony concerts, in school lecture halls, and while religious services are being conducted. Often this happens because people forget to turn their phones off, but not always. Some people consider it vitally important to be accessible at all times and don't care whether they disturb other people. Interestingly enough, however, many people now consider it chic *not* to be reachable by cell phone, that is, they wish to guard their privacy and limit their accessibility to others. Cell phones used to be signifiers of importance, but they are now so common they have lost their cachet.

Howard Rheingold argues that cell phones have had a profound impact on the cultures and societies where they are used and have led to the creation of what he calls "smart mobs."

> On a Spring afternoon in the year 2000 . . . I began to notice people on the streets of Tokyo staring at their mobile phones instead of talking to them. The sight of this behavior, now commonplace in much of the world, triggered a sensation I had experienced a few times before—the instant recognition that a technology is going to change my life in ways I can scarcely imagine. Since then, the practice of exchanging short text messages via mobile telephones has led to the eruption of subcultures in Europe and Asia. At least one government has fallen, in part because of the way people used text messaging.
>
> Adolescent mating rituals, political activism, and corporate management styles have mutated in unexpected ways.
>
> I've learned that "texting" is only a small harbinger of more profound changes to come over the next ten years. My media moment . . . was only my first encounter with a phenomenon I've come to call "smart mobs." When I learned to recognize the signs, I began to see them everywhere—from Napster to electronic bridge tolls.
>
> When you piece together these different technological, economic, and social components, the result is an infrastructure that makes certain kinds of human actions possible that were never possible before: The killer apps of tomorrow's mobile infocom industry won't be hardware devices or software programs but social practices. The most far-reaching changes will come, as they often do, from the kinds of relationships, enterprises, communities, and markets that the infrastructure makes possible. (2003: xi–xii)

So the cell phone, as Rheingold points out, may be used for much more than person-to-person communication and may have significant social and political impacts.

In this chapter I deal with the social impact, in the broadest sense of the term *social*, of the new media technologies on American culture, and consider such topics as computers and the Internet, the development of virtual communities, the video game phenomenon, and new video and audio recording and playing devices.

Consider what has happened to the medium of television as the result of new technologies. At one time we had only three national television networks and some local stations; now there are countless cable and satellite channels available to the people who subscribe to them. Some people have lamented that now "we have five hundred channels but there's nothing on." By this they mean that the same genres that were carried by television networks are now found on the cable networks, except that some cable outlets are now very specialized and only carry programming devoted to specific genres such as music videos, sports, news, old films, or comedy.

To understand what is happening in this brave, new, mass–mediated digital world we live in—the world that has brought us iPods, digital cameras, HDTV, video games, cell phones with digital cameras, and a seemingly endless number of other devices—we must understand what **digital** means.

THE DIGITAL WORLD

The first thing we must come to grips with is that the new media technologies involve the replacement of **analog** technologies with digital ones. Consider what the watches everyone used to wear were like: they had a second hand sweeping around the dial as the seconds

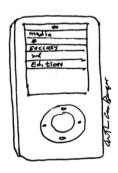

New Media Technologies and Teen Taste

Relatively recent developments in media technology, such as satellite transmission, the remote control, the VCR, and the Internet, have expanded enormously the number of media materials available and have given teens in the United States much more control over when and where they will use them. In the next five years, other technological innovations such as digital compression will bring an estimated three hundred program choices into most U.S. homes; by 2010 most homes will have a thousand channels or "content windows." . . . Other media, such as radio, magazines, and movies are already highly specialized and offer an array of content that appeals to a variety of tastes and interests. Today's teens have the opportunity to select their own media diets from a smorgasbord of possibilities.

Source: Jane D. Brown and Elizabeth M. Witherspoon, "The Mass Media and Health of Adolescents in the United States," in Kamalipour and Rampal 2001, 78.

---

passed and they had a minute hand and an hour hand. These watches were analog watches, based on the notion that things are connected to one another, that time is continuous, and that we live in a world in which there are many degrees of difference. The word *analog* is derived from the same Greek word as *analogy*, which means similar to something, or like something.

In the digital world, by contrast, everything is separated, and with digital watches and clocks, time becomes a series of separate and discrete moments, succeeding one another but not showing that any moment in time is related to any other one. With an analog watch, you can glance at your watch and say, "It's a quarter to five," but with a digital watch, you get a readout saying, in effect, it is now 4:45 P.M. and so many seconds.

Peter Lunenfeld, a scholar who has written a number of books on art and Internet technologies, offers in his book *The Digital Dialectic: New Essays on New Media* an excellent explanation of what the term *digital* means. He writes:

> Digital systems do not use continuously variable representational relationships. Instead, they translate all input into binary structures of 0s

and 1s, which can then be stored, transferred, or manipulated at the level of numbers or "digits" (so called because etymologically, the word descends from the digits on our hand with which we count out those numbers). Thus a phone call on a digital system will be encoded as a series of these 0s and 1s and sent over the wires as binary information to be reinterpreted as speech on the other end. . . . It is the capacity of the electronic computer to encode a vast variety of information digitally that has given it such a central place within contemporary culture. As all manner of representational systems are recast as digital information, then all can be stored, accessed, and controlled by the same equipment. (1999: xv)

Lunenfeld offers the example of the digital photograph, which is composed of a number of *pixels*, cells that form "a grid of cells that have precise numerical attributes associated with them, a series of steps rather than a continuous slope" (1999: xvi). The new media technologies are digital then, and are based on binary oppositions between various combinations of 0s and 1s—that is, ons and offs— and in the case of images, these binary oppositions are incorporated in grids of separate cells with numerical attributes.

The following list shows some important media and the date of their digitization.

Year	Medium
1962	telephone
1967	print
1977	films (segments of *Star Wars*)
1995	complete films (*Toy Story*)
1998	high definition television (HDTV)

We see then that we are in an age of digitalization and that our media are now almost completely digitized, with the exception of television, which is slowly becoming so.

THE COMPUTER AND CULTURE

In the early days when computers were just being developed, a businessman—I think he was the head of IBM—suggested that the entire

United States could use, maybe, five computers. At that time computers cost millions of dollars and filled up large rooms. Now, it isn't unusual to find families with five computers. Originally, people used computers because of so-called killer applications like spreadsheets, word processing programs, and later, image manipulation software. Now of course computers are ubiquitous and can be used to do all kinds of remarkable things.

The price of computers has gone down over the years. I bought my son a Commodore 64 (64K) for $900 around 1980, and $900 then was worth a lot more than it is worth now. In 2001 I bought my wife a Hewlett-Packard desktop PC (personal computer) with 256 MB of RAM, a 40-MB disk drive, a chip speed of 1.1 GHz, a 15-inch color monitor, loads of software, and an inexpensive ink-jet printer, and paid only $650. And the store where I purchased the PC gave me a year of free Internet service, worth approximately $250, which means the PC and printer ended up costing around $400. It is now possible to get desktop PCs for around $300 and laptops for $400, and prices are continuing to drop.

There is also to be considered the matter of what has been called the "knowledge gap." Those with access to computers and other new technologies quite obviously have an advantage over those who do not have access to them. In recent years, however, schools and libraries have purchased computers, so computers are more available now than ever before. Nevertheless, there are many families on the bottom rungs of the socioeconomic ladder that do not have the funds to purchase their own computers and to purchase access to the Internet, so children in these families are seriously disadvantaged.

With the development of and greater access to the Internet, the computer now is seen as an important communication device, and not just something that can be used for databases or spreadsheets or for word processing or manipulating images. In recent years, for example, computers have come to be used for playing video games. People send billions of e-mails to one another, and are bothered by businesses sending them billions of undesired e-mail advertisements (known as "spam"). With the Internet, the world is open to us, but that also means that we are open to the world and vulnerable to all kinds of people whom we will never meet and who don't know who we are—some of whom are criminals and others of whom are malicious.

The growth of the Internet also is changing our media-usage behavior. There are now millions of websites that people visit, for one reason or another. Many companies use websites to sell products and services on the Internet. Many stores with physical outlets (known as "bricks") now also have elaborate websites ("clicks") where they sell their merchandise.

The phenomenon of "cruising," or "browsing," the Internet—that is, looking around—is now worldwide, helped by powerful search engines such as Yahoo! and **Google**. It's instructive to see how many Internet sites Google finds on a random day if we search for keywords involving media:

media	5.1 billion
"mass media"	38 million
"media and society"	533,000
"media effects"	342,000
"media and children"	73,000

We see then that search engines such as this enable us to gain information on the Internet about subjects across a considerable range and that on the Internet there is also a great deal of interest in various aspects of the media. (It's interesting to note that *Google* has now become a verb, "to google," as in "I googled it.")

Figure 6.1   The Internet has increased our computer usage significantly, offering us the capability to e-mail, research, shop, book travel, find dates, check weather forecasts, get real-time sports scores, catch up on the news, and search for jobs.

The number of sites on the Internet otherwise and the subjects they deal with is astounding: everything from sites with online books to fan sites dealing with video games or movie stars, and from sites discussing philosophical movements (a recent Google search for the term *postmodernism* listed over 8.6 million sites) to sites dealing with medical problems or selling books, cameras, groceries, or whatever. In the San Francisco area, two supermarket chains—Safeway and Albertson's—now sell groceries on the Internet, which they deliver to your house for a fee.

The marriage of computers and printing devices has led to the development of digital printing presses that enable publishers to print and bind books on demand. This *print-on-demand* phenomenon has the potential to revolutionize publishing. So the computer is having an incredible impact, not only in publishing and television, but in all kinds of other areas—from medical imaging to music.

The darker side of the computer is that it enables governments to store information about people—and some communications theorists worry that the power of a government to gather and to store information about people will lead to abusive behavior by governmental agencies. And now that we live in an age of terrorism, some people are advocating that the government develop a national identity card with an electronic chip that would provide the government with data about the holder of that card.

It is now possible, for example, to take photographs (digital, of course) of people's retinas and to use these photographs in identity cards, enabling airline passengers who purchase these cards (and pay a yearly fee) to check in for flights and get to waiting rooms for departures very quickly. This technology could be used to warn of terrorists trying to board planes, but it could also be used to check on who is flying where, for whatever purposes the government might have in collecting this information.

The globalization of world communications means, also, that criminals and antisocial individuals with a knowledge of programming can use the Internet to spread destructive computer "viruses" that can disable millions of computers worldwide. Vandalism used to be local, but now, in the age of the Internet, it is global. There is now even "cyber-warfare" as countries fight each other by fighting, so to speak, on the Internet.

New devices for recording television programs or music are continually being developed. One of the fastest-selling devices is the DVD (digital video disk) player. According to a *Video Business* article by Jennifer Netherby in January 2006, nearly 82 million U.S. households had switched from VHS (video home system) video-cassette recorders to DVD by the end of 2005. DVD recording devices are on the market as well, and with economies of scale, the price of these recorders will continue to fall. Consumers can also watch DVDs on other devices, such as video game systems and computers, and some computers can record video on DVDs. As a result of the development of the DVD, sales of VHS are plummeting and more and more people are watching films or TV shows on DVD rather than VHS. The images are much sharper on DVD and the sound is better.

Everywhere we look, devices are being created and technologies that were new just a few years ago are being discarded. Telephones now can take pictures, show television, hook up to the Internet, be used to play games, play music, and do all kinds of things that couldn't be imagined just a few years ago. The world is now

Figure 6.2   New technologies are being created and adapted all the time. Cell phones can now do a variety of additional things, from playing music to taking pictures to connecting online.

"wired," but we do not know, at this time, what changes and effects these new technologies will have on our everyday lives and on our society. On a recent visit to Vietnam, for example, I noticed that the streets of downtown Hanoi were lined with video cafes, and the cafes were full of tourists and Vietnamese sending e-mail and using the Internet. I made use of these video cafes myself to keep in touch with friends and my family. There are now video cafes in most major cities all over the world.

Yet despite all the new developments coming from our new technologies, people in America still spend an average of four hours per day watching television, and our networks, cable systems, newspapers, and magazines are still controlled for the most part by media conglomerates. Though new technologies and also ethnic media outlets may have some role in countering the perspectives promulgated by the media conglomerates, they still are relatively minor voices in the scheme of things.

VIRTUAL COMMUNITIES

There is, I would suggest, something inherently alienating about the digital world that we now live in. The metaphor for digital devices is separation, representing a world of discrete moments and binary oppositions, of on or off, in or out, yes or no. The digital devices we use are increasingly more powerful and are able to connect us to one another in remarkable ways, but at the same time, they seem to be fostering a kind of hyperindividualism and a lack of a sense of community. We say that global communication means you *can* be connected to everyone; the question is, *are* you connected to anyone? Are people less stressed in our new digital world or more stressed? Do they have less time for themselves, their loved ones, and their communities, or more time?

A student of American popular culture, John Fraim, has found something very interesting about this question of the decline of community in the United States. It involves the fact that gamblers now spend more and more time with slot machines and less time with table gambling. He writes:

> Does the long-range movement from tables to slots mirror a similar trend in America as a whole towards less sociability? Harvard professor Robert Putnam argues American culture as a whole has moved towards less sociability in his book *Bowling Alone*. The book argues that America faces a civic crisis in that once social activities such as bowling leagues, dinner parties and community arts performances are slowly vanishing from the American landscape. Increasingly, argues Putnam, Americans are withdrawing from communal life, choosing to live and play alone. They are losing what Putnam calls "social capital" or the "glue" of trust in each other that is so essential to a democratic society.
>
> Does the decline of table gaming and the rise in slot machine gambling suggest that more and more people want to gamble alone? Rather than being a fantasy island set off from the rest of America, Las Vegas gaming trends might offer one of the best laboratories for investigation of large scale American social trends. (unpublished manuscript, 2002)

What Fraim has discovered about changes in gambling in America suggests that our sense of community may be declining—or, as some have suggested, taking new forms.

With the development of the Internet, new kinds of communities known as "virtual communities" are evolving for people with shared interests. There are many people who belong, if that's the correct word, to such communities and who spend many hours each day online, communicating with other members of their virtual community. Within such communities there are often dozens of interest groups where people with mutual interests can send messages to one another. These virtual communities can be looked upon as a **functional alternative** to real communities in which people know one another through face-to-face interaction and shared activities.

While being a member of a virtual community does have some value as far as helping people take care of their need for social interaction—we are, after all, social animals—I can only wonder whether the gratifications people get from being members of these communities are adequate to their needs for social interaction.

Take the matter of our sexual needs. Howard Rheingold, in his book *Virtual Reality*, describes the possibilities for virtual sex in a chapter titled "Teledildonics and Beyond":

> The first fully functional teledildonics system will be a communication device, not a sex machine. You probably will not use erotic telepresence technology in order to have sexual experiences with machines. Thirty years from now, when portable telediddlers become ubiquitous, most people will use them to have sexual experiences with other *people*, at a distance, in combinations and configurations undreamed of by precybernetic voluptuaries. Through a marriage of virtual reality technology and telecommunications networks, you will be able to reach out and touch someone—or an entire population—in ways humans have never before experienced. Or so the scenario goes. (1991: 346)

This telecommunicated sex would be made possible by people wearing close-fitting body suits full of sensory devices (not yet in existence). Rheingold wrote his book in 1991, which means that this kind of sexual activity will be possible around 2021, if his timetable is correct. Woody Allen satirized the notion of mechanical devices providing sexual gratification in his film *Sleeper*, in which characters used devices known as "orgasmatrons."

The question I ask is, Why bother with virtual sex when real sex, between real people, is so much easier? Virtual sex, I would suggest, will probably be like virtual dining—you'll still be hungry after-ward. Perhaps by 2021 we will even have computers that eat food for us and relay sensations to our brains so we can have the experience of having a gourmet dinner without actually having one.

Let me move on to an activity in which our participation in vir-tual realities of one kind or another is much more developed: video games.

VIDEO GAMES:
A BIO-PSYCHO-SOCIAL PERSPECTIVE

In 2004, sales of video games (software) were over $7.1 billion. And the video game industry continues to grow at a phenomenal pace; some experts even suggest that the video game industry (including the games and consoles used to play them, and Internet versions of the games) may reach $31 billion in sales in a few years. So we are dealing with a very important popular culture phenomenon. There are many different genres of video games: sports games, role-playing games, racing games, "first-person shooters," and so on. Some games can be played on computers, but most dedicated video game players purchase game playing consoles such as Sony's PlayStation 2, Micro-soft's Xbox, or the Nintendo GameCube. In the spring of 2002, Sony and Microsoft both lowered the prices of their consoles (by $100) to $199 in a price war for domination of the industry, and in the summer of 2002 they lowered their prices even more, to $149. Since video game consoles cost, on average, around $200 and video games often cost around $50, playing video games can become quite expensive.

In 2005 the video game console wars entered the "next genera-tion." Microsoft announced a new system, the Xbox 360, that was released in November 2005. This system has a 20-GB hard drive and is being positioned as a media "hub" for families because it can play music and show videos. Microsoft has developed a broadband net-work for network gaming by video game players with Xboxes. Sony subsequently announced its PlayStation 3 (PS3), which at this writing was scheduled for release in late 2006. It will be a miniature supercomputer and the most powerful gamebox ever, with "cell" technology and high-resolution video, which Sony claims will narrow the gap between video games and films. And Nintendo has also announced its new system, Wii, due to be released in late 2006 or early 2007. Microsoft sold 20 million copies of its first Xbox, but Sony has sold 100 million copies of PlayStation 2.

Microsoft, Sony, and Nintendo hope that their powerful devices will become the central conduit for media entertainment in the families that purchase them. They are hoping that these devices will become "Trojan horses" that will supplant computers and other devices as the core media device in these families, who will then use them for all (or most of) their media needs.

A news release by the Entertainment Software Association (ESA) in January 2005 offers information about the growth of the video game (software) industry:

> Computer and video game software sales set a new record in 2004, reaching $7.3 billion, according to final data compiled by the NPD Group and announced today by the Entertainment Software Association (ESA). The industry's impact is illustrated further through other data showing that Halo 2®, one of the best-selling titles of 2004, took in more revenue in its first day of sales than any movie has ever taken in its opening day. In addition, according to industry data, Nintendo sold over 1 million units of its new handheld game system, Nintendo DS™, in North America by the end of 2004, a mark that took Apple's iPod® 19 months to achieve.
>
> "In 2004, video games flew off the shelves as eight titles were sold per second per day throughout the year, evidence of the continuing vast popularity of games among consumers of all ages," said Douglas Lowenstein, president of the ESA, the U.S. association representing computer and video game software publishers. "This industry remains strong and poised for renewed double digit growth over the next five years as we enter a new cycle of video game console launches. The future could not be brighter.
>
> According to the data compiled by the NPD Group, overall U.S. video game console software sales reached $5.2 billion (160.7 million units), computer games sales were $1.1 billion (45 million units), and a record $1.0 billion (42.3 million units) in portable software sales. In terms of total units sold, approximately 248 million

computer and video games were sold in 2004—nearly two games for every home in America by ESA estimates. (Note: The numbers released by the ESA today do not include sales of game hardware or accessories.) By way of comparison, 2003 figures were: U.S. video game console sales reached $4.9 billion (149 million units), computer games sales were $1.2 billion (52.7 million units), and portable software sales were $903 million (37.4 million units). In terms of total units sold, 239.3 million computer or video games were sold in 2003. (www.theesa.com/archives/2005/02/computer_and_vi.php)

CRITICISMS OF VIDEO GAMES

It has been suggested that many costs—physiological, psychological, and social—are connected with playing video games. Let me list some of them. You will notice some similarities to the earlier arguments about the potential negative effects of television.

1. Damage to a player's muscles. This comes from repeating the same movements over and over again with joysticks and other input devices. These repetitive stress injuries often are quite serious and need expensive medical attention.
2. Obesity. This comes from a lack of exercise and from excessive snacking on fatty foods while playing video games.
3. Related medical problems. Obesity leads to other medical problems, often involving heart disease, and in a number of cases, juvenile diabetes. Diabetes is a serious disease that can affect kidney function and cause many other serious medical problems that are very expensive to deal with.
4. Decrease in socialization with others. Some game playing is done with others, but even so, children playing video games don't have the experience of being with lots of other children and don't develop the ability to get along with them. This can lead to a sense of alienation from others and from society at large, especially among young people who become addicted to game playing.
5. Hyperactivity. This kind of behavior, manifested when not playing video games, is exacerbated, perhaps, by the incredi-

ble amount of excitement generated by some of these games and the instantaneous gratifications they provide.

6. Violence seen as a means of resolving problems. In many video games, there is an incredible amount of killing going on as players kill aliens, monsters, and other characters. Even though the players know they are playing a game, some of them may conclude that violence is an effective tool for doing things they want to do in real life. There are many video games full of violence and sex: *Grand Theft Auto: San Andreas*; *Resident Evil 4*; *Black*; and countless others.

7. Desensitization. In video games, players perform the actions that lead to virtual fighting, shooting, and killing. This is different from seeing others do these things. It is possible that repeated experiences of being responsible for violence does desensitize some children, which then leads to their acting out and being violent in the real world. While video game playing may not be the cause of this kind of behavior, it seems to be a contributing factor, especially in youths who have psychological problems.

You can see from this list that while individuals (and their friends) may play video games privately, there are widespread, public medical and psychological costs—which translate to social and political costs—involved with the video game phenomenon. Private acts, we must realize, often have public consequences, and while much video game playing is harmless, and some games provide wonderful and intellectually challenging entertainment, there are many negative aspects and social costs that critics contend are connected with this phenomenon.

POSITIVE ASPECTS OF
VIDEO GAME PLAYING

If there are dangers connected to video game playing, there are also benefits worth considering. James Paul Gee, a professor of education at the University of Wisconsin, argues in his book *What Video Games Have to Teach Us about Learning and Literacy* that video games help children learn a new kind of literacy. These games, Gee suggests, do several things for players, such as helping them learn how to establish an identity, how to choose between different ways of solving problems, and how to get information from nonverbal cues. So there are positive attributes to video games, and Gee suggests they will play an important role in education in the future.

A psychologist at the University of California, Los Angeles, Patricia Marks Greenfield, was one of the first scholars to see the beneficial effects of video game playing. As she writes in her book *Mind and Media*:

> Pac-Man and other arcade computer games require the player to induce the rules from observation. Computer games therefore call up inductive skills much more than did games of the pre-computer era. (1984: 111)

The visual dynamism of video games and the fact that players actively participate in the outcomes of these games are the primary sources of their appeal, the author argues, and not the violence found in them. And she adds, games can be developed that teach players how to cooperate rather than compete with one another.

One danger video games do pose, the author concludes, is that they are so responsive to the input of their players that they can lead to players being impatient with the messy way things work in the real world. But this has to be weighed against the positive attributes of video game playing, which involve developing a sense of competence and control as well as certain motor skills involving hand-eye coordination.

The explosive growth of the video game industry in recent years—and it is a global phenomenon—suggests that these games provide numerous and powerful gratifications for video game players. The dilemma these players face involves finding a way to navigate between the addictive and negative aspects of video games and their positive attributes, including their potential for developing new kinds of literacy and new modes of teaching.

The Cultural Significance of *Pac-Man*

Pac-Man was one of the most popular video games of the 1980s. Let me offer here some hypotheses about the hidden meanings found in this game. I do this to suggest that video games might have a greater cultural significance than we might imagine.

In *Pac-Man*, the violence is feminized and is based on biting and ingestion rather than on shooting guns and rockets and using other masculine and **phallic** forms of violence and aggression. From a developmental standpoint, when playing *Pac-Man* we have regressed from a phallic, gun-shooting stage (*Space Invaders*) to a more infantile, oral stage. Freud suggested children go through four stages of development: oral, anal, phallic, and genital. *Pac-Man* and various other versions of the game are, quite obviously, at the oral stage.

Games like *Space Invaders* involve scooting around the universe. *Pac-Man*, however, takes place in a labyrinth, which suggests that we see ourselves as trapped. We have to learn then how to deal with being confined and having limited possibilities. In a sense, the game suggests that we see ourselves as prisoners.

Pac-Man is also a game in which dots eat dots, and this view of life can be a metaphor for capitalist society as characterized by class conflict and a dog-eat-dog mentality. As captives of a labyrinth from which there is no escape, we can either work toward the collective good of everyone or, conversely, try to maximize things for ourselves, and it is this latter goal that is emphasized in *Pac-Man*. *Pac-Man* may have reflected a paradigm shift in the American psyche: trapped in the labyrinth of America, people are now suffering from a loss of nerve and a change of perspective, which makes them focus upon themselves (and how many dots they can gobble) and forget about their social obligations. Clearly, there's more to video games than fingering a joystick furiously, gobbling up dots, or killing aliens.

THE TECHNOLOGICAL IMPERATIVE

One important question we must consider when dealing with technology is whether there is some kind of *technological imperative*. Must all new technologies be allowed to develop as much as they can, regardless of the possible consequences to individuals and to societies?

We can make bombs now that can kill millions of people; should we push ahead and make bombs capable of destroying the earth? Or on a less cataclysmic note, should we allow file-sharing programs to make it possible for people to download songs without paying for them? The U.S. Supreme Court has said this latter process is unlawful, but whether the Supreme Court's decision will have any practical impact remains to be seen.

Many philosophers have suggested that human beings must decide how far to let new technologies develop. For instance, we might be able to clone human beings, but most people think it is a bad idea to try to do so. Some technology theorists are worrying, now, that computers and robots will soon have enough brain power (if that's what you want to call it) to replicate themselves and may someday dominate human beings. We will all become, according to this scenario, *servo-proteins* that exist only to service the new computers and robots that will create themselves. (The fact that Gary Kasparov tied an Israeli-programmed computer in a chess match in 2003 suggests there is hope, but Kasparov is probably the best chess player alive.)

This matter of becoming servo-proteins is probably a far-fetched scenario, but it does pose the question very sharply: Where do we draw the line and say technological development beyond a certain point is not to be allowed? Or can we? Ralph Waldo Emerson said, in the celebrated essay *Ode to W. H. Channing*, "Things are in the saddle, and ride mankind." Perhaps even as I write this, to paraphrase Emerson, technology is in the driver's seat and mankind must go along for the ride. I would like to think that Emerson was pessimistic and not prescient. The technological imperative theory suggests that we cannot stop technology from developing to its logical conclusion, but many philosophers have argued that not only can we keep technology from pushing beyond certain points, we must. The various *Terminator* films deal with this matter in very vivid terms.

Ad agencies are so very useful. They express for the collective that which dreams and uncensored behavior do in individuals. They give spatial form to hidden impulse and, when analyzed, make possible bringing into reasonable order a great deal that could not otherwise be observed or discussed. Gouging away at the surface of public sales resistance, the ad men are constantly breaking through into the Alice in Wonderland territory behind the looking glass which is the world of subrational impulse and appetites. . . . The ad agencies and Hollywood, in their different ways, are always trying to get inside the public mind in order to impose their collective dreams on that inner stage. . . . The ad agencies flood the daytime world of conscious purpose and control with erotic imagery from the night world in order to drown, by suggestion, all sales resistance. (1951: 97)

—Marshall McLuhan, *The Mechanical Bride*

7

THE SOCIAL SIGNIFICANCE OF MASS-MEDIATED TEXTS

Texts—the works carried (and to some degree shaped) by the media—are often neglected in analyses of social aspects of the media made by communications researchers. In part, media analysts and researchers are interested in making generalized statements about the media or in doing statistical analysis on matters such as violence in the media, and texts (that is, specific works) do not fit comfortably into these kinds of studies.

And yet as I have suggested earlier, people do not watch television per se, but rather watch certain programs; and they don't just listen to the radio, but to specific stations that carry the kind of music or other programming to which they are attracted. The same applies to other media—people choose to watch certain television shows, listen to certain radio stations, play certain video games, or go to particular films of interest to them. (In some cases, when people watching television "channel surf" and switch from one program to another rapidly—looking for something to amuse themselves—the composite of all the shows they have glanced at, a pastiche, can be considered a postmodern text.)

Russian theorist Yuri Lotman points out that texts are incredibly complex and function as very rich storehouses of information for those who know how to access this material.

> Since it can concentrate a tremendous amount of information into the "area" of a very small text (cf. the length of a short story by Checkov and a psychology textbook) an artistic text manifests yet another feature: it transmits different information to different readers in proportion to each one's comprehension; it provides the reader with a language in which each successive portion of information may be assimilated with repeated reading. It behaves as a kind of living organism which has a feedback channel to the reader and thereby instructs him. (1977: 23)

This explains why we can read certain novels over again with pleasure—we get different things out of each reading. The same applies to certain films and television programs. The more you know, the more you can find in a given text. Texts may seem simple, but in reality, Lotman argues, they are incredibly complex.

Lotman has also suggested that every aspect of a text is important. As he writes, "The tendency to interpret *everything* in an artistic text as meaningful is so great that we rightfully consider nothing accidental in a work of art" (1977: 17). This means that texts are remarkably complicated, since everything in them is important, and analyzing them and interpreting them is a difficult matter. It is understandable then why certain great texts have fascinated readers, viewers, and critics, who keep finding new things in them over the years, decades, and in some cases—such as *Hamlet* and other classics—centuries.

When we deal with mass-mediated texts such as films and television programs, we have to consider every aspect of these texts as important—not only the dialogue and narrative elements, but also the editing and other aspects of media aesthetics. It's worth considering what texts do, or in a more general sense, what art is and what it does.

THEORIES OF ART: WHAT TEXTS DO

M. H. Abrams, a literature professor, wrote an influential book, *The Mirror and the Lamp*, in which he suggested that there are four important critical orientations to the arts. I use the acronym POEM to deal with these approaches:

1. *Pragmatic*   Art is functional and does things.
2. *Objective*   Art projects its own reality.
3. *Expressive*   Art expresses the reality of the artist.
4. *Mimetic*   Art imitates life.

Debates about what art is and how it functions have been with us since Aristotle's time. Aristotle argued that art is an imitation of life, and this is a key statement of the **mimetic theory of art**. (I will discuss this matter in more detail shortly.) The objective theory of art is the opposite of the mimetic theory, for it suggests that artists create and project their own reality. Another pair of opposites involves the pragmatic theory of art, which argues that art has certain functions, and the **expressive theory of art**, which focuses on the emotional impact of works of art.

Alan Gowans, a professor of the history of art, argues for the pragmatic theory. In his book *The Unchanging Arts* he discusses the functions of art, which from our point of view involves works of art or texts carried by the media. He argues that we shouldn't waste our time debating what art is or, in terms of our interest in the media, whether texts carried by the mass media are art, but should focus

instead on what the functions of the art (and the media) are. As he explains:

> Instead of asking "What is Art?" we need to ask "What kinds of things have been done by that activity traditionally called Art?" And then we will find that activity historically performed four functions: substitute imagery; illustration; conviction and persuasion; and beautification. (1) In cases where the appearance of something needed to be preserved for one reason or another, art made pictures that could be substituted for the actual thing. (2) Art made images or shapes (including pictographs) that could be used in whole or part to tell stories or record events vividly ("illustrate," "illuminate," "elucidate," all come from the same root "lux" = "light"). (3) Art made images which by association of shapes with ideas set forth the fundamental convictions or realized ideals of societies (usually in what we call architectural or sculptural form); or conversely art made images intended to persuade people to new or different beliefs (usually in more ephemeral media). (4) Art beautified the world by pleasing the eye or gratifying the mind; what particular combinations of forms, arrangements, colors, proportions or ornament accomplished this end in any given society depended, of course, on what kinds of illustration or conviction or persuasion a given society required its arts to provide. (1971: 12–13)

So for Gowans, the arts have certain functions: first, they preserve the appearance of things; second, they make images that can be used to tell stories; third, they are used to persuade; and fourth, they help beautify the world. What Abrams and Gowans write about the various theories of the arts, in general, can be applied to the media and raise interesting questions for us to think about.

THE TEXTS THE MEDIA CARRY HAVE POWER

In thinking about the media, we must keep in mind the texts they carry and help shape. These texts have the **power**, I suggested in my discussion of vicious cycles (see chapter 1), to help shape our consciousness and give us notions about how to live, what is right and wrong, and so on. Some people get part of their social identity from television programs. For example, there are people known as "Trekkies" who attend numerous *Star Trek* conventions dressed up in *Star Trek* uniforms and buy various artifacts connected with the TV show and later movies. There are fan groups (and websites) for scores of movie franchises and TV shows, from *Star Wars* and *The X-Files* to *Buffy the Vampire Slayer*, *Alias*; *Lost*; and *24*. Let me focus here on television, since it the medium that dominates our daily media usage. There are many different *kinds* of texts or shows carried by television. Some of the more important of these genres are listed in table 7.1.

Each of these genres or kinds of programs has certain conventions that make it what it is and differentiate it from other genres. The conventions involve such things as the kinds of characters we find in the genre, the actions they are involved in, and the way they speak. As we grow up and watch different kinds of programs, we learn these conventions and become able to distinguish one genre from another. This is a kind of **incidental learning**. After watching a number of episodes of a certain genre, for example, we learn what to expect in that genre, whether it's a soap opera, a cop show, or any of the other popular genres. That is, most genres are formulaic and rely, to a considerable extent, on the knowledge that audiences bring to the shows and the desires these audiences have for certain kinds of entertainment.

CONVENTION AND INVENTION IN TEXTS

A continuum can be drawn between texts that are primarily based on convention and those that are essentially based on invention. In the

Table 7.1   Genres: Kinds of Texts on Television

commercials	action-adventure show	media event
news show	science fiction	sports show
talk show	religious show	horror show
soap opera	cooking show	cop show
situation comedy	music video	play
crime show	documentary	award show

mass media, because radio and television stations want to attract as large an audience as possible, you tend to get texts closer to the convention side of the continuum—texts that audiences can easily understand and that don't challenge them very much. At the opposite end you have works that are very challenging.

Another way to look at the differences between convention and invention is found in John Cawelti's classic study of westerns, *The Six-Gun Mystique*:

> Conventions are elements which are known to both the creator and his audience beforehand—they consist of things like favorite plots, stereotyped characters, accepted ideas, commonly known metaphors and other linguistic devices, etc. Inventions, on the other hand, are elements which are uniquely imagined by the creator such as new kinds of characters, ideas, or linguistic forms. (1971: 27)

For example, think of the difference between a television show like *American Idol* and a novel like James Joyce's *Ulysses*. We can use the diagram in figure 7.1 to think about where certain films and television shows might be placed on a convention–invention continuum. If *American Idol* = 1 and *Ulysses* = 10, it's an interesting problem to consider where any of the following texts might fall: *SportsCenter*; *The Daily Show*; *CSI*; *60 Minutes*; *The Sims*; *Grand Theft Auto*; *King Kong*; *Napoleon Dynamite*; *Pride and Prejudice*; *The Da Vinci Code*; or *Hamlet*.

Most mass-mediated texts are conventional, but that doesn't mean they have to be, and one finds a good deal of experimentation and even so-called avant-garde textual practices in certain genres such as science fiction, music videos, and TV commercials.

Convention									**Invention**
1	2	3	4	5	6	7	8	9	10
American Idol									*Ulysses*

Figure 7.1   The Convention–Invention Continuum

THE POWER OF COMMERCIALS

In the United States the most important television genre by far—from an economic standpoint, that is—is the commercial. It may be somewhat simplistic and reductionistic to put it this way, but as we've seen earlier, many critics argue that from an economic perspective, the essential thing that television does is deliver audiences to advertisers for their commercials. As we have seen, the nature of these audiences is very important, and different genres and different shows within a genre will attract different kinds of audiences with different levels of education, different degrees of sophistication, and different income levels (that is, different demographics).

We've all heard about how much is spent by advertisers on commercials that air during the Super Bowl, but consider this. The annual NCAA basketball tournament (known as "March Madness") brings in more ad money overall than either the Super Bowl or the World Series. TNS Media Intelligence, a company that tracks advertising, revealed that for the 2006 NCAA tournament, more than $500 million was spent on TV commercials, and an ad during the championship game cost $1 million. In addition, about $100,000 went toward online promotions by marketers such as Coca-Cola, Marriott, and Cingular. A vice president at CBS Sports noted that this televised tournament "has the single largest out-of-home viewing," while Marriott's senior vice president of marketing strategy said that online sponsorship and advertising gave the company "a way to interact with our target where they have chosen to be" (Howard 2006).

In the final analysis, the system we have in the United States for financing television is all about attracting audiences for commercials, making money for the companies that advertise their products using those commercials, and thereby making money for the stations and networks that broadcast the commercials. The price we pay in the United States for our so-called free television is advertising; commercials now take up as much as twenty minutes of an hour show in some cases. The average situation comedy is written to take up twenty-two minutes; the remainder of the half hour is for commercials and promos.

It has been estimated that Americans spend approximately nine

years of their lives watching television and one year of their lives just watching television commercials. Typically, American teenagers are exposed to approximately 360,000 television commercials by the time they graduate from high school (some have estimated the number at closer to 500,000). So the television commercial is what makes television, as we know it here in the United States, possible. There are other countries where people pay fees to the government to watch television and aren't exposed to the number of commercials that we are in the United States. Our system of providing free television, which we pay for by allowing commercials on our programs, isn't the only one around.

It is also important to remember that we eventually pay for our free television programs by generally being charged more by the makers of the advertised products and services we purchase; these makers pass their advertising costs on to the consumer. We pay many hundreds of dollars for advertising every time we purchase a new car. And while watching TV we also pay a psychological price by having our attention interrupted by commercials so often.

Commercials not only affect our minds (that is, our decision making about products and services) but also have the power to affect our bodies. As a result of the growth of the fast-food industry—which makes extensive use of commercials—an increasingly large percentage of U.S. children and adolescents, as well as adults, are now obese. Many of them suffer from clogged arteries, other heart problems, and diabetes from eating all those french fries, hamburgers, and other fat- and calorie-laden junk foods that they saw advertised on television. This obesity problem is now found in many other countries as well.

In recent years, prescription drug manufacturers have started advertising, and magazines and the airwaves are now full of advertisements and commercials for various prescription drugs. The people who are exposed to these advertisements then put pressure on their physicians to prescribe the advertised drugs. This has resulted in an incredible growth in the popularity, and also a significant rise in the price, of certain prescription drugs. There is a good deal of support now for doing something to restrain the amount of advertising these drugs companies do, as it is felt that this advertising has a negative effect on the medical industry and the health of Americans.

Television commercials, then, often have a social significance that goes far beyond the products they are advertising. There is a physiological, psychological, and social dimension to commercials; these narratives—or perhaps micronarratives is more correct—have important consequences.

NARRATIVES IN THE MEDIA

Our lives are saturated with the media and the media are saturated with narratives. This point is made by the French scholar Michel de Certeau, who explains in his book *The Practice of Everyday Life*:

> From morning to night, narrations constantly haunt streets and buildings. They articulate our existences by teaching us what they must be. They "cover the event," that is to say, they *make* our legends (*legenda*, what is to be read and said) out of it. Captured by the radio (the voice is the law) as soon as he awakens, the listener walks all day long through the forest of narrativities from journalism, advertising, and television narrativities that still find time, as he is getting ready for bed, to slip a few final messages under the portals of sleep. Even more than the God told about by the theologians of earlier days, these stories have a providential and predestining function: they organize in advance our work, our celebrations, and even our dreams. Social life multiplies the gestures and modes of behavior (*im*)*printed* by narrative models; it ceaselessly reproduces and accumulates "copies" of stories. Our society has become a recited society, in three senses: it is defined by *stories* (*recits*, the fables constituted by our advertising and informa-

tional media), by *citations* of stories, and by the interminable *recitation* of stories. (1984: 186)

What Certeau points out is that these narratives are not simply entertainments; he calls our attention to the fact that they have a powerful social and cultural significance to them. We learn certain physical gestures from them, and we learn how to behave in many cases by imitating those we see in these narratives, who become models for us. These narratives, Certeau argues, even organize our lives and permeate our dreams.

In the last thirty years the amount of television viewing people do on a daily basis has increased, and it is reasonable to suggest that we see more televised narratives now than in earlier times. It is the ability of these narratives, which tend to be full of violence and exploitative sexuality, to powerfully affect our emotions and our ideas about ourselves and life that is of importance here.

ARISTOTLE ON NARRATIVES

We all know what narratives are—stories. But the matter is a bit more complicated. The earliest and one of the most important philosophers to write about narratives was Aristotle. In his *Poetics*, written around 330 BC, Aristotle suggests that literary works—today we would include works such as films, television shows, novels, and plays—are always imitations of reality; that is, they can be thought of as mirrors. When we refer to this type of imitation, we often use the term *mimesis*, which is taken from the Greek.

There are three topics that relate to imitation for Aristotle:

1. *the medium of imitation* (language)
2. *the mode of imitation* (comedy or tragedy)
3. *the objects imitated* (men in action)

Aristotle points out that some works use only language while others use many different media. The mode of imitation, according to Aristotle, depends on whether a work is comic or tragic, or some combination of both. Then Aristotle moves on to the object of imitation, which is men in action. This matter of dealing with men in action he later describes as a plot, namely, the structure of the interactions or arrangement of incidents in a story. So a narrative, for our purposes, is a story of men (and women) in action.

Aristotle offered rules that were observed for centuries, rules requiring that plots have a beginning, a middle, and an end (in which the action is resolved), and rules about the nature of comedy and tragedy, among other things. Aristotle's rules are no longer slavishly observed, but he did offer a description of the basic elements of narrative, and this is useful for our purposes. According to Aristotle, a narrative tells a story by having characters interact with one another, and the narrative can use many different techniques and media—such as lighting, music, sound, scenery, and costuming—toward this end.

TEXTS AND OTHER TEXTS: INTERTEXTUALITY

One of the reasons that narrative texts such as films and television programs have such an emotional impact and affect us so powerfully

Figure 7.2   Imitation, as in *Saturday Night Live*'s parody of newscasts, is one form of intertextuality. What shows or movies can you name that imitate, allude to, adapt, or modify other media texts?

is that they often draw upon (deliberately or accidentally) other texts with which we are familiar—a situation known as **intertextuality**. There is a considerable amount of controversy about what intertextuality means, but for our purposes we will consider it to involve making allusion to, imitating, adapting, or modifying previously created texts, styles of expression, or genres. Often this intertextual borrowing is not done consciously by the creators of texts, I should point out, though sometimes—especially in the case of parodies—it is. Think, for example, of the *Saturday Night Live* spoofs of news programs (see figure 7.2).

In *Understanding Media Semiotics*, Marcel Danesi offers us an excellent example of intertextuality in his discussion of *Blade Runner:*

> The main text of the movie *Blade Runner* . . . unfolds as a science fiction detective story, but its subtext is, arguably, a religious one—the search for a Creator. This interpretation is bolstered by the many intertextual allusions to Biblical themes and symbols in the movie.
>
> The search for replicants in the film also ties it into postmodern thought, which is concerned with simulations of all kinds and their relation to reality. (2002: 63)

Some films pay homage, stylistically, to the works of great filmmakers such as Orson Welles and Sergei Eisenstein; some films are remakes of other films, such as *King Kong*; and some films adapt novels or stories, such as *Brokeback Mountain*. Many other examples of intertextuality can be found in all media.

Texts exist, then, in a kind of limbo—suspended between the past, that is, earlier texts, and the future, or forthcoming texts. All texts, it could be said, are intertextual in that they borrow from, are based on, or are affected by, to varying degrees, texts that have preceded them. These earlier texts have, in different ways, an impact on the psyches and sense of possibility of the creators of later texts. Bakhtin's stress on the importance of dialogue (technically known as *dialogism*) offers us new insights into the creative process; it also shows how important the social and cultural context is for creators of all kinds. That is because the creators of artistic texts are profoundly affected by the social and cultural milieu in which they find themselves—whether they recognize this to be the case or not. And by extension, all texts and other creative works that already exist cast a long shadow, so to speak, and provide a compelling frame of reference for all later texts being created at a given moment.

In many cases, artists and creative people in the media are unaware of the extent to which their work has been influenced by previously created texts; in other cases, in parody for example, artists are aware of earlier works and imitate them in a ridiculous manner. Bakhtin deals with the difficulties of separating one person's speech—or text—from another's:

> The relationship to another's word was equally complex and ambivalent in the Middle Ages. The role of the other's word was enormous at that time: there were quotations that were openly and reverently emphasized as such, or that were half-hidden, completely hidden, half-conscious, unconscious, correct, intentionally distorted, deliberately reinterpreted and so forth. The boundary lines between someone else's speech and one's own speech were flexible, ambiguous, often deliberately distorted and confused. Certain types of texts were constructed like mosaics out of the texts of others. . . . One of the best authorities on medieval parody, Paul Lehmann, states outright that the history of medieval literature and its Latin literature in particular "is the history of the appropriation, re-working and imitation of someone else's property." (1981: 69)

So intertexuality is nothing new. The concept helps us understand why it is that new texts can sometimes seem so familiar, and why texts often have remarkable emotional power: in part, it is because these texts often connect—stylistically or in terms of content—to other texts with which we are familiar.

An interesting example of intertextuality is discussed in *Pulp Politics* by Glenn W. Richardson Jr. He discusses a speech from the 1988 presidential campaign of George H. Bush.

> The appeal of invoking associations drawn from popular culture was not lost on George H. Bush's advisors in 1988 when they considered what turned out to be one of the most important phrases the vice president would ever utter. In August, Bush's speechwriting team was sharply divided over whether to include in his acceptance speech at the Republican National Convention the now infamous line, "Read

my lips: no new taxes." "Read my lips" was a catch-phrase of the
hyper-macho action-film hero "Dirty Harry" Callahan, played by
actor Clint Eastwood. . . . By merely aping the language of a familiar
Hollywood icon, the vice president was able to activate a deep web
of preexisting associations in his audience. Campaign ads can do this
even more effectively, by using audio, visual, and narrative elements
to tap viewers' cognitive maps, literally evoking neural networks in
our brains to communicate campaign themes with emotional force.
(2003: 4–5)

We see here how an intertextual reference to a well-known, popular-
culture text can have enormous consequences, and why political
campaigns often make use of such references in their print advertisements and television commercials.

THE QUESTION OF THE UR-TEXT

If all texts are related to one another—stylistically, in terms of their
adoption of certain technical or genre conventions, or content-wise
(that is, in terms of imitating or alluding to a particular text)—the
question arises as to whether all texts are related to one, primal, **ur-
text**. This text would be a kind of template for all other texts, a
"mother of all" texts.

Let me suggest that the fairy tale is the foundational model of
the narrative, and that fairy tales, which psychoanalytic critics such as
Bruno Bettelheim say are the first important narratives to which we
are exposed, are ur-texts. Fairy tales, collectively, contain all the elements found in the more important contemporary narrative genres,
and a given tale may contain all of them. Consider the following list
of contemporary genres and their fairy-tale elements:

science fiction	characters ride on magic carpets, have magic weapons
horror	various monsters and dragons need to be dealt with
action-adventure	heroes have tasks to do or battles to fight

| detective | characters must solve puzzles and crimes |
| romance | heroes marry princesses |

In modern narratives we generally find these primal elements updated, but even so the origin of our more important genres can be traced back to the fairy tale and to the psychological gratifications and societal instructions that these fairy tales provide.

NEWS ON TELEVISION

The coverage of the 9/11 attack and the events that followed showed that television can perform a valuable service. In times of crisis, it is invaluable. At other times, however, the news falls victim to the same forces that operate on other television programs: the need to maximize profits. At one time, news was considered a service that networks provided to audiences, even if the news shows lost money. Now, news—especially national news broadcasts—have been "lightened" up, and broadcast news in general suffers from having been turned into entertainment, a process we might call "tabloidization." Local television news can, generally speaking, only be described as a disaster.

The tyranny of audience demographics and the quest of advertisers for younger audiences are constantly at work. A friend of mine in the advertising industry told me recently that the hottest demographic is now twelve- to thirty-two-year-olds. Advertisers are after twelve-year-olds especially, hoping to "brand" them and recruit them as life-long customers of their products and services. Young children have also been taught to be brand conscious. We can only wonder what the impact of all this branding will be on American culture and society.

I would suggest that news shows and commercials are—in terms of their social, economic, and political impact—the most important genres carried by television, and that selected texts from these genres can have a significant impact upon our psyches, our bodies, and our society. Curiously, however, it may be that it is the commercials we

Figure 7.3   In the aftermath of Hurricane Katrina, a man carries a baby through the flooded streets of New Orleans outside the Super Dome stadium. How are we affected by viewing hundreds of news images of disasters like Katrina and 9/11?

watch that have the most profound and long-lasting impact on us as individuals—especially commercials for food products, which affect and in some cases shape our food preferences, and political commercials, which play an important role in electing politicians and thus helping determine social policy.

9/11 AND THE SOCIAL IMPACT OF MEDIA IMAGES

When it comes to the matter of the social impact of the mass media, the 9/11 tragedy is of signal importance. For people in the United States, and elsewhere as well, there have been probably no television images in recent history as horrifying as those of the two planes, controlled by terrorists, crashing into the World Trade Center. These images were followed by horrific images of people jumping to their deaths from the buildings, and then of the giant towers collapsing into a gigantic pile of rubble, with smoke from the fires filling the sky. Some people who were asked about viewing these events on television said it looked more like a movie to them.

These images, and the news programs that were on the airwaves for the next few days, changed America in profound ways. There was an immediate sea change in U.S. foreign policy, which went from being quasi-isolationist to internationalist, as Americans suddenly recognized that what was going on in a poor country like Afghanistan, thousands of miles away from American shores, could affect the United States in profound ways.

A new, villainous figure emerged—the international terrorist—and with his emergence, all kinds of things that we used to take for granted, such as superficial examination of our baggage at airports, ended. Suddenly we became conscious of the danger terrorists represented, and made major changes to our law-enforcement practices. The American Muslim community, which had never received much press, suddenly became the subject of intense interest, and a number of atrocities and hate crimes were committed against Muslims or people who were thought to be Muslim.

At the same time, new heroes presented themselves: the firemen and policemen and policewomen who risked their lives trying, valiantly, to save people in the World Trade Center. Many of these brave men and women in the New York City Fire Department and Police Department lost their lives doing so. The attacks on America led to a new sense of nationalism in the American public; all of a sudden, people started displaying the American flag outside their homes, on their automobiles, and wherever else they could.

There have been reports of large numbers of people who watched the 9/11 newscasts later suffering from increased anxiety and post-traumatic shock. (Many young children, I should note, were traumatized by the events of 9/11 and required therapy.) Some psychiatrists even suggested at the time that it would be best if people didn't watch so much television in the immediate aftermath of 9/11, but people's curiosity about the event—who was responsible for it, and its consequences—was so strong that many people watched an enormous amount of the 9/11 news coverage.

We see then how powerful a text can be. In this case, we are dealing with the most serious attack on the American mainland in our history—an attack that cost nearly three thousand lives. The news shows about the 9/11 attack demonstrate how a particular event—and images of that event—can have an enormous impact on individuals and indeed on entire societies. The same applies to the impact of the television coverage of hurricanes Katrina and Rita in September 2005, whose full effect on our economy and collective psyche has yet to be determined.

As we have seen then, particular mass-mediated texts can have enormous consequences. In the case of 9/11, the event itself was most significant, but the media coverage of it on television and cable outlets, in newspapers and magazines, and on countless talk shows played a major role in giving the event the impact it had on the American public and the world. More recently, cartoons of the Prophet Muhammad, first published in Danish newspapers in fall 2005 and reprinted in several publications throughout Europe, sparked protests overseas—some peaceful but many violent—that claimed numerous lives and continued well into 2006.

BY WORDS ALONE?

This chapter has dealt with the power of narratives (including commercials) and of images in texts—especially with respect to the horrific 9/11 tragedy. In narrative texts such as films, television shows, and video games, we find that some acts of violence may be much more important than other acts of violence, so merely counting the number of violent incidents in a text or a given time period, while important, doesn't tell the whole story. We may talk about television in general terms, but it is really the texts carried by television, often in combination with one another during an evening's viewing (which is sometimes called "flow"), that affect our beliefs and emotions; and as we have seen, these beliefs and emotions have considerable economic, social, and cultural significance.

A question now suggests itself. If we did not have television coverage of an event like 9/11, if we didn't *see* all those terrifying images, if we only heard about the attack on the radio or only read about it in newspapers, would such an attack have had the impact it did? Eventually, I would imagine, we would have made the same decisions we made about foreign policy and all the other aspects of our lives affected by the attack, but I don't think that reading about the attack, or even listening to a radio report of it, would have had the same impact as watching the events on television.

Still, words alone can have serious impact. A different mass-mediated text, a 2005 report in *Newsweek* magazine that American troops at the Guantanamo Bay detention site had flushed a copy of the Koran down the toilet, led to riots and several deaths and injuries in Afghanistan. *Newsweek* later repudiated the article, but the damage had been done. There is considerable debate as to what degree *Newsweek* was responsible (if at all) for the riots and deaths, but the event shows how what seems like a minor detail in a news story can have enormous repercussions.

The most comprehensive analysis of violence on television has been conducted in the National Television Violence Study (1996) which analyzed the content of a total of 3,185 programs across 23 television channels from 6 a.m. until 11 p.m., 7 days a week, for the course of a television season. The researchers report that 57% of all programs analyzed had some violence and that one-third of programs presented nine or more violent interactions. This study also examined the context within which the violence was presented and found that rarely was violence punished and rarely were victims shown as suffering any harmful consequences. . . . These patterns led researchers to conclude that not only was violence prevalent throughout the entire landscape, but that it was typically shown as sanitized and glamorized. (1998: 166)

—W. James Potter, *Media Literacy*

8

MEDIA AND VIOLENCE

Many and perhaps most analyses of **media violence** don't pay attention to specific violent acts in specific texts because researchers are looking for generalizations they can make and correlations they can find between the amount of exposure to media of selected populations and the amount of violence members of these populations commit.

There is a distinction between *causality* and *correlation* to be made.

causality	X causes Y. Whenever you have X, you get Y.
correlation	Y comes after X and is possibly connected to it.

We have not been able to do more than find strong relationships or correlations between the amount of television violence viewed and violent behavior in real life; we have had trouble proving that exposure to televised violence actually causes violent behavior. The evidence suggests that viewing violence on television can and probably does lead to violent behavior, but it doesn't seem possible for us to go beyond that assertion. This matter of the relationship between television violence and real-life violence has been of great interest to researchers.

In 1988, for example, Nancy Signorielli and George Gerbner published *Violence and Terror in the Mass Media: An Annotated Bibliogra-*

151

phy, which deals with 784 studies of television violence. It contains brief descriptions of articles from scholarly books and journals, and articles from government reports, popular journals, and conference papers on violence in the media. The book covers areas such as media content, media effects, pornography and the media, and terrorism and the media.

HOW IS MEDIA VIOLENCE DEFINED?

Signorielli and Gerbner offer the following definition of media violence:

> Reliable observation and systematic analysis usually requires limited and objective definitions. Most research studies have defined media violence as the depiction of overt physical action that hurts or kills or threatens to do so. A terroristic act is typically defined as one involving violence by, among, or against states or other authorities in order to spread fear and make a statement, usually political. Media violence and terror are closely related. They depict social relationships and the use of force to control, dominate, provoke, or annihilate. By demon-

---

Websites on Violence and the Media

Some websites that deal with violence and the media are:

Adults and Children Together Against Violence
www.actagainstviolence.com/mediaviolence

American Psychological Association (APA Online)
www.psychologymatters.org/mediaviolence.html

Media Awareness Network (Canada)
www.media-awareness.ca/english/issues/violence

Media Literacy Online Project
http://interact.uoregon.edu/Medialit/mlr/readings/contents/violence.html

---

strating who can get away with what against whom, factual and fictional representations of violence or terror can intimidate people; provoke resistance, aggression, or repression; and cultivate a sense of relative strength and vulnerability as they portray the social "pecking order." (1988: xi)

Signorielli and Gerbner explain their understanding of "cultivate," writing that "for most viewers, television's mean and dangerous world tends to cultivate a sense of relative danger, mistrust, dependence, and—despite its supposedly 'entertaining' nature—alienation and gloom" (1988: xviii). Other researchers, who worked independently of Gerbner and his associates, found the following things about media and violence (I have slightly modified the language of these reports for the sake of readability):

1. Media exposure to violence boosts public estimates of crime and violence.
2. There's a significant relationship between exposure to crime shows and approval of police brutality and bias against civil liberties.
3. Television viewing can be related to feelings of anxiety and fear of victimization.
4. Television viewing tends to cultivate the presumption of the guilt rather than the innocence of a suspect. (1988: xviii)

It is reasonable to argue, based on the above material, that television violence is not, as a number of theorists suggest, a harmless cathartic but has, instead, profound effects upon both individual viewers and society in general. Television may not be the direct and only cause of much of the violence that we find in American society, but it has to be considered a contributing factor. When Signorielli and Gerbner discuss terrorism, it seems like just a minor aspect of the matter, but after the horrendous events of 9/11, terror has become a major factor in analyses of violence. There is little question that people in the United States feel extremely vulnerable now as a result of the destruction of the World Trade Center.

A LONGITUDINAL STUDY OF
TELEVISION VIEWING AND VIOLENCE

A study by the Center for Media and Public Affairs shows that there has been a 17 percent drop in prime-time violence on television, while broadcast violence has decreased 11 percent, and violence on premium cable shows has decreased 65 percent. This may represent a certain amount of progress, but a drop of 17 percent from a very high initial level of violence may not be that important. As noted above, we now have research that suggests a strong connection—that is, a correlation—between viewing television violence and committing aggressive acts in real life.

An article by Nanette Asimov in the *San Francisco Chronicle* deals with a new longitudinal study on the relationship between television viewing and violence. It reports that young teenagers who watch more than an hour of television each day "are nearly four times as likely to commit aggressive acts in later years than those who watch less than an hour." Asimov discusses the findings of a seventeen-year study on the relation between television viewing and violence. She writes:

> The 17-year study, to be published in today's issue of the journal *Science,* studied 707 children from adolescence to early adulthood.

Researchers found a "significant association" between television viewing and later violence by both boys and girls, although the effect was most striking in boys. (March 29, 2002: 2)

Jeffrey Johnson of Columbia University, one of the coauthors of the study, suggested that parents should not let children watch more than an hour of television a day during early adolescence. His study mentions that during an average hour of prime-time television, three to five violent acts are portrayed, while an hour of children's television has twenty to twenty-five violent acts. Most of the violent acts on children's television are comic, but that doesn't mean they don't predispose children toward violent behavior.

One of the more remarkable findings deals with youths who watched three or more hours of television per day at age fourteen and acted in an aggressive manner at sixteen or twenty years of age: it turns out that 45.2 percent of males and 12.7 percent of the females acted aggressively. Of the fourteen-year-olds who watched one hour or less per day, 8.9 percent of the males and 2.3 percent of the females acted aggressively. The authors of the study also argue that television viewing "remained significant" as a factor after accounting for other factors that might generate violent behavior, such as neighborhood violence, neglect, and psychiatric disorders.

Television and Aggression

We saw the jump [in the time children were watching television] was between less than one hour and more than one hour a day. There was a four-fold increase. Parents should try not to let children watch more than one hour a day on the average. We are social beings and we tend to want to try out things that we see other people doing, especially if we see the person rewarded for what they did or portrayed as a hero for it. We found that teenagers who, at mean age fourteen, watched more than three hours a day of television were much more likely than those who watched less than one hour a day to commit subsequent acts of aggression against other people.

Source: Jeffrey Johnson, Columbia University.

In studies of television viewing and violence, the results are generally *correlations* between viewing television violence and violent behavior. This is because it is very difficult to establish causal relations between anything when dealing with human beings. But this does not mean that studies that establish correlations are of little interest. The study I have just cited, which dealt with children over a seventeen-year period, is the first that offers such a long-term view of the relationship between television viewing and violence. Defenders of television often argue that television may be a contributing factor in violence, but it is not the sole factor or a causal one. The important question is, To what degree is television a contributing factor?

KINDS OF VIOLENCE

There are, let me suggest, any number of different aspects of violence. Table 8.1 lists a number of sets of paired opposites that summarize the various kinds of violence that exist in relation to the media, and show how complicated a matter violence can be.

Violence, as this list suggests, is an incredibly complex matter. That helps explain why our responses to violence, as individuals and collectively, depend in certain cases on whether we see the violence as defensive (part of the scheme of things, as in sports), as caused by

Table 8.1   Kinds of Violence Contrasted

Form of Violence	Opposite Form of Violence
1. mass-mediated violence	violence we see directly
2. real mediated violence (war coverage)	fictive mediated violence (stories)
3. comic violence (kids' TV shows)	serious violence (adult films)
4. violence against individuals	violence against groups or society
5. police violence (just)	criminal violence (unjust)
6. verbal violence (insults)	physical violence (hitting someone)
7. violence against humans	violence against animals
8. scripted violence (pro wrestling)	"real" violence (bar brawl)
9. violence against heroes	violence against villains
10. violence against women	violence against men
11. visual images of violence	prose descriptions of violence
12. violence as a sign of depravity	violence as a cry for help

hatred, or as just (violence used by the police) or evil (violence used by murderers and terrorists). We feel differently about violence directed against machines or aliens than we do about violence directed against humans, and about comic violence versus serious violence. I doubt that the typical television viewer has ever articulated all these different kinds and aspects of violence, but it is quite likely that viewers can differentiate between so-called good violence and bad violence and at the same time carry in their heads ideas about many of the aspects of violence listed above.

One problem, for example, involves comic violence. Young children are exposed to a great deal of comic violence on many of the television programs they see. We used to assume that because it was comic, it had no serious effects. Now, a number of researchers have suggested that exposure to comic violence has negative effects on children.

VIOLENCE IN TEXTS:
QUALITY VERSUS QUANTITY

One problem with counting the number of violent incidents in a given time period is that it neglects the specific kinds of violence and the way violence is used in a particular text. One act of violence in a particular text may have a much more powerful impact than a number of acts of violence in a different text. So merely counting the number of acts of violence on television in a given time period may not be very useful. However, because there is no universally accepted way of scaling the impact of different acts of violence in a text, counting the number of acts of violence in a given time period is the best we can do. And as the study cited above suggests, there is a strong correlation between the amount of television viewing children and adolescents do and their tendency to be aggressive and to commit violent acts, regardless of the role the violence might have played in a given text.

There is, of course, violence in many elite texts, that is, classics. Look at Shakespeare's *Hamlet*, for example. At the end of the play, the stage is littered with dead bodies. But the violence in *Hamlet* stems from the plot and is not gratuitous, like the violence in many contemporary films, where cars and buildings are blown up and people are killed, one after another.

In many contemporary films and television programs, there is so much violence that we have, literally speaking, overkill. Violence loses its significance in the plots of these texts, though the impact of this violence on our psyches lingers on, I would suggest, long after we turn off the television set or leave the theater. Many of the violence-filled films of Hollywood are later shown on television, which even without these films is permeated with violence. Consider, for example, local news show reports on community violence, comic violence in children's programs, sports violence (especially in hockey and football), violence in cop shows and other dramatic pieces, and, of course, televised wrestling matches—which really should be seen as theatrical performances and not sport.

In some texts, as I suggested earlier, we may see a number of incidents of violence, but one particular incident may be much more important than others. In the classic western *Shane*, a pathological killer named Jack Wilson (played by Jack Palance) kills a hapless victim in a bar, but the most significant act of violence comes at the end of the film when Shane (played by Alan Ladd) confronts Wilson in a classic shoot-out.

By the time this shoot-out occurs, dramatic tension has built up, and the violence in this scene has much more resonance and power than the other violent scenes in the film. And there is an incredible sense of relief in the audience as Wilson finally crumples to the ground, killed by Shane—a gunslinger even faster than Wilson. So some acts of violence in a text are much more powerful and meaningful than other acts of violence in the same text. In many contemporary films that are permeated by violence—fights, exploding cars, killings—it is often difficult to see which violent scene or event is the most significant.

VIOLENCE IN NEWS BROADCASTS

If we watch a typical local television news show, we see stories about such things as murders, rapes, fires, and automobile accidents. Local

Figure 8.1   Real violence covered in the news, from local violence to the war in Iraq, has a status different from violence in dramas and narratives that is "unreal." Some media critics suggest that it may convince viewers that the world is a very dangerous place and may generate feelings of anxiety and fear.

television news shows, and to some extent national news shows, are filled with violence—in part because there is so much real violence in some cities and regions of the world. In Oakland, California, for example, there were more than one hundred murders during 2002. This meant that the ten o'clock news on KTVU Channel 2, an hour-long local news program from Oakland, had a huge number of news reports that year about murders in Oakland, as well as reports of other murders, rapes, and kidnappings that took place in Oakland and elsewhere.

Television is an audiovisual medium, and television producers are looking for stories that have a strong visual element. Interviews with so-called talking heads don't have the visual power an image of a fire or a dead body has, even though these interviews may have more importance in that some of these talking heads have political power, and their decisions can affect our lives in profound ways.

Because the violence shown on television news is real, because television news captures events that actually happen, news violence has a status different from violence in dramas and narratives that is not real. This real-world violence may affect viewers differently than the violence of dramatic fictions. It may convince viewers, as George Gerbner and others have suggested, that the world is a very dangerous place, and may generate feelings of anxiety and fear.

The question we must ask about local televised news is, Are there other events, of more importance to the well-being of the community, that could be dealt with on these shows instead of an endless succession of murders, rapes, robberies, fires, and automobile crashes? It's important to remember that producers of local news programs select from a number of different possible stories to cover; they don't have to fill their newscasts with gossip and sensationalist stories, but they do so because they believe (and perhaps they know) that by doing this they attract a large audience. In other words, they are giving their television viewers what they want.

This may or may not be true. But should television give people what they want or seem to want (in part, because they have been brought up on a diet of sensationalistic news shows), or rather what they need, that is, information that will make them more informed and more responsible citizens? The question of whether television audiences want (or say they want) what they've been taught to want has not been resolved and is one that still troubles media researchers.

Many critics have suggested that news programs, which once were regarded as a public service to the community (and often lost money), now have become obsessed, like other kinds of television shows, with getting high ratings and making as much money as possible. Critics describe news as having undergone "tabloidization," by which they mean that news shows today have too many stories about celebrities, scandals, and other material of little real importance. In some cases, news show producers feel forced to cover stories that have appeared in tabloid newspapers, which are full of gossip, unsubstantiated celebrity gossip, and in some cases, political scandal. News has become, to a considerable degree, an entertainment, and as such it finds itself continually relying on the crutches found in many other entertainment genres: sensationalism and violence.

In his book *Going Live: Getting the News Right in a Real-Time Online World*, Philip Seib offers a telling indictment of most radio and television news programs:

> Real-time journalism often delivers the news in easily consumable bites. But these are intellectual snacks, not meals; they satisfy only briefly and leave a hunger for more. There is not enough substance to be truly filling. This issue is not relevant to some news reports, since the story topics themselves—especially spot news items—are shallow and inconsequential. More substantive stories—those that have long-term importance—suffer from high-speed, quick-and-dirty coverage. (2002: 58)

What people need to counter such stories, especially the ones found on local news shows, is generally found in newspapers, which can offer context and in-depth coverage. Unfortunately, most Americans don't get this kind of material, since a high percentage of the American public relies on radio and television for all its news.

CHILDREN AND MEDIA VIOLENCE

There are a huge number of websites devoted to media and violence, and a search on Google for the key phrase "media and violence" yields around forty-seven thousand relevant sites, or "hits." Sites such as these offer their readers information discovered by the numerous psychologists, sociologists, and other media scholars who have made serious studies of violence in the media. The findings of a preponderance of media scholars who have studied violence follows (taken from the websites of a number of pediatricians, media researchers, and other interested professionals):

1. Media violence can lead to aggressive behavior in children. Our most recent study (the seventeen-year study discussed above) confirms this fact.
2. By age eighteen, the average American child will have seen 16,000 murders and viewed about 200,000 acts of violence on television.

3. The level of violence on Saturday morning cartoons is higher than the level of violence during prime-time television. There are 3 to 5 violent acts per hour in prime time, versus 20 to 25 acts per hour on Saturday morning.
4. Media violence is especially damaging to young children (under age eight) because they cannot easily tell the difference between real life and fantasy. Violent images on television and in movies may seem real to young children, and they can be traumatized by viewing these images.
5. Media violence also affects children by increasing their aggressiveness, antisocial behavior, and fear of victimization, and by desensitizing them (making them less sensitive to violence and to victims of violence and increasing their appetite for more violence in entertainment and in real life).
6. Media violence often fails to show the consequences of violence. This is especially true of cartoons, toy commercials, and music videos. As a result, children may come to believe that there are few if any repercussions when committing violent acts.

Many media researchers and pediatricians suggest that the amount of television that children are permitted to watch be limited to no more than two hours a day, and that parents monitor the television their children watch.

Experts also suggest that parents should not allow their children to watch violent television programs, videos, or films, and should monitor the video games their children play. In addition, they suggest that parents must help their children distinguish between fantasy and reality by explaining to them that real-life violence has consequences. Unfortunately, a large percentage of parents do not monitor the television their children watch—in part because these parents use television as a baby-sitter, and in part because many children (68 percent according to a Kaiser Family Foundation report, http://kff.org/entmedia/entmedia030905nr.cfm; see chapter 1) have their own television set in their bedroom. The semanticist S. I. Hayakawa once wrote an article titled "Who's Bringing Up Your Children?" His answer was—television.

Figure 8.2   Many children watch television without parental supervision or guidance.

I consulted a neurologist about mass-mediated violence, and he suggested that violent scenarios may affect us by modifying our neurological systems; violent acts may become a form of conditioning, that is, they may create certain pathways and circuits in the brain and affect its neurochemistry. The brain then is alerted by certain acts that function as "red flags," and this can lead to physical violence or other forms of antisocial behavior.

We know that children imitate others, so there is reason to fear that children will imitate the behavior of media characters they identify with, often while not realizing what the outcome of their behavior will be. So there is reason to argue that children before the age of eight should be shielded from mass-mediated violence. We should do the same for young adolescents, and actually for everyone, since watching portrayals of violence can have very negative consequences even for adults. Adults, as many scholars and researchers suggest, also become fearful and anxiety-ridden when exposed to violence, even when they know that the violence is not real.

"KILL 'EM"

When I taught courses on media criticism, I used to ask my students to watch wrestling matches on television. It was not unusual during these matches to see some spectators, including little old ladies, run up to the ring and scream, "Kill him, kill him" to their favorite wrestler—usually a good guy, hero wrestler who was throwing a dirty, bad guy wrestler around the ring according to the script. These fans didn't want their hero to actually kill his opponent, but their behavior shows how violence, even scripted violence, can excite people. *There is a visceral, that is, a physiological, effect from seeing violence, even fake violence*, that leads people to react in different ways: some get very excited, some scream and cheer, some tremble, some avert their eyes.

My point is that even if we think we are old and mature enough to handle violence, we may be fooling ourselves and we may still be affected by it—traumatized, made anxious, made fearful. The word *violence* is very close to the word *violate*, which has many negative denotations and connotations. When we watch violent acts in the media, we may be *violated*, or affected in ways we may not recognize.

The fact that we are probably exposed to fifteen thousand or more murders during the course of our television viewing as we grow up must have some effect on us. This is perhaps not true for most of us, but there are some of us who will have psychological problems and other difficulties, and who will be more influenced than others by their exposure to television violence, film violence, and other forms of mass-mediated violence (music videos and rap music, for example). These individuals would have been much more likely to act out and be violent, sometimes in serious ways, as children, and they will continue to do so as they grow older.

There are several solutions that suggest themselves here. First, the people who make violent television shows and films and other texts must significantly reduce the amount of violence they inject into their works. There is even an aesthetic concern that makes this a reasonable course of action: the law of diminishing returns suggests that the continual use of violence dulls its impact; so producers, directors, and writers would serve their own interests—as well as those of society at large—in reducing the amount of violence in their texts. Second, we must reduce our exposure to violent texts, and especially the exposure of our children to these texts. As I've noted, during the aftermath of the 9/11 tragedy a number of psychiatrists and mental health professionals suggested that it would be a good idea for adults to cut down on the amount of news they were watching, since constant exposure to the horrendous images of the attacks were having powerful and negative effects on viewers, both young and old.

It would also be a good thing if the government or parent groups could find a way to induce the creators of television programs for children to reduce the comic violence in their shows. The airwaves, after all, are owned by the American people, and the networks and stations that use the networks are supposed to be broadcasting in the public interest. I recall once seeing an interview with a television producer who said he wouldn't let his own children watch the shows he made because the shows were too violent.

We ought surely to look in the child for the first traces of imaginative activity. The child's best-loved and most absorbing occupation is play. Perhaps we may say that every child at play behaves like an imaginative writer, in that he creates a world of his own or, more truly, he rearranges the things of this world and orders it in a new way that pleases him better. . . .

Now the writer does the same as the child at play; he creates a world of phantasy which he takes very seriously; that is, he invests it with a great deal of affect, while separating it sharply from reality. Language has preserved this relationship between children's play and poetic creation. It designates certain kinds of imaginative creation, concerned with tangible objects and capable of representation, as "plays"; the people who present them are called "players." The unreality of this poetic world of imagination, however, has very important consequences for literary technique; for many things which if they happened in real life could produce no pleasure can nevertheless give enjoyment in a play—many emotions which are essentially painful may become a source of enjoyment to the spectators and hearers of a poet's work.

—Sigmund Freud, "The Relation of the Poet
to Day-Dreaming"

9

MEDIA ARTISTS

B y *media artists* I mean all the people who create texts—either individually, as in the case of most nonfiction books or works of fiction by novelists, or collectively, as in the case of a film or television show. In a typical film or television show, for example, we have

performance artists:	actors and actresses
production artists:	directors, editors, camera operators, musicians
creative artists:	writers

We may add to these the producers, publicity people, and all those involved in the business side of filmmaking.

Most films involve an incredible number of different kinds of media artists and specialists. After a film concludes and as we get up from our seats in the theater, the credits roll, listing the large number of people who were involved in making that film, from the producer, director, actors, actresses, first assistant director, and second assistant director down to the grips and the makeup artists. Television programs, while usually not as complicated as films, still require many different kinds of artists. For example, there were a dozen writers on the writing team that created the situation comedy *Frasier* each week. The show that we see on television is just the tip of the creation and production iceberg, so to speak. A simple program, such as a cooking show, could easily have fifteen or twenty people involved in actually making the program.

There is a difference between writing books, which tends to be an individual effort, and making films and television shows, which require collaborative effort. But writers of books, while they may write alone, still must take the wishes and desires of others—namely publishers and editors, and sometimes people such as marketing directors—into consideration. And of course writers, like anyone else doing creative work, must consider their audiences.

In order to show how complicated the process of creating media texts is, let me take a relatively simple kind of text—a scholarly book—as an example. For other kinds of texts such as television programs, films, and video games, you can assume that matters are even more difficult.

PUBLISHING A SCHOLARLY BOOK: A CASE STUDY

Let's say that someone writes a book on a scholarly subject—a book that may also be used in courses at colleges and universities. I make a distinction here between scholarly books that are written on some subject and may be used as texts in courses, and textbooks, which are written only for use in courses and which generally have a great deal of teaching apparatus: study questions, extensive bibliographies, learning exercises, and so on. In some cases, the distinction between scholarly books and textbooks is hard to make.

Writers of scholarly books always face the problem of finding publishers who will agree to publish their books. In many cases, the writer must prepare a substantial proposal that describes the book, lists the chapters, discusses the competition, and offers a sample chapter. This is sent to editors at various publishers who publish the kind of book the author wishes to write. Let us suppose an acquiring editor at XYZ Books likes a submitted proposal and asks to see the book manuscript. Generally speaking, writers of scholarly books send off their proposals for books before they have actually written them, so they won't write a book that nobody will publish. Let us assume now that the scholar has written a book-length manuscript based on the proposal submitted earlier.

The acquiring editor, who is responsible for finding books to publish, must then convince an editorial committee at his or her publishing house—a committee often made up of editors, marketing directors, and others—that the book (now in manuscript form) is worthwhile. By this I mean it is a good book, well-written, backed by sound scholarship, and will probably find a suitable audience. It takes a considerable amount of money to publish a book, and publishers, like any business, must make a profit if they are to survive. So every book published is, in a sense, a bet made by the publisher that the book will find enough of an audience to make publishing it profitable. Publishers realize they can't win every bet, but if they don't win enough bets, and sell enough books, they go out of business.

My experience has been that editors often have many useful suggestions to make about what is dealt with in a book—about how much weight should be given to certain subjects and about what might be added to a book or deleted from it. It is not unusual for an author to get a manuscript back with long notes, questions, and suggestions on many pages of the manuscript. Then once the manuscript for the book is revised to the satisfaction of the editor, he or she often sends it to a number of scholars and professors who are thought to be experts in the subject, to see whether there are errors of fact or interpretation in the manuscript and whether there are topics that have been missed or not explained well. So it is not unusual for an author to receive several (sometimes four or five) anonymous reviews of the manuscript, each suggesting what should be done to make the book better, or in some cases, even advising that the manuscript not be published.

This means that there is another step that must be taken: dealing with these scholarly and professorial reviews of the manuscript, some of which may be constructive and valuable and others of which may be mean-spirited and extremely hostile. Such reviews, even the negative ones, can be helpful, since they point out areas that might need work and problems readers might face in reading the book. The author then must take the various suggestions into consideration and revise the manuscript again, where revisions are called for.

Let us suppose that this has been done to the satisfaction of the book's editor. Soon after, the book is sent to a copyeditor, who goes through the book doing things like checking for typing mistakes the author has made, smoothing the prose here and there, asking questions about facts, and checking footnotes and bibliographical citations. I have found copyeditors to be extremely helpful in the course of my career. In the old days, copyeditors wrote their questions on sticky notes, and you'd get your manuscript back with perhaps three or four notes, with questions or suggestions on them, per page. Now copyeditors tend to ask their questions and make their changes in bold type right in the electronic file of the manuscript (taken from the disk or CD that has the manuscript on it), and then they send a printout—or simply the electronic files—marked with their questions and suggestions for the writer to consider. The copyedited manuscript is then sent back to the writer, who answers the questions the copyeditor asks, makes sure the copyeditor hasn't changed the meaning of the text, and approves any changes the copyeditor has made.

When the manuscript has been copyedited and examined by the author, it is then shepherded (usually by a production editor) through typesetting. The edited manuscript first goes to book designers who decide on the typography of the book—what typefaces are to be used, what size the text block should be, how much spacing there should be between lines of type, and where illustrations are to go and how large or small they should be. The production editor generally tells the designer how many pages the book should be, and the designer works within those guidelines. A cover must also be designed for the book. Sometimes the typography and cover design are done by artists who work for the publisher, and other times the typography and cover design are sent out to freelance book designers and cover artists.

When the manuscript has been typeset into what are often called page proofs, it is checked by a proofreader and the author, who look for errors made by the typesetter and for errors that the copyeditor and author missed earlier. The author then must make an index or have the page proofs sent to a professional indexer. Once the index is typeset and all proofreading corrections are made, the page proofs can be sent to the printer and the book is manufactured.

You can see, then, that while it only took one person to write the book, it took a number of people to move the book manuscript into production and to actually publish the book. This process is less complicated with novels, but editors often play an important role with novel writers as well—getting them to cut or expand their manuscripts, and to make various changes here and there—so novelists often work closely with their editors. One reason editors are important is that writers become so involved with their manuscripts that, in a sense, they can't see them clearly, and a person who is not so emotionally tied to a book can often see the things that need to be done to make it better.

Writing scholarly books and novels is a lonely occupation. You sit in front of a computer (it used to be a typewriter) and spend hours putting words down, one after another. But once you have a manuscript that has been accepted by a publisher, you find yourself dealing with many book publishing professionals, with different areas of expertise, who work with you in turning your manuscript into a book.

THE BOOK BUSINESS

It's interesting to compare the audiences for books and other mass media, such as television programs. We can make a distinction between trade books, which are produced for the general public and sold in bookstores; scholarly books, which are written by and for scholars but are often used in university courses; and textbooks, which are produced for students, and are generally only sold in university bookstores. Publishers sell scholarly books and textbooks by printing catalogs describing their books and sending them to professors who may find a certain book of personal interest and may also want to use it in a course they are teaching. Most publishers now have sites on the Internet where their books are described and where buyers can purchase them. Trade books generally only have a three-month "window of opportunity." This means that if they don't sell well during that period, they are typically remaindered, or sold to companies that grind them up and reuse the paper pulp.

A trade book that sells 100,000 copies is considered a great success, while a network television show that *only* attracts 6 million or 8 million viewers (and thus has poor ratings) is often considered a failure. Some trade books, of course, sell in the millions, but the average book is lucky if it sells 5,000 or 10,000 copies, and the average scholarly book doesn't sell anywhere near that number. Textbooks are a different matter, and a good textbook in a core subject (such as introductory economics or freshman English) can sell tens of thousands, hundreds of thousands, or even millions of copies.

New technology has now come to the aid of the writers and publishers of scholarly books. The minimum pressrun for a scholarly book (i.e., a pressrun that makes economic sense) is between 500 and 1,000 copies, though in many cases the pressruns are much larger. But some scholarly books don't sell anywhere near 1,000 copies, which means that publishers—usually university presses—often end up with stacks and stacks of previously published scholarly books in their warehouses, which costs them money. Now as a result of the development of new print-on-demand printers that can print a cover and the text of a book from a CD-ROM in just a short period of time, scholarly book publishers can print their books as they are needed. That is, they can print books when they get orders for them and so avoid holding large inventories of books, many of great scholarly importance, that may or may not find purchasers. And inventories of previously published books can be disposed of, without the books going out of print.

Several commercial print-on-demand publishers, such as IUniverse (www.iuniverse.com) and Xlibris (http://xlibris.com), enable authors to publish a book for as little as $500 or $600. For this money, authors get their book set into type (from an electronic file the author provides) with a cover designed for the book. When anyone orders one or more copies of a specific book, the copies are printed.

A new competitor to IUniverse and Xlibris has appeared: a website called Lulu that can be found at www.lulu.com. Lulu allows writers to publish books at no cost. It provides a fully automated means of publishing books, as long as the manuscript is written on a computer file and can be uploaded to the Lulu website. Authors only pay for the cost of printing copies of their books, which generally amounts to nine or ten dollars per copy.

What this means is that anyone with a computer can now publish a book with companies such as Xlibris, IUniverse, and Lulu. These books are available to the general public and are in some cases described and listed on sites such as www.amazon.com and www.barnesandnoble.com. It isn't a way to make a great deal of money, but people who write books that may not be commercially viable can still publish them at very low cost. Before print-on-demand machines were developed, authors who couldn't find a regular publisher for their books used vanity publishers (in reality, printers who specialized in publishing books for authors who couldn't find regular publishers), and it generally cost thousands of dollars to have a book manufactured in this way.

Recently, for example, I published two mysteries on Lulu: one is about interpreting film, *The Rashomon Case*, and the other is about writing compositions, *Terminal Papers*. These books, including a small royalty payment for each book, cost nine dollars each per copy.

SCRIPT WRITING AND
ABERRANT DECODING

Let us move from books to television. Using communication jargon, we can say that writers of scripts for televised programs such as sitcoms, dramas, or documentaries encode a communication, assuming or hoping that their audiences will decode their communication correctly—that is, that audiences will "get" what the writers wanted them to get and will interpret the text the way the writers wanted them to interpret it. These terms—*encode* and *decode*—come from linguist Roman Jakobson's model of communication: a sender encodes a message and sends it, using some medium, to a receiver who decodes it. This applies to films as well and to all kinds of other mediated texts.

We sometimes find, in our everyday lives, that in a conversation we say something to someone who, for one reason or another, doesn't correctly interpret what we said. This misinterpretation could be caused by any number of things: our receiver didn't know some of the words we were using, couldn't hear everything we said, didn't notice the tone in which we said it, or wasn't playing attention and missed some of it.

When it comes to the mass media, where the sender of a text is the writer of a film or television show (or a member of a team of writers) for example, the opportunities for receivers (that is, audiences) to misinterpret what's in a text grow exponentially. This misinterpretation is known as **aberrant decoding**. Umberto Eco, a semiotician who has written extensively on popular culture, has suggested that aberrant decoding tends to be the rule when it comes to the mass media. That is, people generally don't decode texts the way the media artists who create them expect them to be decoded. He writes, in his essay "Towards a Semiotic Inquiry into the Television Message":

> Codes and subcodes are applied to the message [the text] in the light
> of a general framework of cultural references, which constitutes the
> receiver's patrimony of knowledge: his ideological, ethical, religious
> standpoints, his psychological attitudes, his tastes, his value systems,
> etc. (1972: 115)

This problem becomes widespread in the mass media since there is
often a considerable difference between the class and educational levels of the writers of mass-mediated texts and those of the audiences
for these texts. For example, writers may mention artists, philosophers, or works of art that most members of their audience have
never heard of, or writers may make allusions to historical events that
members of the audience do not know about.

This means that writers for the mass media have to be very careful that they don't write material that's "over the heads" of their
audiences. They must keep their target audience in mind, though this
doesn't mean that everything on television has to be "dumbed-
down" so it will appeal to, and be understood by, the so-called lowest
common denominator viewing public. In some cases, the target
audience can be a relatively small (in percentage terms) number of
people, for example, those who watch elite programming on public
television channels or on regular television networks or cable. These
particular target audiences may not be large, but the people in these
audiences tend to be affluent opinion makers whose influence is considerable and whose purchasing power is of interest to select advertisers.

MEDIA ETHICS AND JOURNALISTS

Ethics is that branch of philosophy that has to do with what might be
described as right conduct. There are many different philosophical
arguments that have been made about what is and what isn't ethical
behavior, and what ethics should deal with. When we come to the
media, there are a number of different concerns involving ethics.

Consider journalists. Journalists are supposed to work under a
code of ethics that requires them to report the news honestly and
accurately—by which we generally mean not putting their own

Product Placement and the News

As the result of time-shifting devices such as TiVo and changes in the way people use media, the thirty-second television commercial, once the dominant form of television advertising, is now seen as an endangered species. To counter this development, advertising agencies have further embraced "product placements," in which they integrate their products into the narratives of texts such as television shows, films, and other visual media, assuming that when people see these products they will, at the very least, be induced to *consider* trying them.

One incredible wrinkle in this matter of product placement involves placing products into local television news shows, especially morning shows and newsmagazine formats, many of which have so-called lifestyle segments. Placement strategies have included holiday spots on last-minute gifts, makeovers or other giveaways to viewers, and logos in the crawls at the bottom of the screen during newscasts. Local news programs have long been shifting to a kind of entertainment rather than a serious attempt to report on events of social and political significance. They can be seen, more and more, as half-hour commercials with reportage, usually of sensational events, mixed in here and there. Even national news is not immune. In 2004, CNN received complaints when a sponsor's product, Total cereal, appeared in a health segment of *American Morning*. CNN said it was an accident; regardless, the network found itself facing angry critics worried that an advertiser may have crossed the editorial line.

In the end, for local news shows, there is danger that whatever little credibility they may have had will be destroyed by their desperate attempts to gain more revenue by doing product placements—and the irony is that the product placements may not be successful for the advertiser either.

Sources: Gail Schiller, "Advertisers Get Piece of Local News Shows," *Hollywood Reporter*, March 16, 2006, www.hollywoodreporter.com; Stuart Elliott, "A Sponsor's Product Appears on a CNN Segment, and Some See a Weaker News-Advertising Division," *New York Times*, February 10, 2004, www.nytimes.com.

interpretation, or "spin," on what they cover. Some critics have suggested that all news involves interpretation, even when reporters wish to be accurate. Reporters also are expected to avoid even the appearance of any conflict of interest. For example, a journalist who covers the stock market for a newspaper should not write an article praising a company in which he or she has an investment.

To give another example, in recent years it was discovered that a number of reporters were being paid by the government and thus weren't being objective when they reported on certain topics. They had become, in effect, public relations workers and were not being honest with audiences and with their colleagues.

Journalists may face a different problem when reporting about events that cast a negative light on a major advertiser with the newspaper or television station that employs them. This problem is often faced by editors who have to decide whether to run a story that they know one of their important advertisers doesn't want them to run. Some editors deal with negative stories about such advertisers by burying them in the back pages of their newspapers, or on news shows by just mentioning them in passing.

Journalists often face other ethical dilemmas. Those who get information about a case being tried in the courts have often refused to give this information to prosecutors or even to reveal who gave them the information. Many journalists have spent time in jail for refusing to hand this kind of information over. That is because they have given their word to their informants that they wouldn't hand the information over or reveal who gave it to them. The notes a journalist has taken, for example, are considered private and privileged. The same applies to footage shot by television journalists when interviewing people for news programs.

Ideological and financial matters also generate ethical problems for journalists. The news editors at newspapers and radio and television stations have to decide what stories to run out of all the stories they could run. Is a story about a murder-suicide more important than a story about a speech by a senator or congressperson? And how should that speech be presented? What should be included and what left out? In many cases, ideological matters may be even more important than financial ones. Political partisanship colors what stories are run and the perspective a reporter takes. Newspapers and radio and television stations are generally owned today by giant corporations, which have their own political agendas.

ETHICS AND ADVERTISING

Selling Cancer

Media artists (in advertising they are often called *creatives*) face ethical problems of all sorts. For example, think of the dilemma copywriters and art directors face in advertising agencies that have tobacco accounts. These artists and copywriters are asked to use their talents to sell a product that medical evidence has proven leads to cancer. It may be legal to purchase cigarettes, but is it moral for copywriters to use their literary and artistic skills to convince people to purchase such dangerous products?

In other cases, copywriters are asked to sell products that don't work (such as diet remedies), aren't good for people (certain foods, chewing tobacco), or are dangerous (certain sport utility vehicles). On the other hand, people who work in advertising agencies often have families to support, and they may feel that they cannot put their jobs or the welfare of their families at risk. Advertising executives often argue that they are only providing people with information,

Figure 9.1   What are the ethical implications of creating advertisements for cigarettes?

and it is up to each individual to decide what to do with the information the advertising agency has provided. Others say, less convincingly, "If we don't do tobacco ads, some other agency will, so we'll do these ads even if we really don't want to do them." There are, of course, some agencies that refuse to handle these kinds of accounts—especially tobacco accounts—which, I would argue, is the moral thing to do.

Portrayal of Women

Advertising agencies (and the companies that employ them) have frequently been attacked for the way they portray women in print advertisements and commercials. An overwhelming number of the female models we see in the glossy advertisements in magazines and on newspaper pages are unusual physical specimens who look as if they are anorexic or close to being so. The images of these models give other women the notion that they must be slender if they are to be glamorous and beautiful. These models also perpetrate the notion that women should define themselves as sex objects to be gazed at and lusted after by men and not as active, forceful individuals. Women are frequently portrayed in narrative texts as victims who are saved by male heroes.

As Anthony J. Cortese writes in *Provocateur: Images of Women and Minorities in Advertising*:

> Attraction is both socially constructed and biologically shaped to be an instantaneous decision. Whether a female is attracted to a male or vice versa is based on biological unconscious signals of sexual interest. Just as female animals are attracted to power and exhibitions of strength in males of the same species as signs of health and fertility, human females are drawn toward displays of masculine power and strength. . . . For females, a small waist . . . and a high-pitched voice are signs of vulnerability which appeal to a male's self-identification, through cultural transmission, as a protector.
>
> Large pupils are sexually appealing, and this dilation occurs unconsciously during arousal. . . . Youth is also a sign of health and sex appeal. . . . Women use foundation makeup to hide small wrinkles, because eliminating any signs of aging contributes toward a more

desirable and attractive image. Skin tones are warmed up in order to project a healthy sexual glow.

An exaggerated leg length appears to be more adult and, there-fore, more sexual. . . . Hair grooming is also an important component of attraction and gender display. . . . A smile symbolizes approval or attraction. . . . Unconscious blushing is considered to be very sexual. . . . How female breasts are displayed is a key part of sexual attraction. The cleavage area between the breasts is perhaps the epicenter of dis-play and stimulation of interest. In fact, breast cleavage and the cleav-age of the buttocks are considered to be very sexual. In truth, there is a great similarity between the appearance of the two types of cleavage. (2004: 26, 28)

Cortese points out that our notions of what makes a woman beautiful are culturally and socially determined, though he reminds us that there is also a biological component to sexual attraction.

At different times through history, our notions of what makes a woman beautiful have changed; at one time we liked curvaceous and full-bodied women, but in recent years we have favored very slim, almost boyish-looking women. Attitudes about what makes a woman beautiful are also connected to socioeconomic class, ethnicity, and a number of other variables.

This exploitation of the female body has been attacked by femi-nist critics, social scientists, and others as having negative effects on both men and women. Men and women both are given unreal images of what an ideal woman is like: young, long-legged, glamor-ous, wasp-waisted, satin-skinned, and inflamed with a sexual desire that is generally shown by their body language, display of cleavage, and facial expressions. In recent years, advertisers have found that they can use close-ups and images of only parts of women to create the sexual tension and excitement they seek to generate, a device known technically as *synecdoche* (the part stands for the whole, and vice versa).

Political Commercials

Over the past fifty years, the practice of running attack ads in political campaigns has grown considerably. In these highly negative

Figure 9.2 The woman in the skin care advertisement (top illustration) has normal-sized pupils. In the makeup ad, (bottom illustration) the model's pupils are partially dilated. Large pupils are often used in advertising to suggest sexual appeal.

commercials and print advertisements, candidates are attacked for something they did, something they said, or for some policy they supported or vote they cast. That is, the ad doesn't say what the politician responsible for it believes in but instead attacks his or her opponent. In many cases, the makers of these attack ads play fast and loose with facts and the truth—for political advantage. The general public always says, when polled, that they hate these ads, but attack ads, especially commercials, have been shown to be very effective.

As Montague Kern writes in *30-Second Politics*:

> By 1986 negative advertising, which focuses on the opponent rather than a candidate in terms of both issues and character, was . . . considered to be a necessary evil by representatives of all the schools [of media consultants]. (1989: 208)

And negative advertising in attack commercials is with us today more than ever.

One danger of these attack ads is that the politicians who use them are thought to be mean-spirited and nasty; and a corollary danger—in not responding to such ads with attack ads of one's own—is that candidates will allow these attack ads to give voters a picture of themselves that they can't live down. Politicians who use attack ads often find surrogates to do the attacking, and the same applies to politicians who respond to attack ads with their own "counterattack ads."

Those who are attacked in these negative political ads have learned to go on the offensive immediately, before a specific attack ad can take hold of voters' imagination. These counterattack ads often attack the credibility and truthfulness of the politician behind the original attack ad. What this means is that political campaigns have become very negative in recent years, with politicians and their parties attacking and counterattacking one another.

Political scientists have suggested that one of the reasons politicians use attack ads is that they want to get average voters (who often vote for Democratic candidates) so fed up with the process of political campaigns that they don't vote. This would mean that Republican politicians might do better because a very high percentage of their constituents tend to vote consistently.

One of the most famous attack ads was one known as the "Revolving Door," which was broadcast during the 1988 presidential campaign and suggested that Michael Dukakis, the Democratic candidate, was "soft" on crime. The title of the ad was "The Dukakis Prison Furlough Program," and it was made by Frankenberry, Laughlin and Constable. The ad showed prison guards walking along a barbed-wire fence. It then showed a close-up of prisoners going through a revolving door, with a caption superimposed on the screen: "268 escaped." Next came a medium shot of prisoners going through the revolving door. The next caption read: "And many are still at large." Then there was a dissolve to a wide shot of the prison wall, the guards, and the guard-tower.

As the images of the prisoners in the revolving door and the guards showed on the screen, the announcer in a voice-over read a dialogue that attacked Dukakis:

> As governor, Michael Dukakis vetoed mandatory sentence for drug dealers. He vetoed the death penalty. His revolving-door prison policy gave weekend furloughs to first-degree murderers not eligible for parole. While out, many committed other crimes, like kidnapping, rape. And many are still at large. Now Michael Dukakis says he wants to do for America what he's done for Massachusetts. America can't afford that risk.

Dukakis didn't respond immediately to this commercial, and as a result found himself on the defensive during the rest of his campaign. He had allowed the Bush campaign to define him as "soft on crime" by using these very gripping and, it turned out, long-lasting images that stuck in voters' minds.

The people who make these attack ads—the political consultants, copywriters, art directors, and others—must realize that their behavior can be construed as highly questionable from an ethical point of view. Perhaps they justify it by thinking that "All's fair in love and war"—and by then defining political campaigns as a kind of war.

Or perhaps they think that it is so important to get their candidates elected that other matters, such as whether an attack is fair, are not considered important. But this seems very close to arguing that

A Questionable Republican TV Commercial

One of the most notorious television commercials of the 2000 U.S. presidential campaign was run by the Republicans and referred to a drug prescription plan offered by the Democrats. In the commercial, one screen still—just on the screen for a brief moment—used the word *RATS*.

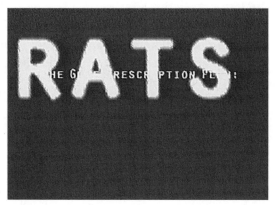

Figure 9.3

Some media critics have suggested that the Republicans were using **subliminal** suggestion to connect, in the minds of those who were exposed to these commercials, Democrats and rats. The people who made this commercial denied that this was their intent. A neurologist I asked about subliminal suggestion said he thought it had been proven to be effective.

the ends justify the means, which is a philosophical position that says, "Anything goes." Such a position is counter to our American belief that the means are implicitly tied to their ends, and that using immoral means for good ends only corrupts those good ends.

Jeffrey Scheuer makes an important point about political advertising in his book *The Sound Bite Society: Television and the American Mind*. He writes:

> It is a truism of our media-dominated age that television has largely usurped the traditional role of political parties. Power flows to those

who control (or can afford to buy access to) the airwaves. The gate-keepers are the arbiters of visibility, such as Ted Koppel and Larry King, and their corporate media-masters; party bosses have been replaced by pollsters, media advisers, and direct-mail consultants. Virtually all political actions and communications—not just political ads but also floor speeches by legislators, news conferences, debates, and party conventions—are designed expressly for consumption as sound bites by a TV audience. (1999: 29)

In his book, Scheuer also describes the degree to which conservative political forces dominate television and other media.

We now "sell" politicians and presidents the way we sell laundry detergent, and I can't help but think that this development has had very negative consequences for our country—as shown, for instance, in the relatively small percentage of eligible voters who actually vote. When people don't vote in large numbers, small and highly disciplined minorities, often organized around single issues, can have a great impact on the political process, an impact far beyond what their numbers would suggest.

Media artists, we see, have tremendous power: their words, their images, the narratives they create, and the songs they write have audiences that often number in the millions. The same, of course, applies to those who perform the works that media artists create. But with this power comes a great responsibility, and one that too many writers and artists (and others connected with creating and performing texts in the various media) do not, so it seems, want to accept.

In the dictionary the mass is defined as the great body of the people of a nation, as contrasted to some special body like a particular social class. Lazarsfeld and Kendall use such a definition when they write "The term 'mass' then, is truly applicable to the medium of radio, for it more than the other media, reaches all groups of the population uniformly." This notion of the mass merely implies that a mass communication may be distinguished from other kinds of communication by the fact that it is addressed to a large cross-section of a population rather than only one or a few individuals or a special part of the population. It also makes the implicit assumption of some technical means of transmitting the communication in order that the communication may reach at the same time all the people forming the cross-section of the population. (1953: 313)

—Eliot Freidson, "Communication Research
and the Concept of the Mass"

There is no "mass" communication because there is no "mass" audience. Instead, there are many audiences, some with structures and leadership and others without these characteristics. Some audiences last only a few hours (Super-bowl viewers) while others last for a whole season (diehard football fans). Some audiences are based on a need for immediate information (viewers of CNN), some on in-depth information (readers of news magazines), some on a need for a religious experience (viewers of the PTL Club), some on a need for political stimulation, musical entertainment, romantic fantasy, and on and on. . . . Each of us is a member of multiple audiences. You are a member of a local community that the local newspaper and cable TV franchise targets. You are a member of virtual communities when you are on the Internet—communities that quickly form and may last for only one evening. You are a member of certain hobby groups that are targeted by certain magazines. (1998: 246–47)

—W. James Potter, *Media Literacy*

10

THE MASS CULTURE /
MASS SOCIETY HYPOTHESIS

In this chapter I deal with an argument that was very popular a number of years ago: that the mass media are turning America into what can be called a "mass society." I will call this the mass culture / mass society hypothesis. The hypothesis is that mass culture inevitably leads to a mass society in which individualism is destroyed and a slavelike "mass man" (and now we'd add "mass woman") is created. Although this theory about mass culture stems from the 1950s, it is still relevant today—and perhaps, due to the increased power of the media, it is even more important now than it was when it was originally propounded.

THE MASS CULTURE HYPOTHESIS:
MYTH OR REALITY?

In America there is, I would suggest, a kind of diffuse obsequiousness regarding European philosophers, culture critics, and theorists of one sort or another. Culturally speaking, we still see ourselves, I would argue, as spiritual orphans, as "sons and daughters" who have abandoned their intellectual motherlands and fatherlands in Europe and elsewhere in a desperate but futile attempt to escape from history, or more precisely, historical consciousness (though today we probably have half the historians in the world in America).

Our intellectuals and deep thinkers on cultural matters, espe-

cially those found in university literature and communications departments, now bend their knees more to French cultural theorists than to those from other countries. (In the fifties it was mainly German thinkers, many of whom were escaping from the Nazis, who dominated our theorizing, as I shall explain shortly.) Today we derive many of our concepts and ideas, as far as cultural criticism is concerned, from the likes of Roland Barthes, Claude Lévi-Strauss, Jean Baudrillard, Jacques Derrida, Jean-François Lyotard—one could go on and on here—with a few Russians, Bulgarians, Italians, Germans, and others bringing up the rear, so to speak.

ROUND UP THE USUAL INDICTMENTS, OR, THE LANGUAGE OF CRITICISM IN THE FIFTIES

In recent years the critics of American media and culture don't seem to be as certain about things as they were in earlier times. Perhaps the demise of Communism and the questions many now raise about Marxism have contributed to this feeling. In the fifties, however, many American intellectuals and others interested in media, culture, and society learned and became indoctrinated by, one might say, the jargon of a number of social theorists and culture critics who had fled from Germany and other countries in Europe. Let me cite two examples.

In an important collection of essays, *Mass Culture: The Popular Arts in America* (Rosenberg and White 1957), Gunther Anders explains to us in his essay "The Phantom World of TV" that "modern mass consumption is a sum of solo performances: each consumer, an unpaid homeworker employed in the production of the mass man" (358). This leads, he adds, to the creation of mass-produced hermits who don't want to renounce the world, but instead want "to be sure they won't miss the slightest crumb of the world as image on a screen" (359). Eventually, he predicts, tongue-in-cheek perhaps, we will lose our ability to talk. "Because the receiving sets speak in our place, they gradually deprive us of the power of speech, thus transforming us into passive dependents" (361).

T. W. Adorno is represented in the same book with an essay, "Television and the Patterns of Mass Culture," that suggests that "popular culture is no longer confined to certain forms such as novels or dance music, but has seized all media of artistic expression" (Rosenberg and White 1957: 475). The media, for Adorno, seem all-powerful. He describes modern mass culture as repetitive, boring, and ubiquitous, and suggests that these aspects of modern mass culture "tend to make for automated reactions and weaken the force of individual resistance" (476). Eventually, he adds, people not only lose their ability to see reality as it is, but their capacity for life experience may be dulled.

WHERE ARE THE MASS MEN AND MASS WOMEN THE CRITICS OF THE FIFTIES WARNED US ABOUT?

The theorists we have been discussing believed that popular culture and the mass media would automatically generate mass culture, and it, in turn, would lead to the development of mass man and mass woman: the cretinized, dehumanized, moronized, kitsch-loving, de-individuated inhabitants of mass societies that, as an additional and ominous feature, would lend themselves to becoming totalitarian. This would happen because—and this is implicit in the arguments of the early elitists—the media affects everyone more or less the same way. According to these theorists, individuals living in mass societies are essentially isolated or atomized and thus are highly susceptible to messages from the media.

This theory, that the media not so much affect or shape but actually determine the consciousness of individuals, is very close to what used to be called the hypodermic theory or magic bullet theory of the media, a theory that is now generally discredited and considered simplistic. According to this theory, as we discussed in chapter 4, messages in the media are interpreted in essentially the same way by everyone, and these messages generate responses that are direct and more or less automatic and immediate.

Media scholars now recognize that things are not as simple as the hypodermic theorists thought they were, and that such matters as race, religion, age, ethnicity, gender, education, values, personality, and a host of other variables affect our decisions about the media we will watch or listen to and the way we respond to the texts carried by the media. This does not mean that the media don't have effects on large numbers of people, but there is good reason to argue that the effects are not universal and that not everyone is affected the same way.

There is some question in my mind as to whether mass culture actually exists or can exist. Of course there are countries, such as America, where an enormous amount of media are available to people, but is that the same thing as mass culture? Eastern-European societies, under the thumb of Russia and their national Communist parties, were subjected to forty years of totalitarian rule, continual propaganda, and a rigidly controlled mass media, but the people in these countries ditched the Communists with hardly a second thought when they discovered that the Red Army wouldn't be invading them.

DOES POPULAR CULTURE DESTROY OUR ABILITY TO ENJOY ELITE CULTURE?

According to Adorno and a number of other theorists of mass culture, popular culture drives out elite culture, and as people become more and more exposed to popular culture, they lose their interest in the elite arts and their capacity to enjoy them. This may sound plausible in theory, but in practice it doesn't seem to work out very well.

Let me offer a hypothetical situation here that most people have some experience with, and put the theory to the test. Take fast foods and, in particular, McDonald's hamburgers: one of the most important symbols of American culture. As the theory goes, because McDonald's is fast and relatively cheap, this chain of restaurants (or others like it) will drive out other kinds of restaurants that are less technologically advanced and involve individual choice (delicatessens, coffee shops, regular restaurants, and ethnic restaurants, for example), and eventually, following the logic of the elitist theorists, we will have only McDonald's and other fast-food restaurants in America and then all over the world because we have lost our taste for good food. (Those interested in the impact of McDonald's on society might consult two books by sociologist George Ritzer: *The McDonaldization of Society* [1993], which he wrote, and *McDonaldization: The Reader* [2002], which he edited.)

I think we can see, from our own experience, that fast-food restaurants have not driven other restaurants out of business. These fast-food restaurants do have a social cost, however, which I alluded to earlier. As a result of the popularity of these restaurants, childhood and adult obesity is now growing at an alarming rate, and with it many diseases tied to obesity such as diabetes and heart disease. Fast-food restaurants are now trying to cope with the anxiety many people feel about eating fast food by experimenting with upscale and less fatty foods.

People use fast-food restaurants for their own purposes, and do not necessarily lose their capacity to enjoy other kinds of foods. Just the opposite happens frequently. In the San Francisco area where I live, for example, there has been an explosion of Thai and Vietnamese restaurants, and as other ethnic groups settle in America, other ethnic foods become increasingly popular. The same applies to upscale French and Italian restaurants.

I wrote an essay forty years ago, "The Evangelical Hamburger," in which (somewhat tongue-in-cheek) I suggested that the dynamics of McDonald's hamburger restaurants were similar to those of evangelical Protestantism, and that McDonald's would spread all over the world. Many people thought these ideas simply ridiculous. I also suggested, playing with the Marxist concept of *embourgeoisement* (which argues that capitalism generates bourgeois, middle-class mentalities), that McDonald's involved "hambourgeoisement" and functioned so as to convince people that they were middle class because they had ready access to ground meat. We now see a similar evangelical thrust in the incredible growth of Starbucks coffee shops. The argument that popular culture will destroy the so-called elite arts—and in this case, French, Italian, and other ethnic restaurants—doesn't appear to have come true.

ARE WE BECOMING HOMOGENIZED?
ARE THE MASS MEDIA UNIFORM?

One assumption of mass culture theorists is that the mass media are uniform, in some way, and thus can perform their task of destroying our sense of individuality and of making Americans (and people in

other countries) mass men and women. But a look at the media shows us that there is a great deal of competition in any given medium, such as television or the magazine industry, and among the media, an equally vigorous competition for the attention of people. The growth of video games, for example, has been explosive. (There has also, of course, been a great deal of consolidation in the media—a subject I deal with in chapter 11.) The networks are continually battling one another for viewers since they must deliver audiences to their advertisers if they want to make money.

Most of what the networks carry is highly formulaic junk, but even formulaic genres can be done well from time to time. And there are many wonderful dramas and comedies on television and cable and in film. It is not the media themselves that are the problem but the beliefs of many of the people running the media about what kind of material will be popular. This is what is responsible, to a great degree, for the low level of entertainment in most of the media. I might note, however, that the arts are always risky, and it is fair to say that many of our serious novels and plays today, though thought to be elite forms of art, are in fact second-rate.

In the world of magazines, we find incredible diversity. There are magazines for every interest conceivable, and some that are not conceivable. In addition to regularly published magazines, there are also huge numbers of "zines": small specialty publications on everything from ecology to Zen that are put out by individuals or groups. Now that computers and laser printers are inexpensive, it is easy and cheap for people to publish their own zines or even make their views known on their own websites.

As we saw in chapter 9, individuals now have become Internet publishers of their creations, or texts. The sites I mentioned earlier, such as www.lulu.com, allow these writers to publish their books at minimum expense. And *weblogs*, or *blogs*, have become another very important part of the Internet, with hundreds of thousands of blogs, of all kinds, to be found there.

So there is good reason to question the assumption that we are undergoing **cultural homogenization** at the hands of the media and that the media can perform the needed "mobilization" of people required to create a mass society. Rather than finding a mass society

Figure 10.1 There are magazines for every interest, including business, sports, cooking, fashion, travel, arts, politics, and entertainment.

in America (and the same would apply to many other countries), we find just the opposite: what might be described as cultural and pop-cultural pluralism, with large numbers of subcultures and groups putting out their own publications, making their own films, and broadcasting their own radio and television shows. This does not mean, however, that these groups all see themselves as estranged from American culture.

MASS CULTURE AND THE MELTING POT

With this discussion of popular culture, the mass media, and the theory of mass society as a background, we can now gain some insight into the question of whether there have been fundamental changes in American society and culture in the last few decades, and if so, what role the media might have played in this matter.

If the mass media are as powerful as some elitists believe they are, how do we explain the fact that American society has so many subcultures and different groups based on everything from race, religion, or ethnicity to political persuasion and geographic location? We are not diminished by having these various social entities, but enriched.

A knowledge of urban geography is helpful in gaining an understanding of what America was like fifty or seventy-five years ago. When we look at cities then (and today, as well) we find that they were often divided up into enclaves in which the population would be predominantly Italian, Jewish, black, Irish, Vietnamese, Chinese, or another ethnic group. At the time, these groups often had publications written in their native languages and directed toward their particular interests. Today, many of these groups have television stations that broadcast in their native languages. It would seem that the fabled melting pot is more a theory of what some analysts think happened or would have liked to have seen happening than a true description of what America was like when your parents or grandparents were born—or even today, in many cases.

Many different ethnic groups were thrown, so to speak, into the melting pot (American society) but they didn't melt into one smooth homogenous mass and instead maintained their identities, even while they went about finding their place in America and realizing or trying to realize the American Dream.

Proponents of the mass society thesis would have to argue that though America may not be monolithic now, it once was because of the exposure of immigrants and others to America's ubiquitous and all-powerful mass media. But if the media are as powerful as they are supposed to be, how did the earlier American immigrant resist becoming unified into a mass society, a resistance evident in the ethnic enclaves of American cities fifty or seventy-five years ago? Or why haven't we remained a mass society?

It could be argued, perhaps, that the mass media no longer are as effective as they once were in unifying Americans and providing them with a common frame of reference, and with some kind of a consensus and national consciousness. But Americans are exposed to more media today than ever before. We watch enormous amounts of television, the most powerful medium, and have VCRs to capture

other shows, so we can do *time-shifting* (watching a program at a time other than its original time of broadcast). DVDs are still wildly popular, and devices such as TiVo enable us to time-shift with great ease too. The growth of cable and satellite television means there are huge numbers of channels available to viewers, and new technologies are being developed that in the near future will open as many as five hundred channels to viewers. (What all these channels of communication will carry is another matter, as we have seen, and will be essentially the same old genres found in the movies and on television, with an occasional mixture of genres, such as MTV, or single-genre stations, such as all-news stations.)

We don't know what impact the explosive growth of the Internet will have on our society, nor do we know what the long-range impact will be of new technological developments such as cell phones, iPods, and Blackberrys. Now people use Google every day and cannot imagine a world without it, or without eBay, or the various Internet dating services, or Internet travel services, which are putting nonelectronic travel agents out of business.

The pace of technological change grows faster with each year as computer chips grow more powerful and less expensive. As we saw earlier from Howard Rheingold's experience in Tokyo—where people weren't using their cell phones to talk but were thumbing messages to one another with them—sending text messages by cell phones can have profound social and political effects. We don't know what will happen when the world is completely wired, but from past experience, we can say it is unlikely to create a homogenized society full of mass men and women.

The existence of a society full of subcultures, and characterized by what I've described as pop-cultural pluralism (some might say near-anarchy), suggests the media are not as all-powerful as we, or more precisely, some communications theorists, once thought they were, and also suggests that our notion of America as a huge melting pot was more an illusion (of consensus among historians and conservative social scientists) than a reality. Though various groups in the melting pot didn't melt, they were still in the same pot. Some have suggested that "beef stew" would be a better metaphor than a melting pot where everything blends together into an amorphous mass.

Societies are always evolving, so it would be incorrect to argue that there have not been changes in America. The question is whether these changes mark radical new directions in which our society is moving or whether they are more evolutionary. America, it has often been said, is a country continually undergoing revolution, and thus change is the constant. This notion, that we are continually undergoing change, differs from a conservative perspective that argues, as I see it, that there have been no fundamental changes in American culture and society, or that any such changes have been minimal.

My argument would be that in America, everything is always in the process of change and evolution. The question is, What is the nature of the changes, and how do these changes relate to continuities in American society and culture?

MASS CULTURE AND AMERICAN SOCIETY: THE MYTH OF THE MONOLITH

In an essay in the *Public Perspective*, "The Polarization of America: The Decline of Mass Culture" (Sept./Oct. 1992), Paul Jerome Croce argues that mass culture has lost its ability to shape consensus and suggests that this decline is a fundamental cause of what he sees as an increasingly polarized America. He writes, "Through their popularity, the mass culture's productions shaped taste, established goals and values, and defined the kind of people most people thought they should be." This consensus has now broken down, he adds, and we now find ourselves in a post–mass culture society in which mass culture has "metasticized, with individuals still pursuing distant styles, but doing so in clusters broken off from a single massive standard."

I don't believe we ever had the "single massive standard" Croce thinks we had, or that the mass media ever had the power he suggests it had to shape a society. And I don't think we ever were as unified as Croce thinks. Mass media tends to reinforce values we already have—such as individualism, equality, freedom, and achievement. The media tend to reflect the societies in which they are found, although, of course, they also affect them. There's always been a great deal of conflict in American society between classes, races, geographic sections of the country, and to some degree among religious groups.

People who burn with "passionate intensity" and belong to subcultures, and groups that attack this or that aspect of our society, are nothing new: we have a long history of utopian communities and of

Figure 10.2   Cities all across America have distinct ethnic communities. Many include grocery stores, restaurants, or other businesses run by and for ethnic citizens, such as this tortilleria in Lafayette, Colorado. Lafayette, a town of about 25,000, is approximately 16 percent Hispanic.

morally defined groups such as the Abolitionists. (We still have forty thousand people living in communes, it turns out.)

What the mass media do, I would suggest, is reflect the changes going on in society at a given point in time. They may add impetus to the changes and speed things up, they may help set agendas, they may increase our awareness and show us things many of us don't like, but I find it hard to believe that they have ever had the ability to homogenize us the way they allegedly did. We never were unified to the extent Croce believes, except, perhaps, in terms of our basic values, so the media are being attacked for not continuing to do what they never did and could not do. There are plenty of reasons to find fault with our mass media, but we can dismiss as false the charge against them that they no longer unify our society. If anything has ever unified Americans, it is the public school system, not the media.

America, if the postmodernist theorists are correct, is a society in which elite art and popular culture no longer are seen as distinct or different from one another, and in which eclecticism and fragmentation are the norms. Earlier we noted Jean-François Lyotard's example of someone who "listens to reggae, watches a western, eats McDonald's food for lunch and local cuisine for dinner," and so on. This doesn't sound like the homogenized culture that mass culture theorists predicted. And this has been the case since around 1960 when, it has been suggested, the postmodernist mind-set took over.

What all this suggests is that American society is one in which diversity is celebrated, and in which differences are accepted—as part of the scheme of things. Rather than splitting apart, everything in American society is getting mixed up, yet different groups still are able to maintain their identities. That, in fact, is the story of America—a country of immigrants, where people from many different nations come in search of the American Dream. Different groups may have different versions of this dream, may take different paths to realize this dream, and may be different in many ways, but there is a commonality behind these differences.

As evidence of this, let me mention a recent poll that was taken of Hispanics in America. The poll discovered that Hispanics want to assimilate into America, that they believe there's too much immigration to America, that they think residents of America should learn to speak English, and that Hispanics are, in fact, not as unified as we used to believe they were. "A large majority of Hispanics born in the United States speaks English better than Spanish," as a matter of fact, and there's a high degree of English literacy among foreign-born immigrants who prefer to speak Spanish. The Latino National Political Survey, in a report titled *Latino Voices*, concludes that "the [survey's] results should dispel any notions that [Hispanics'] political attitudes separate them from the majority of the American population or define them as a monolithic interest group."

What this survey suggests is that the United States is truly a multicultural society in which various subcultures exist, and that multiculturalism doesn't mean separateness and alienation but rather, a different kind of coexistence. Our mass media and popular culture have turned us into neither a mass society (on the road to totalitarianism) nor a society in which "the center cannot hold." But political decisions in recent years have caused great difficulties for many Americans, and our faith in the American Dream is now weakening.

The tensions and anxieties found in America have been generated in large measure and exacerbated by an unfair and grossly distorted (some would say obscene) distribution of wealth that has occurred here, especially since 1980, with the poorest segments of our society actually losing ground and large numbers of people in the middle classes not gaining any ground. Since 2000, the inequities in the distribution of wealth in America have become worse, with many members of the middle class now finding it difficult to maintain that status and with many poor people sinking deeper into poverty and despair.

An editorial in the *New York Times* with the subtitle "New Hope for the Fabulously Wealthy" (June 7, 2005) points out that since 2000, the income of the top 0.1 percent of American society, the super rich, has more than doubled, while the share earned by the top 10 percent rose a great deal less and the bottom 90 percent's share actually declined. The middle class, the upper-middle class, and even the wealthy, it seems, are being left behind, "in the dust," by the super wealthy as a result of tax policies. Hurricane Katrina revealed to many Americans just how desperate the situation was for many poor people living in New Orleans and elsewhere in America.

It is politics, not popular culture, that is most responsible for our social disorganization, and it will be political decisions—not our popular culture or the mass media—that must correct how we distribute our wealth and lead to the amelioration of the situation in which we find ourselves.

What I am calling the Electronic Right comprises a broad alliance of elected officials, journalists, broadcasters and intellectuals, whose access to the media is supported by deep conservative reservoirs such as the Sarah Scaife and Carthage foundations (both controlled by Richard Mellon Scaife) and Olin, Smith-Richardson, J.M., and Bradly foundations. This policy-marketing machine sponsors an assortment of leading think tanks (such as the Heritage Foundation, American Enterprise Institute, Cato Institute, Hudson Institute, Manhattan Institute, and the Hoover Institution); various newspapers, magazines, journals and media pressure groups; conferences and seminars, books and articles, research studies, speaking engagements, editorial briefing sessions, and Internet projects; "astroturf" (fake grassroot) campaigns; radio and TV shows, including the public television programs of William F. Buckley, Peggy Noonan, William Bennett, and Ben Wattenberg among others; and sundry antitax and antiregulatory organizations. Foundations on the left have vastly inferior resources. (1999: 42–43)

—Jeffrey Scheuer, *The Sound Bite Society:*
Television and the American Mind

11

MEDIA IN SOCIETY

Wᵉ have just examined the mass society hypothesis of certain social critics, who suggest that the mass media are leading to a society in which there is no sense of community and that mass culture will lead, inevitably, to a breakdown of democracy. This critique is, I suggested, a highly suspect one and not based on convincing evidence. The following chapter will deal in a more general way with the media in society—with topics such as media consolidation (and its possible consequences), the cultural imperialism hypothesis, the problem of pornography, and government regulation.

MEDIA CONSOLIDATION

Robert McChesney has argued in the essay "The Global Media Giants" that there has been a continual and accelerated process of concentration in the media in the United States and globally as well. He writes:

> The global media system is now dominated by a first tier of nine giant firms. The five largest are Time Warner (1997 sales: $24 billion), Disney ($22 billion), Bertelsmann ($15 billion), Viacom ($13 billion), and Rupert Murdoch's News Corporation ($11 billion). Besides needing global scope to compete, the rules of thumb for global media giants are twofold: First, get bigger so you dominate markets and your competition can't buy you out. Firms like Disney and Time Warner

have almost tripled in size this decade. Second, have interests in numerous media industries, such as film production, book publishing, music, TV channels and networks, retail stores, amusement parks, magazines, newspapers and the like. The profit whole for the global media giant can be vastly greater than the sum of the media parts. A film, for example, should also generate a soundtrack, a book, and merchandise, and possibly spin-off TV shows, CD-ROMs, video games and amusement park rides. Firms that do not have conglomerated media holdings simply cannot compete in this market. (www .fair.org/extra/9711.gmg.html)

The five media giants McChesney cites control an enormous amount of the media produced and spread throughout the world by the corporations they control. And they have numerous advantages over companies that cannot match their global reach.

There are, McChesney adds, four other "first tier" media conglomerates: enormous in their own right, but not comparable to the first five media giants. Among these are Sony (1997 sales: $48 billion), which owns Columbia and TriStar Pictures and major recording interests; and Seagram (1997 sales: $14 billion), which owns Universal and various music interests. And there are a number of second-tier media conglomerates, as well. These two tiers of transnational global media conglomerates control most of the media in the world.

Ben Bagdikian, former dean of the School of Journalism at the University of California, Berkeley, was one of the first scholars to call our attention to this matter. As he explains:

In 1982, when I completed research for my book, *The Media Monopoly*, 50 corporations controlled half or more of the media business. By December 1986, when I finished a revision for a second edition, the 50 had shrunk to 29. The last time I counted, it was down to 26. [When the latest edition of *The Media Monopoly* was published in 1993, the number was down to 20.—ed.] A number of serious Wall Street media analysts are predicting that by the 1990s, a half-dozen giant firms will control most of our media.

Of the 1,700 daily papers, 98 percent are local monopolies and **fewer than 15 corporations** control most of the country's daily circulation. A handful of firms have most of the magazine business, with **Time**, Inc. alone accounting for about 40 percent of that industry's

revenues. (www.fair.org/extra/best-of-extra/corporate-ownership
.html; emphasis in original)

The **consolidation** of media companies that Bagdikian and
McChesney talk about has taken place in other areas connected to
the media. There are, for example, just four or five giant global
advertising corporations that own most of the important advertising
agencies. Companies that want to hire advertising agencies now
demand, in many cases, that they be part of these global conglomerates so their advertisements can have a global reach.

The question that arises now is, What difference does it make?
McChesney offers an answer:

> On balance the system has minimal interest in journalism or public
> affairs except for that which serves the business and upper-middle
> classes, and it privileges just a few lucrative genres that it can do quite
> well—like sports, light entertainment and action movies—over other
> fare. Even at its best the entire system is saturated by a hyper-com-
> mercialism, a veritable commercial carpet bombing of every aspect of
> human life. As the CEO of Westinghouse put it (*Advertising Age*,
> 2/3/97), "We are here to serve advertisers. That is our raison d'etre."
> (www.fair.org/extra/9711.gmg.html)

McChesney mentions that the fifty corporations that control the
media have connections with many other media organizations,

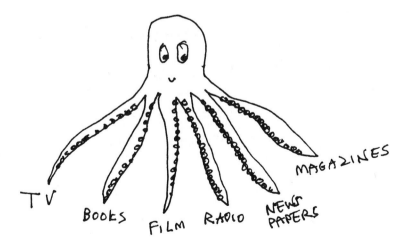

TV   BOOKS   FILM   RADIO   NEWS PAPERS   MAGAZINES

which helps the media giants consolidate their power. The media giants also have political goals and interests that affect their programming and the editorial stances they take in their publications.

It may be that the giant media organizations counterbalance one another on certain political issues and that they do serve the public in certain areas: fighting racism and promoting safe sex to counter the AIDS epidemic, for example. It is also possible that their size makes it possible for them to take chances with artists and filmmakers that others cannot afford to take. For example, poetry books do not sell well, and if all publishers only put out books that had a good chance of making a profit, very few poetry books would be published. Publishing poetry books by serious poets can be looked upon as a public relations gesture by these companies, more than anything else.

ON CULTURAL IMPERIALISM: THE "COCA-COLONIZATION" HYPOTHESIS

The **cultural imperialism** theory, or Coca-Colonization hypothesis, holds that the United States and a few other First World countries that export their films, television programs, and other popular culture to the rest of the world are also exporting their capitalist ideologies and value systems with this material. It isn't that America is con-

---

The Quality of Newscasts

Television stations owned by big, out-of-town companies tend to produce lower quality newscasts than those owned by smaller groups, a study by a journalism think tank has concluded. Newscasts at stations owned by large television networks fared poorly in the study. It was released Sunday by the Project for Excellence in Journalism, affiliated with the Columbia University School of Journalism. . . . The five-year study, which examined roughly one-quarter of the nation's local TV stations, gave an "A" grade to only 11 percent of the stations owned by the 10 biggest media companies. Thirty-one percent of stations owned by small groups earned the top grade.

Source: Associated Press, Feb. 17, 2003.

sciously trying to indoctrinate people in the Third World; what happens is that American writers, filmmakers, and television producers quite naturally make works that reflect their values—values they learned while growing up in America. But these values, such as a belief in the self-made man or woman and the importance of consumption, then are spread all over the globe.

Most Third World countries can't afford to make films and television programs. It is much cheaper to import works from First World countries, and with these works they are also getting, without recognizing it, First World ideologies and values. Thus, American and other First World cultures are not only dominating more fragile Third World cultures, they are destroying them. The spread of our films, television shows, McDonald's hamburger restaurants, and Starbucks coffee shops is, according to this theory, leading to a kind of worldwide cultural homogenization. Eventually, according to the logic of this argument, every place will look like every other place: people everywhere will drink Coca-Cola or Pepsi, eat at the same fast-food restaurants, dress the same, and watch the same films and television shows.

The cultural imperialism theory assumes that the media are extremely powerful; if they weren't, then the effects of the media would not be significant, and American media would be essentially just a source of entertainment and not a force for Americanizing and changing the fundamental value systems of these cultures.

Herta Herzog-Massing dealt with this question in some research she conducted on how people in Germany decoded, or made sense of, the widely popular (at the time) television series *Dallas*. As she explained in her article "Decoding *Dallas*":

> Critics of popular culture, and of things American in particular, have concerned themselves with the question of whether the worldwide diffusion of programs such as "Dallas" made possible by the growth of the new media technologies may eventually result in worldwide cultural assimilation at the expense of indigenous diversity. (*Society* 24 [1986]: 74)

Herzog-Massing's study of the way *Dallas* was interpreted in Germany led her to write, "The answer to my initial question—do viewers in different countries read popular culture differently?—must be answered affirmatively" (1986: 77).

Figure 11.1   How much influence do American media and advertising have on other countries? In early 2006, Indian film actor Aamir Khan (*right*) celebrated the launch of his new movie—*Rang De Basanti*—by posing with Coca-Cola India's vice president of marketing (*left*) and a model of the movie's special edition Coke bottle.

Herzog-Massing was dealing with the way one First World country, Germany, interpreted a text from another First World country, the United States. But her finding, that people in different cultures interpret texts in different ways, is a compelling reason to suggest that the media imperialism theory may be a bit overblown and that the impact of our media and popular culture on other cultures may be somewhat superficial. In recent years many countries have been putting American television shows on at late hours, replacing them in earlier time-slots with their own shows that are more closely tied to the culture involved. But American movies still are dominant everywhere.

A NOTE ON IDEOLOGY AND THE MEDIA

What's really important, critics of the media argue, is the way media giants can dominate political discourse and gain their ends—making

further expansion and consolidation possible, and shutting out competition. As the saying goes, "He who pays the piper, calls the tune."
The owners of the media are the ones who call the tunes, nowadays.
They publish their "tunes" in the newspapers, magazines, and
through the book publishers they own; they broadcast their "tunes"
on their radio stations and television stations and cable networks;
they make CDs of their "tunes"; they make video games of their
"tunes"; and since we only hear their "tunes," for the most part,
theirs are the ones that stick in our minds and that we find ourselves
humming.

By "tunes" I mean something much broader than songs, namely,
political viewpoints and ideological positions, attitudes, notions, and
ideas. **Ideology** is generally defined as a system of logically coherent
beliefs about the social and political order. The giant media conglomerates can help shape our ideologies in a number of different ways.
First, their newspapers and radio and television stations function as
gatekeepers and determine which stories they want to cover and
which ones they will exclude or to which they will give scant attention. Second, the *way* the news media organizations cover stories also
affects the opinions of readers, viewers, and listeners to news programs. As I mentioned earlier, what we see on television is always
something that someone has determined we will see (just as what we
won't see has been determined for us).

THE PROBLEM OF PORNOGRAPHY

Beauty, as they say, is in the eye of the beholder, and so, it seems, is
the determination of what is and what is not pornography. Where do
we draw the line between the increasingly more explicit sexual content of the advertisements and commercials that flood our magazines,
airwaves, and cable media and so-called soft-core pornography, and
then between soft-core pornography and hard-core pornography?

There is also the question of whether pornography is harmful to
children or others who are exposed to it, children who, as is often
the case, go seeking it. The Internet is full of pornographic sites, and
older children and preteens, who are curious about sexual matters,

may often go to these pornographic sites. But as I've suggested, one of the problems involved in dealing with pornography is that it is difficult to find a definition of pornography that everyone can agree upon. Pornography is, like many concepts, hard to pin down.

In a government paper, "U.S. Media in the 1990s: III. The Media and Society," Fredric A. Emmert writes:

> Although the courts have long held that media publishing or broadcasting obscenity and pornography do not enjoy First Amendment protection, it remains hard for a judge to define those terms. Consequently, in the 1973 "Miller versus California" and "Paris Adult Theater versus Slaton" cases, the U.S. Supreme Court rejected the notion of a national obscenity standard and left the definition and regulation of obscenity up to "contemporary community standards defined by the applicable state law." (http://usinfo.state.gov/usa/infousa/media/files/media3cd.htm)

The Supreme Court concluded, then, that there was no way to define obscenity in a manner that everyone could accept, and left the matter of defining up to local communities. Obviously, cultural matters come into play, and in large, international cities such as New York and San Francisco, people may have a much different notion of what is obscene than the people in more conservative rural communities.

Emmert does explain how the Supreme Court believed communities could determine whether a text was obscene or not.

> The Court . . . proclaimed a general test for obscenity to be:
> 1) whether the "average person, applying contemporary community standards" would find that the work, taken as a whole, appeals to the prurient [sexually exciting] interest;
> 2) whether the work depicts or describes, in a patently offensive way, sexual conduct specifically defined by the applicable state law; and
> 3) whether the work, taken as a whole, lacks serious literary, artistic, political or scientific value.

As you can see, there are a great many loopholes here—which probably explains why the Supreme Court decided to let cities and states fight the matter out. For one thing, a text has to be prurient when "taken as a whole," and it also, as a whole, must lack "serious literary, artistic, political or scientific value." This means that parts of a text may be "prurient," but if the whole text isn't, or if the text is a serious work of art, the work cannot be considered pornographic. In addition, a text must depict or describe sexual conduct "in a patently offensive way," and the depicted or described conduct must be sexual conduct that is defined as illegal by state law.

A U.S. SUPREME COURT DECISION ON VIRTUAL CHILD PORNOGRAPHY

On April 16, 2002, the U.S. Supreme Court rendered a verdict involving virtual child pornography and struck down a bill, the Child Pornography Prevention Act of 1996, as infringing on the First Amendment rights of artists and writers. This bill had made it criminal to create "virtual child pornography, distribute it or possess it." The Supreme Court, by a vote of 6 to 3, argued that the bill was an infringement on the rights of free expression guaranteed by the First Amendment of the Constitution. The First Amendment reads, "Congress shall make no law . . . abridging the freedom of speech."

Justice Anthony Kennedy, who wrote the opinion for the majority, explained that the prohibition in the Child Pornography Prevention Act of 1996 involved "any visual depiction" and was not concerned about how an image was produced.

> The section [in the law] captures a range of depictions, sometimes called "virtual child pornography," which include computer-generated images, as well as images produced by more traditional means. For instance, the literal terms of the statute embrace a Renaissance painting depicting a scene from classical mythology, a "picture" that "appears to be of a minor engaging in sexually explicit conduct." The statute also prohibits Hollywood movies, filmed without any child actors, if a jury believes an actor "appears to be" a minor engaging in "actual or simulated . . . sexual intercourse." (*Ashcroft v. Free Speech Coalition*, 122 S. Ct. 1389 [2002])

Justice Kennedy's point, then, which he developed at length in his statement, is that the law could be used to prevent people from having access to great works of art or even lesser works that have sexual content that some people find objectionable. He also wrote that "the government has shown no more than a remote connection between speech that might encourage thoughts or impulses and any resulting child abuse."

We can see then that deciding what is obscene or pornographic is not an easy thing to do, and that attempts by the government to protect children may, unwittingly, dampen free expression and so have very negative consequences.

One of the problems legal experts face in dealing with artistic texts is that these texts are often complicated, difficult to analyze, and elusive, and whether we're critics, moralists, or concerned citizens, we cannot easily reach a consensus on them. As I pointed out earlier, there are all kinds of aesthetic factors involved in such texts, so it is hard for anyone to prove that a work is obscene, especially since in postmodern societies the barriers between everything seem to have been obliterated. We must remember that James Joyce's *Ulysses*, one of the greatest novels of the twentieth century, was once held to be obscene and only was allowed into the country after a lawsuit brought by Bennett Cerf of Random House.

In 2002 a museum in New York City had an exhibit on contemporary art. In the exhibit was a work of art called *Cloaca*, which I heard about on a report on National Public Radio. *Cloaca* is, its creator says, a work of art. It is a machine that is fed food, which it then grinds up, passes through its various tubes, and finally "defecates." I believe *Cloaca* was created in the Netherlands, where its "excrement" was packaged in plastic and sold to people—until it was found that the excrement could not be protected from bacteria and started putrifying. Some people consider *Cloaca* to be a cosmic joke, and others think it is a wonderful work of art. In an art world in which almost anything goes, who is to say what is serious art and what isn't? And in a similar sense, who is to say, in our postmodernist society, what is pornography and what isn't?

THE SPIRAL OF SILENCE: PUBLIC OPINION AND POLITICAL IDEOLOGY

There is a theory of communication that might help us understand how certain ideas become dominant in society. It was developed by a German scholar, Elisabeth Noelle-Neumann, who wrote, in an important article in the *Journal of Communication*, that people who believe—correctly or not—that they represent the majority opinion have a tendency to make their views known, while those who believe they represent the minority opinion have a tendency to keep quiet. This is because people don't wish to be isolated, and those who hold what they think is a minority view often convince themselves that their view is wrong. As she explains,

> He may find himself on one of two sides. He may discover that he agrees with the prevailing (or winning) view, which boosts his self-confidence and enables him to express himself with an untroubled mind and without any danger of isolation, in conversation, by cutting those who hold different views. Or he may find that the views he holds are losing ground: the more this appears to be so, the more uncertain he will become of himself, and the less he will be inclined to express his opinion. ("The Spiral of Silence: A Theory of Public Opinion," *Journal of Communication* 24, no. 2 [1974]: 44)

When some people speak up and others remain silent, there starts "a spiraling process which increasingly establishes one opinion as the prevailing one" (1974: 44). This is exacerbated by the fact that we often underestimate the number of people who share our views and overestimate the number of people who oppose them.

It is quite obvious that the media play an important role in shaping public opinion, since what we read in the newspapers, hear on the radio, and see on television news programs (where many people in America get most of their news) has an effect on what we believe is the prevailing opinion on many different issues. Noelle-Neumann's theory suggests, then, that the media help shape public opinion rather than just reflect it.

As we have seen, however, there is some question about how effective the media actually are in shaping public opinion. Although a small number of giant corporations control the media, countervailing forces often play an important role in shaping public opinion. We find, for example, that many groups aligned on important issues—especially issues based on race, ethnicity, gender, or religion—are increasingly making their voices heard, and their beliefs often are critical of the agendas and practices of the giant corporations and media conglomerates. These groups are often able to use and exploit the press for their own purposes. In addition, political parties have an important role in affecting public opinion, especially in regard to political and ideological issues.

Specific events often play an important role in shaping public opinion. For example, the collapse and bankruptcy of Enron Corporation, at one time the seventh-largest corporation in the United States, exposed the degree to which it and other energy producers had helped shape the government's energy policy. It also showed that a giant accounting firm, Arthur Anderson, wasn't correctly monitoring Enron and giving honest reports about its financial status. In February 2003, a congressional committee discovered that Enron had also found a way, in collusion with banks and other financial institutions, to avoid paying its fair share of taxes. This led to the suggestion by many politicians that we change our tax system so corporations cannot find ways to avoid paying taxes. Shaping public opinion isn't quite as simple as it might seem, and the spiral of silence may not always function the way Noelle-Neumann thought it would.

Two terrible hurricanes in September 2005 in the United States, which were covered superbly and nonstop by the media, exposed the shocking degree to which the federal government was unprepared to deal with wide-scale emergencies. The television coverage also showed how much poverty there was in New Orleans, which was a blow to our belief that we were creating a just society in which poverty was being eliminated. Statistics reveal that poverty has been increasing in the United States in recent years, but statistics don't have much of an emotional impact. It was the power of the images of the poor people, mostly African Americans, and of the desperate conditions in which they lived, that made the existence of this poverty much more real to Americans. Many residents of New Orleans hadn't left the city before hurricane Katrina devastated the city because they didn't have cars and were too poor to leave. This media coverage severely damaged the reputation of the president and other high-ranking members of the government. The director of the Federal Emergency Management Agency (FEMA), who was a political appointee and not qualified for the job, was forced to resign.

The coverage of hurricanes Katrina and Rita exposed the inability of our government, at all levels, to cope with disasters. The media, in covering these disasters, played an important role in affecting public opinion. The television coverage of these storms will probably have major political consequences.

GOVERNMENT REGULATION AND DEREGULATION OF BROADCASTING

Congress established an agency in 1934, the Federal Communications Commission (FCC), to regulate the broadcasting industry subject to the "public interest, convenience and necessity." The purpose of the agency is to promote diversity in broadcasting, and so it has issued, over the years, a number of different rules about corporate ownership of radio and television stations, and other rules about newspaper ownership of television stations.

With the growth of cable, which does not use the public airwaves, the FCC has started relaxing its rules on newspaper ownership of radio and television stations, consolidation of radio and television stations, and television network and media organization ownership of cable television systems. The FCC has also decided to stop enforcing the Fairness Doctrine, which mandated that broadcasters provide equal time for different points of view on issues of importance. Some members of Congress have tried to reinstate the Fairness Doctrine but have been unable to do so.

In his book *The Sound Bite Society: Television and the American Mind*, Jeffrey Scheuer discusses recent developments in the broadcast industry relevant to the matter of deregulation:

> The modest balancing mechanism of the Fairness Doctrine was rescinded in 1987; and the public interest standard, as a basis for relicensing stations, has become a national joke; the fox rules the chicken coop. Mark S. Fowler, the first FCC chairman under Reagan who theorized that television is just "a toaster with pictures," deregulated with a vengeance, even lifting rules prohibiting program-length commercials aimed at children. (1999: 43)

Scheuer goes on to discuss the giveaway to the broadcasting industry of the new digital frequency spectrum, a resource also owned by the

Fighting Media Conglomerates

There are many organizations that attempt to fight the power of the media conglomerates. What follows is a call by the Union for Democratic Communications (UDC) for papers for the conference Democratic Communications and Global Justice. The subjects the UDC wishes to have discussed will give you an idea of its interests:

> The Union for Democratic Communications invites the submission of paper and panel proposals, media projects, and workshops addressing the role of democratic communications in the struggle for global justice. We seek submissions with a critical* perspective on existing media structures and practices, such as the continuing global concentration of the media, the commercialization of new media technologies, the creeping influence of advertising from the classroom to the newsroom, and the distortion and suppression of news and information by the mainstream media. We also seek submissions that highlight struggles for global justice from the local to the global level; from preserving communities and cultures to protesting meetings of the world's rich and powerful.
>
> . . . The Union for Democratic Communications is a group of communications researchers, theorists, educators, journalists, media producers, policy analysts, and activists. The UDC is dedicated to the critical study of communications establishments and its policies; the production and distribution of democratically controlled media; the fostering of alternative, oppositional, independent, and experimental production; and the development of democratic communications systems at local, regional, national and international levels. (Union for Democratic Communications, www.udc.org/conf2002/conf20-02call.html)

*The term *critical* here means that the UDC is concerned with offering an ideological critique of the media and the government agencies and media conglomerates that control the media.

public, valued at $70 billion. This outraged some conservatives like Senator Bob Dole, who called it "the biggest single gift of public property to an industry in this century." Scheuer continues:

> I should add that under the George W. Bush administration, deregulation is moving ahead very rapidly and it looks like the broadcasting industry and the media conglomerates will get just about everything that they want in the way of relaxed rules and regulations from the FCC. There are ideological implications to this relaxation of control over the media conglomerates, which we can see, for example, when it comes to television. (1999: 45)

Scheuer also discusses the so-called liberal bias of the press and points out that, in reality, the networks and public television really have a conservative bias. He writes:

> For all their alleged liberal bias, in recent decades, the networks and public television have been decidedly more hospitable to the show-casing of centrist and conservative voices. With rare exceptions, guests on public affairs programs are fonts of conventional wisdom, typically powerful Beltway insiders with views running the gamut from right to center. The fulcrum of debate on the talk shows is even further to the right: for every centrist or moderate liberal on the left side of the screen (e.g., Shields, Germond, Carlson, Clift, Caraville, Stephanopolous), there is a crowd on the right and center-right: Barnes, Bay Buchanan, Pat Buchanan, Buckley, Gergen, Glassman, Kondracke, Krauthammer, Kristol, Limbaugh, McLaughlin, Matalin, Novak, Safire, Snow, Stassinopolous, Sununu, Wattenberg, Will, et al. (1999: 47)

Scheuer points out that the mainstream media tend to interview people from conservative and centrist think tanks more than people from equivalent organizations on the left, and that newspaper opinion pages tend to be conservative as well. He cites an interesting statistic in this respect: Richard Nixon in the 1968 presidential election and George W. Bush in the 2000 presidential election each received somewhere between 60 percent to 80 percent of the endorsements in daily newspapers. We can see, then, that media conglomeration has social and political implications and is not just an economic matter. But we must remember that despite all the endorsements he received, George W. Bush received fewer votes in 2000 than his opponent, Al Gore.

There are now a number of liberal talk shows on radio designed to counter the domination of the radio waves by conservative (and in some cases right-wing) talk show hosts. We have to realize that radio talk shows are political entertainment, and the people working on the liberal talk shows have to demonstrate that they can be as entertaining as their conservative counterparts. There is now a fledgling liberal network of talk shows, but it has yet to match the conservatives in terms of the popularity and impact of its shows.

ETHNIC MEDIA:
A COMPLICATING FACTOR

As America becomes ever more multicultural, with large numbers of people from Asia, Africa, Europe, and South and Central America moving here, we find that the power of ethnic media is growing. As I suggested earlier, the notion that America is a melting pot in which ethnic groups quickly lose their ethnic identities and become Americanized doesn't seem to be accurate—at least in the short run—and a better **metaphor** for the United States would be something like a beef stew, in which each component (that is, each ethnic group) retains its identity, while being part of something bigger than itself.

What has happened is that people from various ethnic groups move into areas where there are other people from their ethnic groups, establishing what a *Wall Street Journal* article on the growth of ethnic media calls "islands of ethnic communities." The article, by Pui-Wing Tam, reports on a survey on ethnic media use in California:

> Ethnic media are pervasive: Fully 84% of the survey's Hispanic, Asian-American and African-American respondents say they get information through ethnic television, radio and publications. Ethnic-media consumers are loyal: 68% of respondents say they prefer ethnic TV stations to English channels for watching news. ("Ethnic Media Muy Popular in California," April 23, 2002)

Figure 11.2 Media organizations like Telemundo provide ethnic communities with programming in their native language and a perspective different from mainstream U.S. media. A 2005 report by New California Media found that 87 percent of Hispanic American adults access Spanish-language television, radio, or newspapers on a regular basis.

These various ethnic media outlets provide perspectives different from those of the major U.S. media outlets. But the U.S. conglomerate GE (General Electric) already owns Telemundo, a major Hispanic network, and other media conglomerates either own or will in time purchase other ethnic media organizations, lest these conglomerates not be able to reach increasingly larger ethnic sectors of American society.

The relationship between the media and society, as we have seen, is a very complicated matter, and it is not easy to make generalizations about this relationship. There is, as I've pointed out, considerable evidence of increasing consolidation of control of the media by giant corporations, but it isn't easy to assess what impact this consolidation has had (or will have) on our culture, our political order, and our society in the long run.

GLOSSARY

aberrant decoding When audiences decode, make sense of, or interpret texts in ways that differ from the ways the creators of these texts expect them to be decoded, we have aberrant decoding. Aberrant decoding is the rule, rather than the exception, when it comes to the mass media, according to the semiotician Umberto Eco.

administrative research Administrative research concerns ways of making communication by organizations and other entities more efficient and more effective. It makes use of statistics and other empirical means of collecting data. Administrative research contrasts with critical research, which has more of an interest in social and economic justice, politics, and related considerations.

aesthetics *See* media aesthetics.

agenda setting This theory argues that the institutions of mass communication don't determine what we think but do determine what it is that we think about. In so doing, they set an agenda for our decision making and thus influence, in important ways, our social and political lives.

artist For our purposes, an artist is not only someone who paints or sculpts or plays a musical instrument, but anyone involved in the creation or performance of any kind of text—especially mass-mediated texts.

attitudes Social psychologists use this term to refer to a relatively enduring state of mind in a person about some phenomenon or aspect of experience. Attitudes usually are either positive or negative, have direction, and involve thoughts, feelings, and behaviors (tied to these attitudes).

audience When we speak of the audiences of the mass media, we mean the people who watch a television program, listen to a radio program, or attend a film or some kind of artistic performance (symphonies, rock concerts, etc.). The members of an audience may be together in one room or in many differ-

221

ent places. In the case of television, we often have families in which each member of the family watches different programs on his or her own set. In technical terms, audiences are *addressees* who receive *mediated texts* sent by an *addresser.*

broadcasting   We use the term *broadcasting* to deal with texts that are made available over wide areas by using radio or television signals. Broadcasting differs from other forms of text distribution such as cable casting, which uses cables, and satellite transmission, which requires dish antennas to capture signals sent by the satellites.

class   A class, from a linguistic standpoint, is any group of things that has something in common. We use the term *class* to refer to social classes, or more literally, socioeconomic classes: groups of people who are similar in terms of income and lifestyle. Marxist theorists argue that there is a ruling class that shapes the ideas of the proletariat, the working class.

codes   By codes we mean systems of symbols, letters, words, sounds, and so forth that generate meaning. Language is a code. It uses combinations of letters (words) to signify certain things. The relation between a word and the thing the word stands for is arbitrary and based on convention. In some cases, the term *code* is used to describe hidden meanings and disguised communications.

cognitive dissonance   Dissonance refers to sounds that clash with one another, are unpleasant, and cause pain and anxiety in the hearer. According to social scientists, people wish to avoid ideas that challenge the ones they hold—that is, ideas that create conflict and other disagreeable feelings. Cognitive dissonance refers then to ideas that conflict with the ideas people hold and therefore generate psychological anxiety and displeasure. People seek to avoid cognitive dissonance.

collective representations   The great French sociologist Emile Durkheim used this concept to address the fact that people are both individuals, pursuing their own aims, and social animals, who are guided by the groups and societies in which they find themselves and from which they take their ideas. Collective representations are, broadly speaking, texts that reflect the beliefs and ideals of groups and other collectivities.

communication   For our purposes, communication is a process that involves the transmission of messages from senders to receivers. We often make a distinction between communication using language, that is, verbal communication, and communication using facial expressions, body language, and other means, which is nonverbal communication.

communications   *Communications*, the plural of the term *communication*, refers to messages, or, what is communicated, in contrast to the process of communication described above.

concept   A concept is a general idea or notion that explains or helps us understand some phenomenon or phenomena. For example, Freud uses the concepts id, ego, and superego in his psychoanalytic theory to explain the way the human psyche operates.

consolidation   This is the term we use for the process in which the control of media companies is transferred to an increasingly smaller number of giant corporations.

critical research   Critical approaches to the media are essentially ideological; they focus on the social, economic, and political dimensions of the mass media and the way the mass media are allegedly used by organizations and others to maintain the status quo rather than enhance equality. This contrasts with administrative research.

cultivation theory   Cultivation theory argues that television dominates the symbolic environment of its audiences and gives them false views of what reality is like. That is, television cultivates or reinforces certain beliefs in its viewers, such as the belief that society is permeated by violence and we live in a dangerous world.

cultural homogenization   This term refers to the destruction of Third World culture and regional cultures in specific countries by the mass media, leading to a cultural sameness and standardization, or, homogenization.

cultural imperialism (media imperialism)   Supporters of this theory, sometimes known as "Coca-Colonization," argue that the flow of media products (such as films and television programs) and popular culture from the United States and other capitalist countries in Western Europe to the Third World is colonizing people in these countries. Along with texts and popular culture, values and beliefs (and most importantly, capitalist ideology) are also being transmitted, leading to the domination of people in Third World countries by these influences.

culture   From an anthropological perspective, culture involves the transmission from generation to generation of specific ideas, arts, beliefs, ways of living, behavior patterns, institutions, and values. When the term *culture* is applied to the arts, it generally is used to specify elite kinds of art works such as opera, poetry, classical music, and serious fiction.

decoding   The process by which audiences make sense of or understand a received text.

defense mechanisms   In Freud's psychoanalytic theory, defense mechanisms are methods used by the ego to defend itself against pressures of the id or impulsive elements in the psyche and superego, elements such as conscience and guilt. Some of the more common defense mechanisms are repression (barring unconscious, instinctual wishes or memories from consciousness), regression (returning to earlier stages in one's psychological development), ambivalence (a simultaneous feeling of love and hate for a person), and rationalization (offering excuses to justify one's actions).

demographics   These are similarities found in selected groups of people in terms of characteristics such as religion, gender, social class, ethnicity, occupation, place of residence, and age.

deviance   Individuals who are deviant, or who are members of deviant groups, have values, beliefs, or behavior patterns that are different (that is, they deviate) from those of most people in society.

digital   "Digital systems," according to Peter Lunenfeld (1999: xv), "translate all input into binary structures of 0s and 1s, which can then be stored, transferred, or manipulated at the level of numbers or 'digits' (so called because etymologically, the word descends from the digits on our hand with which we count out those numbers)."

dysfunctional (disfunctional)   Something is dysfunctional if it contributes to the breakdown or destabilization of the entity in which it is found.

ego   In Freud's theory of the psyche, the ego functions as the executant of the id and as a mediator between the id and the superego. The ego is involved with the individual's perception of reality and adaptation to reality.

ethical criticism   Ethics is that branch of philosophy that involves our sense of what is moral and correct, and ethical criticism analyzes texts in terms of the moral aspects of what happens in those texts and its possible impact on others.

ethnocentrism   This term refers to the notion that the ideas, customs, beliefs, and way of life of one ethnic group are inherently better than those of other ethnic groups.

expressive theory of art   The expressive theory of art holds that the principle function of art is to express the feelings, beliefs, and emotions of the creators of texts and works of art.

false consciousness   For Marxists, false consciousness refers to mistaken ideas that members of the proletariat (and other classes as well) have about their class, status, and economic possibilities. These ideas help maintain the status quo and are of great use to the ruling class, which wants to avoid changes in the social structure. Marx argued that the ideas of the ruling class are always the controlling ideas in a society.

feminist criticism   Feminist criticism, generally speaking, focuses on the portrayal of women and the roles given to them in texts of all kinds, but especially mass-mediated ones. Feminist critics argue that women are typically used as sex objects and are portrayed stereotypically in most texts, and that this has negative effects not only on women but also on men.

focal points   These are the five general topics or subject areas we concentrate on in studying mass communication. They are the work of art (or text), the artist, the audience, America (or another society), and the medium.

formula   In narrative theory, the term *formulaic* refers to a text with conventional characters and actions that audiences are familiar with. In other words, the text follows a formula. Genre texts such as westerns, sitcoms, detective stories, science fiction adventures, and romances are highly formulaic.

functional   In sociological theory, the term *functional* refers, broadly speaking, to the contribution an institution makes to the maintenance of society. Something is functional if it helps maintain the system in which it is found.

functional alternative   The term *functional alternative* refers to an entity that can be used as an alternative to something—that is, it takes the place functionally of something else. For example, watching a professional football game on Sunday could be seen as a functional alternative to attending religious services.

gatekeepers   In the news world, gatekeepers are editors and all those who determine what stories are covered by newspapers, magazines, television news programs, or on the electronic media. Literally speaking, a gatekeeper is someone who stands at a gate and determines who or what goes through it. Thus, these gatekeepers determine what news stories we get, and in a broader sense, they also decide what we see in news shows, what films we see, what books we read, what songs we hear, and so on.

gender   Gender is the sexual category of an individual: male or female. It also refers to behavioral traits customarily associated with each category.

genre   *Genre* is a French term that means "kind" or "class." In this book, genre refers to the kind of formulaic texts found in the mass media: soap operas, news shows, sport programs, horror shows, and detective programs, for example.

hegemonial ideological domination   This is the term for the domination by the ruling classes of the thinking of the masses, who cannot locate the source of their beliefs because these beliefs are so widespread as to seem to be "that which goes without saying." It is a form of domination more subtle than ideological manipulation or indoctrination. *See also*, hegemony.

hegemony   This term, which in Greek means "rule," was used by the Italian Marxist thinker Antonio Gramsci (1891–1937) to explain how the masses are convinced by the ruling classes to accept the ideas of the ruling class and to remain dominated by them. According to Gramsci, when a capitalist cultural perspective becomes all-pervasive in a society, the masses develop a false consciousness and are led to believe that the class system is natural and thus cannot be changed.

hypodermic needle theory   The hypodermic theory, generally discredited now, holds that all members of an audience decode a text in the same way and get the same things out of it. The media are seen as a hypodermic needle, injecting the same message into one and all. Some theorists also talk about *interpretive communities*, which suggests that groups of people can get similar messages from texts.

hypothesis   A hypothesis is a notion that is assumed to be true for the purposes of discussion, argument, or further investigation. It is, in a sense, a guess or supposition that is used to explain some phenomenon.

id   In Freud's theory of the psyche (technically known as his *structural hypothesis*) the id is that element of the psyche that is the representative of a person's drives. Freud called it, in *New Introductory Lectures on Psychoanalysis*, "a chaos, a cauldron of seething excitement" (quoted in Hinsie and Campbell 1970: 372). It also is the source of psychic energy, but lacking direction, it needs the ego to harness and control it. In popular thought, the id is connected with impulse, lust, and an "I want it all now" kind of behavior.

ideology   An ideology is a logically coherent, integrated explanation of social, economic, or political matters that helps establish the goals and direct the actions of an individual or a group or political entity. People act (and vote or don't vote) on the basis of an ideology they hold, even though they may not have articulated or thought much about that ideology.

image   Defining what we call an image is extremely complicated. We might say that an image is a combination of signs and symbols—what we find when we look at a photograph, a film still, a shot of a television screen, or a print advertisement, for example. The term is used for mental as well as physical representations of things. Images often have historical significance and powerful emotional effects on people (see chapter 7 and my discussion of 9/11). Two recent books that deal with images in some detail are Kiku Adatto's *Picture Perfect: The Art and Artifice of Public Image Making* (1993) and Paul Messaris's *Visual Literacy: Image, Mind, and Reality* (1994).

incidental learning   This refers to the information we gain as a result of our everyday experiences—that is, in non-formal, outside of the classroom, situations. It contrasts with the kind of learning we experience in educational institutions of all kinds.

intertextuality   Intertextuality is a reference to previously created texts, styles of expression, or genres by subsequently created texts through the use of allusion, imitation, adaptation, or modification.

latent functions   Latent functions are the hidden, unrecognized, and unintended functions of some activity, entity, or institution. They are contrasted by social scientists with manifest functions, which are recognized and intended.

lifestyle   This term refers to the way people live, and to the decisions they make about such matters as how to decorate their apartment or home (and where it is to be located), what kind of car to drive, what kind of clothes to wear, what kind of foods to eat (and which restaurants to dine at), and where to go for vacation.

limited effects (of media)   Some mass communication theorists argue that the mass media have limited or relatively minor effects in the scheme of things. They cite research that shows, for example, that effects from the media don't tend to be long lasting, and they argue that the notion that the mass media have strong effects has not been demonstrated. This argument is no longer as prominent as it once was.

manifest functions   The manifest functions of some activity, entity, or institution are those functions that are obvious and intended. Manifest functions contrast with latent functions, which are hidden and unintended. The manifest function of television broadcasting might be entertainment, while the latent function might be the encouragement of materialism.

mass   For our purposes, *mass* as in *mass communication* refers to a large number of people who are the audience for a specific communication. There is considerable disagreement about how to understand the term *mass*. In earlier years, theorists said a mass is comprised of individuals who are heterogeneous, do not know one another, are alienated, and do not have a leader. Others have attacked these distinctions, saying they are not based on fact or evidence but on speculative theories that have not been verified.

mass communications   This refers to the transfer of messages, information, texts, and so forth from a sender of some kind to a large number of people, or, mass audience. This transfer is done through the technologies of the mass media: newspapers, magazines, television programs, films, computers, CD ROMs, and so on. The sender often is a person in some large media organization, the messages are public, and the audience tends to be large and varied.

mass culture   Mass culture, sometimes called mass-mediated culture, refers to theories about the impact of the mass media on culture. Many mass culture theorists argue that the media will lead to a mass culture in which we will all lose our sense of individuality and our identities and will be easily manipulated by those who control the media.

media aesthetics   When applied to the media, aesthetics involves the way the technical characteristics of a text such as lighting, sound, music, camera work, and editing affect the way audiences react to the text.

media ethics   This is that branch of ethics that deals with moral questions relating to the media, especially in terms of the media's impact on individuals and their influence on culture and society.

media violence   According to Signorelli and Gerbner, media violence can be described as "the depiction of overt physical action that hurts or kills or threatens to do so" (1988: xi). Varying kinds and aspects of violence have to be considered in dealing with media portrayals of violence.

medium (plural: **media**)   A medium is understood to be a means of delivering messages, information, or texts to audiences. There are different media classifications. Some of the most common are print (newspapers, magazines, books, billboards), electronic (radio, television, computers, CD ROMS), and photographic (photographs, films, videos). Other ways of classifying the media are described in this book.

metaphor   A metaphor is a figure of speech that conveys meaning by analogy. We must realize that metaphors are not confined to poetry and literary works but, according to some linguists, are a fundamental way in which we make sense of things and find meaning in the world. A simile is a weak form of metaphor that uses either *like* or *as* in making an analogy. Metaphors can be communicated by visual images; they aren't dependent upon language.

metonymy   According to linguists, metonymy is a figure of speech that conveys information by association and is, along with metaphor, one of the most important ways people convey information to one another. We tend not to be aware of our use of metonymy, but whenever we use association to express an idea about something (Rolls Royce = wealthy) we are thinking metonymically. A form of metonymy that involves seeing a whole in terms of a part or vice versa is called synecdoche. Referring to the presidency as *the White House* is an example of synecdoche. Like metaphors, metonymies can be communicated visually.

mimetic theory of art   This theory, dating from Aristotle's time, suggests that art is an imitation of reality. Art, then, is a mirror of life, which explains why we can find so much about society and people in art (texts). Some theorists suggest that art is not a mirror but a lamp that projects the reality of the creators behind the texts.

model   In the social sciences, models are abstract representations that show how some phenomenon functions. Theories are typically expressed in language, but models tend to be represented graphically and often use statistics or mathematics. In *Communication Models for the Study of Mass Communications*, Denis McQuail and Sven Windahl define *model* as "a consciously simplified description in graphic form of a piece of reality. A model seeks to show the main elements of any structure or process and the relationships between these elements" (1993: 2).

modernism   *Modernism* is the term used by critics when discussing the arts (architecture, literature, painting, dance, music, and so on) of the period from approximately 1900 until the 1960s. The modernists rejected a rigid narrative structure for simultaneity and montage, and they explored the paradoxical nature of reality. Some of the more important modernists were T. S. Eliot, Franz Kafka, James Joyce, Pablo Picasso, Henri Matisse, and Eugene Ionesco. The period after modernism is called postmodernism.

narrowcasting   A medium like radio, which has stations that tend to focus on discrete groups of people, is said to be a narrowcasting medium. This contrasts with a broadcasting medium like television that tries to reach as large an audience as possible.

nonverbal communication   A great deal of communication comes from nonverbal phenomena. Our body language, facial expressions, style of dress, style of wearing our hair, and so on are examples of our communicating feelings and attitudes (and a sense of who we are) without using words. Even in conversations, a great deal of the communication comes from our body language.

phallic symbol   An object that resembles either by shape or function the penis is described as a phallic symbol. Symbolism is a defense mechanism of the ego that permits hidden or repressed sexual or aggressive thoughts to be expressed in a disguised form. For a discussion of this topic see Freud's book *The Interpretation of Dreams* (1965). Many print advertisements and television commercials make use of phallic symbols to excite people emotionally.

political cultures   According to the late political scientist Aaron Wildavsky, all democratic societies have four political cultures and need these four cultures to counterbalance one another. The political cultures Wildavsky identified are individualists, elitists, egalitarians, and fatalists. A political culture is made up of people who are similar in terms of their political values and beliefs—and for Wildavsky, those as well who observe similar group boundaries, rules, and prescriptions.

popular   The term *popular* is one of the most difficult terms used in discourse about the arts and the media. Literally speaking, *popular* means appealing to large numbers of people. It comes from the Latin term *popularis*, which means "of the people."

popular culture   *Popular culture* is a term that identifies certain kinds of mass-mediated texts that appeal to large numbers of people—that is, texts that are popular. But mass communication theorists often identify (or should we say confuse?) *popular* with *mass* and suggest that if something is popular, it must by necessity be of poor quality, thereby appealing to the mythical "lowest common denominator." Popular culture is generally held to be the opposite of elite culture: those arts that require certain levels of sophistication and refinement to be appreciated, such as ballet, opera, poetry, and classical music. Postmodern theorists reject this popular culture / elite culture polarity.

pornography   This term is almost impossible to define. Generally speaking, pornography is held to be material that is sexually explicit and is meant to arouse sexual excitement. The root of the Greek term *porne* means "prostitute."

postmodernism   We Americans are, some theorists suggest, living in a postmodern era, and have been since the 1960s. Literally speaking, the term *postmodernism* (sometimes written *post-modernism*) means "after modernism," modernism being the period from approximately 1900 to the 1960s. As a leading theorist of the subject Jean-François Lyotard puts it, postmodernism is characterized by "incredulity toward metanarratives" (1984: xxiv). By this Lyotard means that the old philosophical belief systems or metanarratives that once helped people order their lives and societies no longer are accepted or given credulity. This has lead to a period in which, some have suggested, anything goes.

power   Power is, politically speaking, the ability to implement one's wishes with respect to social policy. When we use the term to discuss texts, we are using it to describe the ability of texts to have an emotional impact upon readers, viewers, or listeners, and their ability sometimes to have social, economic, and political consequences.

psychoanalytic theory   Freud's psychoanalytic theory is based on the notion that the human psyche has what he called an unconscious that is ordinarily inaccessible to individuals (unlike consciousness and the preconscious) and that continually shapes and affects our mental functioning and behavior. We can symbolize this by imagining an iceberg: the tip of the iceberg, showing above the water, represents consciousness; the part of the iceberg we can still see just below the surface of the water represents the preconscious; and the rest of the iceberg (which cannot be seen but we know it is there) represents the unconscious. We cannot access the unconscious of our psyches because of repression. Freud also emphasized matters such as sexuality and the role of the Oedipus complex in our lives and social relations.

psychographics   In marketing, the term *psychographics* refers to the distinguishing characteristics of groups of people who have similar psychological profiles. The VALS (values and lifestyles) typology is an example of a marketing system based on psychographics. Psychographics differ from the demographics that marketers use to focus upon the social and economic characteristics that people have in common.

public   Instead of the term *popular culture*, some media theorists use phrases such as *the public arts* or *public communication* to avoid the negative connotations of the terms *mass* and *popular*. A public is a group of people, a community. We can contrast public acts—those meant to be known to the community—with private acts, which are not meant to be known. But private acts often have social and public consequences.

rationalization In Freudian thought, a rationalization is a defense mechanism of the ego that creates an excuse to justify some action (or inaction when an action is expected). Ernest Jones, who introduced the term, used it to describe the logical and rational reasons that people give to justify behavior that is really caused by unconscious and irrational determinants.

reader response theory (reception theory) Reader response theory suggests that *readers* (a term used very broadly to cover people who read books, watch television programs, go to films, listen to the radio, etc.) play an important role in the realization of texts. Texts, then, function as sites for the creation of meaning by readers, and different readers interpret a given text differently. How differently is a matter of considerable conjecture.

relativism In philosophical thought, relativism refers to the belief that truth is relative and not absolute, and that there are no universally accepted objective standards. In ethical thought, relativism suggests that there are no absolutes of morality or ethics. Thus for relativists, different cultures have different ways of living and practices that are as valid as any other culture's way of living and practices. That is, morality and ethical behavior are relative to particular groups and cannot be generalized to include all human beings. This contrasts with the notion that there are ethical absolutes, or universals, that can and should be applied to everyone.

responsive chord theory Tony Schwartz developed this theory, which argues that the best way to understand how the media work is to recognize that they do not transport information to audiences, but instead strike a responsive chord with information individuals already possess. As Schwartz writes in his book *The Responsive Chord*, "The critical task is to design our package of stimuli so that it resonates with information already stored within an individual and thereby induces the desired learning or behavioral effect" (1973: 25).

role A *role*, as sociologists use the term, is a way of behavior that we learn in a given society and that is held to be appropriate to a particular situation. A person generally plays many roles during a given day such as spouse, parent, or worker.

secondary modeling systems Language, according to Yuri Lotman, is our primary modeling system. Works of art that use phenomena such as myths and legends function as secondary modeling systems; that is, systems that are secondary to language.

selective attention (selective inattention) We all have a tendency to avoid messages that conflict with our beliefs and values. One way we do this is by using selective attention: avoiding or not paying attention to messages that might generate cognitive dissonance.

semiotics   Literally, *semiotics* means "the science of signs." *Semeion* is the Greek term for "sign." A sign is anything that can be used to stand for anything else. According to C. S. Peirce, one of the founders of semiotics, a sign "is something which stands to somebody for something in some respect or capacity."

serial texts   We refer to texts that continue for long periods of time as serial texts. Good examples would be comic strips and soap operas. Serial texts pose a problem for critics: What exactly is the text, and how do we deal with it?

sign   In semiotic theory, a sign is a combination of a signifier (a sound or an object) and a signified (a concept). The relationship between the signifier and the signified is arbitrary and based on convention. Signs are anything that can be used to stand for something else.

social controls   Social controls are the ideas, beliefs, values, and mores that people get from their societies and that shape their behavior. People are both individuals, with certain distinctive physical and emotional characteristics and desires, and also, at the same time, members of societies, as Emile Durkheim pointed out. People are shaped, to a certain degree, by the institutions found in these societies.

socialization   Socialization refers to the processes by which societies teach individuals how to behave: what rules to obey, what roles to assume, and what values to hold. Socialization has traditionally been done by the family, educators, religious figures, and peers. The mass media seem to have usurped this function to a considerable degree nowadays, with consequences that are not always positive. Anthropologists use the term *enculturation* to refer to the process by which an individual is taught cultural values and practices.

socioeconomic class   Socioeconomic class is a categorization of people according to their income and related social status and lifestyle. In Marxist thought, the ruling classes shape the consciousness of the working classes, and history is, in essence, a record of class conflict.

spiral of silence   This theory, developed by German scholar Elisabeth Noelle-Neumann, argues that people who hold views that they think are not widely held (whether this is true or not) tend to keep quiet, while those who hold views that they believe are widely accepted tend to state their views strongly, leading to a spiral in which certain views are suppressed while others gain increased prominence.

stereotypes   Commonly held, simplistic, and inaccurate group portraits of categories of people are called stereotypes. These stereotypes can have a positive, negative, or mixed viewpoint, but they usually are negative. Stereotyping always involves making gross generalizations.

subculture   Subcultures are cultural subgroups whose religious practices, ethnicity, sexual orientation, beliefs, values, behaviors, and lifestyles vary in certain ways from those of the dominant mainstream culture. In any complex society, it is normal to have a considerable number of subcultures.

subliminal   This is the term used for images that are shown on television or on film screens for only a fraction of a second and are therefore generally not consciously recognized by the viewer, but are said to have an effect on the viewer.

superego   In Freud's theory of the psyche, the superego is the agency in our psyches related to conscience and morality. The superego is involved with processes such as moral approval or disapproval of wishes, critical self-observation, and sense of guilt over wrong-doing. The functions of the superego are largely unconscious and are opposed to id elements in our psyches. Mediating between the two, and trying to balance them, are our egos.

text   The term *text* is used in academic discourse to refer, broadly speaking, to any work of art in any medium. The term is used by critics as a convenience—so they don't have to name a given work all the time or use various synonyms. There are problems involved in deciding what a text is when we deal with serial texts such as soap operas and comics.

theory   A *theory*, as the term is conventionally understood, is expressed in language, and systematically and logically attempts to explain and predict phenomena being studied. Theories differ from concepts, which define phenomena that are being studied, and from models, which are abstract, usually graphic in nature, and explicit about what is being studied.

typology   A typology is a classification scheme or system of categories that we use to make sense of phenomena. Classification schemes are important because the way we classify things affects the way we think about them.

ur-text   An ur-text is a template for other texts, a foundational model from which other texts are derived.

uses and gratifications theory   The uses and gratifications theory argues that researchers should pay attention to the way members of audiences use the media (or certain texts or genres of texts) and the gratifications they get from their use of the media. In other words, uses and gratifications researchers focus on how audiences use the media and not on how the media affect audiences.

values   Values are understood to be abstract and general beliefs or judgments about what is right and wrong (and what is good and bad) that have implications for individual behavior and for social, cultural, and political entities. There are a number of problems with values from a philosophical point of view. First, how do we determine which values are correct or good and which aren't, that is, how do we justify values, and are values objective or subjective?

Second, what happens when there is a conflict between groups, each of which holds a central value that conflicts with that of a different group?

video games   Video games are electronic games that are interactive, that is, they allow players to participate in the action and outcome of the game. They are played, generally speaking, on specialized consoles that have very powerful graphic and sound capabilities, though many video games can also be played on computers.

violence (mass-mediated)   *See* media violence.

youth culture   A youth culture is a subculture formed by young people around some area of interest usually connected with leisure and entertainment, such as for example, surfing, skateboarding, rock music, or an aspect of computers (games, hacking). Typically, members of youth cultures adopt distinctive ways of dressing, and develop institutions that cater to their needs.

SELECTED BIBLIOGRAPHY

Abrams, M. H. 1958. *The Mirror and the Lamp: Romantic Theory and the Critical Tradition*. New York: W. W. Norton.

Adatto, Kiku. 1993. *Picture Perfect: The Art and Artifice of Public Image Making*. New York: Basic Books.

Adorno, Theodor W. 1991. *The Culture Industry: Selected Essays on Mass Culture*. London: Routledge.

Bakhtin, M. M. 1981. *The Dialogic Imagination*. Edited by Michael Holquist. Translated by Caryl Emerson and Michael Holquist. Austin: University of Texas Press.

Barker, Martin, and Ann Beezer. 1992. *Reading into Cultural Studies*. London: Routledge.

Barthes, Roland. 1972. *Mythologies*. Translated by Annette Lavers. New York: Hill and Wang.

———. 1988. *The Semiotic Challenge*. Translated by Richard Howard. New York: Hill and Wang.

Baudrillard, Jean. 1983. *Simulations*. Translated by Paul Foss et al. New York: Semiotext(e).

———. 1996. *The System of Objects*. Translated James Benedict. London: Verso.

Bennett, Tony, and Janet Woollacott. 1987. *Bond and Beyond: The Political Career of a Popular Hero*. New York: Methuen.

Berger, Arthur Asa, ed. 1991. *Media USA: Process and Effect*. 2nd ed. New York: Longman.

———. 2001. *Jewish Jesters*. Cresskill, NJ: Hampton Press.

———. 2002. *The Mass Comm Murders: Five Media Theorists Self-Destruct*. Lanham, MD: Rowman & Littlefield.

————. 2002. *Video Games: A Popular Culture Phenomenon.* New Brunswick, NJ: Transaction.

————. 2004. *Ads, Fads, and Consumer Culture: Advertising's Impact on American Character and Society.* 2nd ed. Lanham, MD: Rowman & Littlefield.

————. 2005. *Shop 'Til You Drop: Consumer Behavior and American Culture.* Lanham, MD: Rowman & Littlefield.

Berman, Marshall. 1982. *All That Is Solid Melts into Air: The Experience of Modernity.* New York: Touchstone Books.

Best, Steven, and Douglas Kellner. 1991. *Postmodern Theory.* New York: Guilford.

Bettelheim, Bruno. 1976. *The Uses of Enchantment.* New York: Knopf.

Blau, Herbert. 1992. *To All Appearances: Ideology and Performance.* London: Routledge.

Bogart, Leo. 1985. *Polls and the Awareness of Public Opinion.* New Brunswick, NJ: Transaction.

Bolter, Jay David, and Richard Grusin. 2000. *Remediation: Understanding New Media.* Cambridge, MA: MIT Press.

Boorstin, Daniel. 1975. *The Image: A Guide to Pseudo-Events in America.* New York: Atheneum.

Bowlby, Rachel. 1993. *Shopping with Freud: Items on Consumerism, Feminism, and Psychoanalysis.* London: Routledge.

Brenkman, John. 1993. *Straight Male Modern: A Cultural Critique of Psychoanalysis.* New York: Routledge.

Brenner, Charles. 1974. *An Elementary Textbook of Psychoanalysis.* Garden City, NY: Anchor Books.

Brown, Mary Ellen, ed. 1990. *Television and Women's Culture: The Politics of the Popular.* Newbury Park, CA: Sage.

————. 1994. *Soap Opera and Woman's Talk: The Pleasure of Resistance.* Thousand Oaks, CA: Sage.

Buck-Morss, Susan. 1989. *The Dialectics of Seeing: Walter Benjamin and the Arcades Project.* Minneapolis: University of Minnesota Press.

Burton, Graeme. 1990. *More Than Meets the Eye: An Introduction to Media Studies.* London: Arnold.

Butler, Judith. 1993. *Bodies That Matter.* New York: Routledge.

Cantor, Muriel G. 1988. *The Hollywood TV Producer.* New Brunswick, NJ: Transaction.

Cantor, Muriel G., and Joel M. Cantor. 1991. *Prime-Time Television: Content and Control.* Thousand Oaks, CA: Sage.

Carey, James, ed. 1988. *Media, Myths, and Narratives: Television and the Press.* Newbury Park, CA: Sage.

Cawelti, John G. 1971. *The Six-Gun Mystique*. Bowling Green, OH: Bowling Green University Popular Press.

Certeau, Michel de. 1984. *The Practice of Everyday Life*. Translated by Steven Rendall. Berkeley: University of California Press.

———. 1986. *Heterologies: Discourse on the Other*. Translated by Brian Massumi. Minneapolis: University of Minnesota Press.

Clarke, John. 1992. *New Times and Old Enemies: Essays on Cultural Studies and America*. London: Routledge.

Cohen, Jodi R. 1998. *Communication Criticism: Developing Your Critical Powers*. Thousand Oaks, CA: Sage.

Collins, Richard, James Curran, Nicholas Garnham, and Paddy Scannell, eds. 1986. *Media, Culture, and Society: A Critical Reader*. Newbury Park, CA: Sage.

Cortese, Anthony J. 2004. *Provocateur: Images of Women and Minorities in Advertising*. 2nd ed. Lanham, MD: Rowman & Littlefield.

Coward, Rosalind, and John Ellis. 1977. *Language and Materialism: Developments in Semiology and the Theory of the Subject*. London: Routledge and Kegan Paul.

Crane, Diane. 1992. *The Production of Culture: Media and the Urban Arts*. Newbury Park, CA: Sage.

Creed, Barbara. 1993. *The Monstrous-Feminine: Film, Feminism, Psychoanalysis*. London: Routledge.

Creedon, Pamela J., ed. 1993. *Women in Mass Communication*. 2nd ed. Thousand Oaks, CA: Sage.

Crook, Stephen, Jan Pakulski, and Malcolm Waters, eds. 1992. *Postmodernization: Change in Advanced Society*. London: Sage.

Cross, Gary. 1993. *Time and Money: The Making of a Consumer Culture*. London: Routledge.

Culler, Jonathan. 1975. *Structuralist Poetics: Structuralism, Linguistics, and the Study of Literature*. Ithaca, NY: Cornell University Press.

———. 1981. *The Pursuit of Signs*. Ithaca, NY: Cornell University Press.

———. 1982. *On Deconstruction*. Ithaca, NY: Cornell University Press.

———. 1986. *Ferdinand de Saussure*. Revised ed. Ithaca, NY: Cornell University Press.

Danesi, Marcel. 1994. *Messages and Meanings: An Introduction to Semiotics*. Toronto: Canadian Scholars Press.

———. 2002. *Understanding Media Semiotics*. London: Arnold.

Danesi, Marcel, and Donato Santeramo, eds. 1992. *Introducing Semiotics: An Anthology of Readings*. Toronto: Canadian Scholars Press.

Davis, Robert Con, and Ronald Schleifer. 1991. *Criticism and Culture: The Role of Critique in Modern Literary Theory*. London: Longman.

Denney, Reuel. 1989. *The Astonished Muse*. New Brunswick, NJ: Transaction.

Denzin, Norman K. 1991. *Images of Postmodern Society: Social Theory and Contemporary Cinema.* London: Sage.

Doane, Mary Ann. 1991. *Femmes Fatales.* New York: Routledge.

Donald, James, and Stuart Hall, eds. 1985. *Politics and Ideology.* Bristol, PA: Taylor and Francis.

Douglas, Mary. 1975. *Implicit Meanings: Essays in Anthropology.* London: Routledge and Kegan Paul.

———. 1992. *Risk and Blame: Essays in Cultural Theory.* London: Routledge.

———. 1997. "In Defence of Shopping." In *The Shopping Experience.* Edited by Pasi Falk and Colin Campbell. London: Sage.

Duncan, Hugh Dalziel. 1985. *Communication and the Social Order.* New Brunswick, NJ: Transaction.

Dundes, Alan. 1987. *Cracking Jokes: Studies in Sick Humor Cycles and Stereotypes.* Berkeley, CA: Ten Speed Press.

Durkheim, Emile. 1967. *The Elementary Forms of the Religious Life.* New York: Free Press.

Dyer, Richard. 1993. *The Matter of Images: Essays on Representations.* London: Routledge.

Eagleton, Terry. 1976. *Marxism and Literary Criticism.* Berkeley: University of California Press.

———. 1983. *Literary Theory: An Introduction.* Minneapolis: University of Minnesota Press.

Easthope, Antony. 1991. *Literary into Cultural Studies.* London: Routledge.

Eco, Umberto. 1972. "Towards a Semiotic Inquiry into the Television Message." In *Working Papers in Cultural Studies.* University of Birmingham, Centre for Contemporary Cultural Studies.

———. 1976. *A Theory of Semiotics.* Bloomington: Indiana University Press.

———. 1984. *The Role of the Reader.* Bloomington: Indiana University Press.

Elam, Keir. 1980. *The Semiotics of Theatre and Drama.* London: Methuen.

Entertainment Software Association. 2005. "Computer and Video Game Software Sales Reach Record $7.3 Billion in 2004." News release, January 26.

Ettema, James S., and D. Charles Whitney, eds. 1994. *Audiencemaking: How the Media Create the Audience.* Thousand Oaks, CA: Sage.

Ewen, Stuart. 1976. *Captains of Consciousness.* New York: McGraw-Hill.

Ewen, Stuart, and Elizabeth Ewen. 1982. *Channels of Desire: Mass Images and the Shaping of American Consciousness.* New York: McGraw-Hill.

Featherstone, Mike. 1991. *Consumer Culture and Postmodernism.* London: Sage.

Fiske, John. 1989. *Reading the Popular.* London: Routledge.

———. 1989. *Understanding Popular Culture.* London: Routledge.

Fiske, John, and John Hartley. 1978. *Reading Television.* London: Methuen.

Fjellman, Stephen M. 1992. *Vinyl Leaves: Walt Disney World and America*. Boulder, CO: Westview.

Franklin, Sarah, Celia Lury, and Jackie Stacey. 1992. *Off-Centre: Feminism and Cultural Studies*. London: Routledge.

Freud, Sigmund. 1908. "The Relation of the Poet to Day-Dreaming." In *Freud: Character and Culture*. Edited by Philip Rieff. New York: Collier, 1963.

———. 1960. *A General Introduction to Psychoanalysis*. Translated by Joan Riviere. New York: Washington Square Press.

———. 1963. *Jokes and Their Relation to the Unconscious*. Translated by James Strachey. New York: W. W. Norton.

———. 1965. *The Interpretation of Dreams*. Translated by James Strachey. New York: Avon.

Freidson, Eliot. 1953. "Communication Research and the Concept of the Mass." *American Sociological Review* 18 (June): 313–17.

Frith, Simon. 1981. *Sound Effects: Youth, Leisure, and the Politics of Rock 'n' Roll*. New York: Pantheon.

Fry, William F. 1968. *Sweet Madness: A Study of Humor*. Palo Alto, CA: Pacific Books.

Gandelman, Claude. 1991. *Reading Pictures, Viewing Texts*. Bloomington: Indiana University Press.

Garber, Marjorie. 1993. *Vested Interests: Cross-Dressing and Cultural Anxiety*. New York: HarperPerennial.

Garber, Marjorie, Jann Matlock, and Rebecca Walkowtiz, eds. 1993. *Media Spectacles*. New York: Routledge.

Garber, Marjorie, Pratibha Parmar, and John Greyson, eds. 1993. *Queer Looks: Perspectives on Lesbian and Gay Film and Video*. New York: Routledge.

Gee, James Paul. 2004. *What Video Games Have to Teach Us about Learning and Literacy*. New York: Palgrave Macmillan.

Gertner, Jon. 2005. "Our Ratings, Ourselves." *New York Times Magazine*, April 10, 34–41, 56–58, 64–67.

Gitlin, Todd. 1985. *Inside Prime Time*. New York: Pantheon.

———. 2001. *Media Unlimited: How the Torrent of Images and Sound Overwhelms Our Lives*. New York: Metropolitan Books.

Goldstein, Ann, Mary Jane Jacob, Anne Rorimer, and Howard Singerman. 1989. *A Forest of Signs: Art in the Crisis of Representation*. Cambridge, MA: MIT Press.

Gowans, Alan. 1971. *The Unchanging Arts: New Forms for the Traditional Functions of Art in Society*. Philadelphia: J. B. Lippincott.

Greenblatt, Stephen J. 1992. *Learning to Curse: Essays in Early Modern Culture*. New York: Routledge.

Greenfield, Lauren. 2002. *Girl Culture.* San Francisco: Chronicle Books.

Greenfield, Patricia Marks. 1984. *Mind and Media: The Effects of Television, Video Games, and Computers.* Cambridge, MA: Harvard University Press.

Grossberg, Lawrence. 1992. *We Gotta Get Out of This Place: Popular Conservatism and Postmodern Culture.* New York: Routledge.

Grossberg, Lawrence, Cary Nelson, and Paula Treicher. 1991. *Cultural Studies.* New York: Routledge.

Grotjahn, Martin. 1966. *Beyond Laughter: Humor and the Subconscious.* New York: McGraw-Hill.

Guiraud, Pierre. 1975. *Semiology.* London: Routledge and Kegan Paul.

Gumbrecht, Hansl Ulrich. 1992. Translated by Glen Burns. *Making Sense in Life and Literature.* Minneapolis: University of Minnesota Press.

Habermas, Jurgen. 1987. Translated by Frederick G. Lawrence. *The Philosophical Discourse of Modernity: Twelve Lectures.* Minneapolis: University of Minnesota Press.

———. 1989. Translated by Shierry Weber Nicholsen. *The New Conservatism: Cultural Criticism and the Historians' Debate.* Minneapolis: University of Minnesota Press.

Hall, Stuart. 1988. *The Hard Road to Renewal.* London: Verso.

———. 1991. *New Times: The Changing Face of Politics in the 1990s.* London: Routledge.

Hall, Stuart, and Tony Jefferson, eds. 1990. *Resistance through Rituals: Youth Subcultures in Postwar Britain.* London: Routledge. (This was originally published in *Working Papers in Cultural Studies* 7/8 from the Centre for Contemporary Cultural Studies at the University of Birmingham. For an in-depth study of Stuart Hall's work, see *Journal of Communication Inquiry,* Summer 1986, which is devoted to him.)

Hall, Stuart, and Paddy Whannel. 1967. *The Popular Arts: A Critical Guide to the Mass Media.* Boston: Beacon.

Hartley, John. 1992. *The Politics of Pictures: The Creation of the Public in the Age of Popular Media.* London: Routledge.

———. 1992. *Tele-ology: Studies in Television.* London: Routledge.

Haug, W. F. 1971. *Critique of Commodity Aesthetics: Appearance, Sexuality, and Advertising in Capitalist Society.* Translated by Robert Bock. Minneapolis: University of Minnesota Press.

———. 1987. *Commodity Aesthetics, Ideology, and Culture.* New York: International General.

Henry J. Kaiser Family Foundation. 2005. *Generation M: Media in the Lives of 8–18-Year-Olds.* www.kff.org.

Herzog-Massing, Herta. 1986. "Decoding Dallas." *Society* 24, no. 1, 74–77.

Heuscher, Julius E. 1974. *A Psychiatric Study of Myths and Fairy Tales: Their Origin, Meaning, and Usefulness.* Springfield, IL: Thomas.

Hinsie, L. E., and R. J. Campbell, eds. 1970. *Psychiatric Dictionary.* New York: Oxford University Press.

Hoggart, Richard. 1992. *The Uses of Literacy.* New Brunswick, NJ: Transaction.

Hoover, Stewart M. 1988. *Mass Media Religion: The Social Sources of the Electronic Church.* Newbury Park, CA: Sage.

Howard, Theresa. 2006. "Advertisers Place \$500M Bet on NCAA." *USA Today,* March 17, 1B.

Hutcheon, Linda. 1989. *The Politics of Postmodernism.* London: Routledge.

Iser, Wolfgang. 1988. "The Reading Process: A Phenomenological Approach." In *Modern Criticism and Theory: A Reader.* Edited by D. Lodge. New York: Longman.

Jacobs, Norman, ed. 1992. *Mass Media in Modern Society.* New Brunswick, NJ: Transaction.

Jakobson, Roman. 1985. *Verbal Art, Verbal Sign, Verbal Time.* Edited by Krystyna Pomorska and Stephen Rudy. Minneapolis: University of Minnesota Press.

Jally, Sut, and Justin Lewis. 1992. *Enlightened Racism: The Cosby Show, Audiences, and the Myth of the American Dream.* Boulder, CO: Westview.

Jameson, Frederic. 1981. *The Political Unconscious.* Ithaca, NY: Cornell University Press.

———. 1991. *Postmodernism, or, the Cultural Logic of Late Capitalism.* Durham, NC: Duke University Press.

———. 1992. *The Geopolitical Aesthetic: Cinema and Space in the World System.* Bloomington: Indiana University Press.

———. 1992. *Signatures of the Visible.* New York: Routledge.

Jauss, Hans Robert. 1982. *Toward an Aesthetic of Reception.* Translated by Timothy Bahti. Minneapolis: University of Minnesota Press.

Jensen, Joli. 1990. *Redeeming Modernity: Contradictions in Media Criticism.* Newbury Park, CA: Sage.

Jones, Steve. 1992. *Rock Formation: Music, Technology, and Mass Communication.* Thousand Oaks, CA: Sage.

Jones, Steven G., ed. 1994. *Cybersociety: Computer-Mediated Communication and Community.* Thousand Oaks, CA: Sage.

Jowett, Garth, and James M. Linton. 1989. *Movies as Mass Communication.* Newbury Park, CA: Sage.

Jowett, Garth S., and Victoria O'Donnell. 1992. *Propaganda and Persuasion.* 2nd ed. Thousand Oaks, CA: Sage.

Jung, Carl G., ed. *Man and His Symbols.* New York: Dell.

Kamalipour, Yahya R., and Kuldip R. Rampal, eds. 2001. *Media, Sex, Violence, and Drugs in the Global Village.* Lanham, MD: Rowman & Littlefield.

Kellner, Douglas. 1992. *The Persian Gulf TV War*. Boulder, CO: Westview.

Kern, Montague. 1989. *30-Second Politics: Political Advertising in the Eighties*. New York: Praeger.

Korzenny, Felix, and Stella Ting-Toomey, eds. 1992. *Mass Media Effects across Cultures*. Newbury Park, CA: Sage.

Lacan, Jacques. 1966. *Ecrits: A Selection*. Translated by Alan Sheridan. New York: Norton.

Laurentis, Teresa de. 1984. *Alice Doesn't: Feminism, Semiotics, Cinema*. Bloomington: Indiana University Press.

———. 1987. *Technologies of Gender: Essays on Theory, Film, and Fiction*. Bloomington Indiana University Press.

Lazere, Donald, ed. 1987. *America Media and Mass Culture: Left Perspectives*. Berkeley: University of California Press.

Lefebvre, Henri. 1984. *Everyday Life in the Modern World*. Translated by Sacha Rabinovitch. New Brunswick, NJ: Transaction.

Lévi-Strauss, Claude. 1967. *Structural Anthropology*. Garden City, NY: Doubleday.

Levy, Mark R., and Michael Gurevitch, eds. 1994. *Defining Media Studies: Reflections on the Future of the Field*. New York: Oxford University Press.

Lipsitz, George. 1989. *Time Passages: Collective Memory and American Popular Culture*. Minneapolis: University of Minnesota Press.

Lotman, Yuri M. 1976. *Semiotics of Cinema*. Ann Arbor, MI: Michigan Slavic Contributions.

———. 1977. *The Structure of the Artistic Text*. Translated by Gail Lenhoff and Ronald Vroon. Ann Arbor, MI: Michigan Slavic Contributions.

———. 1991. *Universe of the Mind: A Semiotic Theory of Culture*. Bloomington: Indiana University Press.

Lull, James. 1991. *Popular Music and Communication*. Thousand Oaks, CA: Sage.

Lunenfeld, Peter, ed. 1999. *The Digital Dialectic: New Essays on New Media*. Cambridge, MA: MIT Press.

Lyotard, Jean-François. 1984. *The Postmodern Condition: A Report on Knowledge*. Minneapolis: University of Minnesota Press.

MacCannell, Dean, and Juliet Flower MacCannell. 1982. *The Time of the Sign: A Semiotic Interpretation of Modern Culture*. Bloomington: Indiana University Press.

MacDonald, J. Fred. 1994. *One Nation under Television*. Chicago: Nelson-Hall.

Mandel, Ernest. 1985. *Delightful Murder: A Social History of the Crime Story*. Minneapolis: University of Minnesota Press.

Mannheim, Karl. 1936. *Ideology and Utopia: An Introduction to the Sociology of Knowledge*. New York: Harcourt, Brace.

Marx, Karl. 1964. *Selected Writings in Sociology and Social Philosophy.* Edited and translated by T. B. Bottomore. New York: McGraw-Hill.

Mattelart, Armand, and Michele Mattelart. 1992. Translated by James A. Cohen and Marina Urquidi. *Rethinking Media Theory.* Minneapolis: University of Minnesota Press.

McCarthy, Thomas. 1991. *Ideals and Illusions: On Reconstruction and Deconstruction in Contemporary Critical Theory.* Cambridge, MA: MIT Press.

McCue, Greg, with Clive Bloom. 1993. *Dark Knights: The New Comics in Context.* Boulder, CO: Westview.

McGuire, William. 1991. "Who's Afraid of the Big Bad Media." In *Media USA: Process and Effect.* Edited by Arthur Asa Berger. 2nd ed. New York: Longman.

McLuhan, Marshall. 1951. *The Mechanical Bride: Folklore of Industrial Man.* New York: Vanguard Press.

———. 1965. *Understanding Media: The Extensions of Man.* New York: McGraw-Hill.

———. 1970. *Culture Is Our Business.* New York: McGraw-Hill.

McLuhan, Marshall, and Quentin Fiore. 1967. *The Medium Is the Massage.* New York: Bantam Books.

McQuail, Denis. 1992. *Media Performance: Mass Communication and the Public Interest.* Thousand Oaks, CA: Sage.

———. 1994. *Mass Communication Theory: An Introduction.* 3rd ed. Thousand Oaks, CA: Sage.

McQuail, Denis, and Sven Windahl. 1993. *Communication Models for the Study of Mass Communications.* 2nd ed. New York: Longman.

Mellencamp, Patricia. 1990. *Indiscretions: Avant-Garde Film, Video, and Feminism.* Bloomington: Indiana University Press.

———, ed. 1990. *Logics of Television: Essays in Cultural Criticism.* Bloomington: Indiana University Press.

Messaris, Paul. 1994. *Visual Literacy: Image, Mind, and Reality.* Boulder, CO: Westview.

Metz, Christian. 1982. *The Imaginary Signifier: Psychoanalysis and the Cinema.* Translated by Celia Britton et al. Bloomington: Indiana University Press.

Mindess, Harvey. 1971. *Laughter and Liberation.* Los Angeles: Nash.

Mitchell, Arnold. 1983. *The Nine American Lifestyles: Who We Are and Where We're Going.* New York: Macmillan.

Modleski, Tania. 1984. *Loving with a Vengeance: Mass-Produced Fantasies for Women.* New York: Routledge.

———, ed. 1986. *Studies in Entertainment: Critical Approaches to Mass Culture.* Bloomington: Indiana University Press.

———. 1988. *The Women Who Knew Too Much: Hitchcock and Feminist Theory.* New York: Routledge.

Moores, Shaun. 1994. *Interpreting Audiences: The Ethnography of Media Consumption*. Thousand Oaks, CA: Sage.

Morley, David. 1988. *Family Television: Cultural Power and Domestic Leisure*. London: Routledge.

———. 1993. *Television Audiences and Cultural Studies*. London: Routledge.

Mulvey, Laura. 1989. *Visual and Other Pleasures*. Bloomington: Indiana University Press.

Nash, Christopher, ed. 1990. *Narrative in Culture*. London: Routledge.

Navarro, Desiderio, ed. 1993. "Postmodernism: Center and Periphery." *South Atlantic Quarterly* (Summer).

Netherby, Jennifer. 2006. "Ho-Hum 2005 Due to Slowed DVD." *Video Business*, January 20, www.videobusiness.com.

New California Media. 2005. "The Ethnic Media in America: The Giant Hidden in Plain Sight." www.npr.org/documents/2005/jul/ncmfreport.pdf.

New York Times. 2005. "The Bush Economy: New Hope for the Fabulously Wealthy." Editorial, June 7, A22.

Nichols, Bill. 1981. *Ideology and the Image: Social Representation in the Cinema and Other Media*. Bloomington: Indiana University Press.

———. 1992. *Representing Reality: Issues and Concepts in Documentary*. Bloomington: Indiana University Press.

O'Shaughnessy, Michael. 2002. *Media and Society: An Introduction*. New York: Oxford University Press.

Penley, Constance. 1989. *The Future of an Illusion: Film, Feminism, and Psychoanalysis*. Minneapolis: University of Minnesota Press.

Phelan, James, ed. 1989. *Reading Narrative: Form, Ethics, Ideology*. Columbus: Ohio State University Press.

Poster, Mark. 1998. "Postmodern Virtualities." In *The Postmodern Presence: Readings on Postmodernism in American Culture and Society*, edited by Arthur Asa Berger. Walnut Creek, CA: AltaMira.

Potter, W. James. 1998. *Media Literacy*. Thousand Oaks, CA: Sage.

Powell, Chris, and George E. C. Paton, eds. 1988. *Humour in Society: Resistance and Control*. New York: St. Martin's.

Prindle, David. F. 1993. *Risky Business: The Political Economy of Hollywood*. Boulder, CO: Westview.

Propp, Vladimir. 1973. *Morphology of the Folk Tale*. 2nd ed. Austin: University of Texas Press.

———. 1984. *Theory and History of Folklore*. Translated by Ariadna Y. Martin and Richard P. Martin. Minneapolis: University of Minnesota Press.

Radway, Janice A. 1991. *Reading the Romance: Women, Patriarchy, and Popular Literature*. Chapel Hill: University of North Carolina Press.

Ramet, Sabrina Petra, ed. 1993. *Rocking the State: Rock Music and Politics in Eastern Europe and the Soviet Union.* Boulder, CO: Westview.

Real, Michael R. 1989. *Supermedia: A Cultural Studies Approach.* Newbury Park, CA: Sage.

———. 1996. *Exploring Media Culture: A Guide.* Thousand Oaks, CA: Sage.

Reinelt, Janelle G., and Joseph R. Roach, eds. 1993. *Critical Theory and Performance.* Ann Arbor: University of Michigan Press.

Rheingold, Howard. 1991. *Virtual Reality.* New York: Summit Books.

———. 2003. *Smart Mobs.* New York: Perseus.

Richardson, Glenn W., Jr. 2003. *Pulp Politics: How Political Advertising Tells the Stories of American Politics.* Lanham, MD: Rowman & Littlefield.

Richter, Mischa, and Harald Bakken. 1992. *The Cartoonist's Muse: A Guide to Generating and Developing Creative Ideas.* Chicago: Contemporary Books.

Ritzer, George. 2004. *The McDonaldization of Society.* Rev. New Century ed. Thousand Oaks, CA: Sage.

Rosenberg, Bernard, and David Manning White, eds. 1957. *Mass Culture: The Popular Arts in America.* Glencoe, IL: Free Press.

Ryan, John, and William M. Wentworth. 1998. *Media and Society: The Production of Culture in the Mass Media.* New York: Allyn and Bacon.

Ryan, Michael, and Douglas Kellner. 1988. *Camera Politica: The Politics and Ideology of Contemporary Hollywood Film.* Bloomington: Indiana University Press.

Sabin, Roger. 1993. *Adult Comics: An Introduction.* London: Routledge.

Saussure, Ferdinand de. 1966. *Course in General Linguistics.* Translated by Wade Baskin. New York: McGraw-Hill.

Schechner, Richard. 1993. *The Future of Ritual: Writings on Culture and Performance.* London: Routledge.

Scheuer, Jeffrey. 1999. *The Sound Bite Society: Television and the American Mind.* New York: Four Walls Eight Windows.

Schneider, Cynthia, and Brian Wallis, eds. 1989. *Global Television.* Cambridge, MA: MIT Press.

Schostak, John. 1993. *Dirty Marks: The Education of Self, Media, and Popular Culture.* Boulder, CO: Westview.

Schwartz, Tony. 1973. *The Responsive Chord.* Garden City, NY: Anchor Press.

Schwichtenberg, Cathy, ed. 1993. *The Madonna Connection: Representational Politics, Subcultural Identities, and Cultural Theory.* Boulder, CO: Westview.

Sebeok, Thomas, ed. 1977. *A Perfusion of Signs.* Bloomington: Indiana University Press.

———, ed. 1978. *Sight, Sound, and Sense.* Bloomington: Indiana University Press.

Seib, Philip. 2002. *Going Live: Getting the News Right in a Real-Time Online World.* Lanham, MD: Rowman & Littlefield.

Seldes, Gilbert. 1994. *The Public Arts*. New Brunswick, NJ: Transaction.

Sherman, Barry L. 1995. *Telecommunications Management: Broadcasting/Cable and the New Technologies*. 2nd ed. New York: McGraw-Hill.

Shukman, Ann. 1977. *Literature and Semiotics: A Study of the Writings of Yuri M. Lotman*. Amsterdam: North-Holland Publishing.

Signorielli, Nancy, and George Gerbner. 1988. *Violence and Terror in the Mass Media: An Annotated Bibliography*. New York: Greenwood.

Silverman, Kaja. 1983. *The Subject of Semiotics*. New York: Oxford University Press.

Skovman, Michael, ed. 1989. *Media Fictions*. Aarhus, Denmark: Aarhus University Press.

Smith, Gary, ed. 1991. *On Walter Benjamin: Critical Essays and Recollections*. Cambridge, MA: MIT Press.

Standage, Tom. 2006. "The Culture War: How New Media Keeps Corrupting Our Children." *Wired*, April 2006, www.wired.com/wired/archive/14.04/war_pr.html.

Steidman, Steven. 1993. *Romantic Longings: Love in America 1830–1980*. New York: Routledge.

Stephenson, William. 1988. *The Play Theory of Mass Communication*. New Brunswick, NJ: Transaction.

Szondi, Peter. 1986. *On Textual Understanding*. Translated by Harvey Mendelsohn. Minneapolis: University of Minnesota Press.

Theall, Donald F. 2001. *The Virtual Marshall McLuhan*. Montreal: McGill-Queen's University Press.

Todorov, Tzvetan. 1975. Translated by Richard Howard. *The Fantastic: A Structural Approach to a Literary Genre*. Ithaca, NY: Cornell University Press.

———. 1981. *Introduction to Poetics*. Translated by Richard Howard. Minneapolis: University of Minnesota Press.

Traube, Elizabeth G. 1882. *Dreaming Identities: Class, Gender, and Generation in the 1980s Hollywood Movies*. Boulder, CO: Westview.

Turner, Bryan S., ed. 1990. *Theories of Modernity and Postmodernity*. London: Sage.

Van Zoonen, Liesbet. 1994. *Feminist Media Studies*. Thousand Oaks, CA: Sage.

Volosinov, V. N. 1987. *Freudianism: A Critical Sketch*. Translated by I. R. Titunik. Bloomington: Indiana University Press.

Weibel, Kathryn. 1977. *Mirror Mirror: Images of Women Reflected in Popular Culture*. Garden City, NY: Anchor Books.

Wernick, Andrew. 1991. *Promotional Culture: Advertising, Ideology, and Symbolic Expression*. London: Sage.

Wildavsky, Aaron. 1982. "Conditions for a Pluralist Democracy, or, Cultural Pluralism Means More Than One Political Culture in a Country." Unpublished paper.

Willemen, Paul. 1993. *Looks and Frictions: Essays in Cultural Studies and Film Theory*. Bloomington: Indiana University Press.

Williams, Raymond. 1958. *Culture and Society: 1780–1950*. New York: Columbia University Press.

———. 1976. *Keywords*. New York: Oxford University Press.

———. 1977. *Marxism and Literature*. New York: Oxford University Press.

Williams, Rosalind. 1990. *Notes on the Underground: An Essay on Technology, Society, and the Imagination*. Cambridge, MA: MIT Press.

Williamson, Judith. 1978. *Decoding Advertisements: Ideology and Meaning in Advertising*. London: Marion Boyars.

Willis, Paul. 1990. *Common Culture: Symbolic Work at Play in the Everyday Cultures of the Young*. Boulder, CO: Westview.

Wilson, Clint C., and Felix Gutierrez. 1985. *Minorities and Media: Diversity and the End of Mass Communication*. Thousand Oaks, CA: Sage.

Winick, Charles. 1994. *Desexualization in American Life: The New People*. New Brunswick, NJ: Transaction.

Wollen, Peter. 1972. *Signs and Meaning in the Cinema*. Bloomington: Indiana University Press.

———. 1993. *Raiding the Icebox: Reflections on Twentieth-century Culture*. Bloomington: Indiana University Press.

INDEX

24, 135
30-Second Politics, 182
60 Minutes, 136

Abrams, M. H., 2, 132–33
Adatto, Kiku, 36, 37
Adorno, T. W., 189, 191
advertising: amount of time spent
    watching commercials, 138; politi-
    cal commercials, 180–85; portrayal
    of women, 179; power of commer-
    cials, 137–39; problem of clutter,
    61; product placement and news,
    60, 176; "RATS" Republican
    commercial, 184; "Revolving
    Door" political commercial, 183;
    selling cancer, 178–79; Super
    Bowl, 137
Alias, 135
Allen, Woody, 122
American character: individualism and
    egalitarianism, 18–19; problem of
    individualism, 18
American Idol, 136
Anders, Gunther, 189

Annenberg School for Communica-
    tion at the University of Southern
    California, 6
Aristotle, 133, 140–41
artists, 167–85; aberrant decoding
    problem, 173–75; book business
    and, 171–73; ethics and advertising,
    178–85; Freud on artists, 166;
    kinds of media artists, 167–68;
    media ethics and journalists,
    175–78; publishing a scholarly
    book, 168–71
Asimov, Nanette, 154
audiences, 59–83; categories of,
    59–83; demographics and, 66–70;
    demographics defined, 59; effects,
    85–109; hypodermic needle the-
    ory, 77–78; narrowcasting and
    broadcasting, 60; as political cul-
    tures, 74–77; psychographics and,
    70–77; psychographics defined, 59;
    reader-response theory (reception
    theory), 78–79; uses and gratifica-
    tions, 79–82; uses and gratifications
    and genres, 82–83

Bagdikian, Ben, 204–5
Bakhtin, M., 143
Barthes, Roland, 188
Baudrillard, Jean, 188
Blade Runner, 55, 56, 142
Blue Velvet, 55
Brokeback Mountain, 142
Brown, Jane D., 114
Buffy the Vampire Slayer, 135
Burton, Graeme, 58, 79
Bush, George H., 143

Cawelti, John, 136
cell phones: impact of, 111–13; "smart mobs" and, 112
Cerf, Bennett, 212
Certeau, Michel de, 139–40
Claritas: importance of zip codes, 68–70; lifestyle groupings, 68–69, 70
Clark, Walter von Tilburg, 103
Cohen, Jodi R., 58
communication: defined, 26; interpersonal, 28; intrapersonal, 28; Jakobson model, 29; Lasswell model, 30; mass-mediated, 28; small group, 28. *See also* media
Communication Criticism: Developing Your Critical Powers, 58
computers: cost of, 116; digital divide, 116; government surveillance and, 118–19; growth of Internet, 117–20; print-on-demand and publishing, 118; social and cultural impact of, 115–20; technological imperative and, 128–29; video cafes, 120; virtual communities, 120–22
Cooper, Gary, 36
Cortese, Antony J., 179–80

Course in General Linguistics, 39
Crimes and Misdemeanors, 55
Croce, Paul Jerome, 197–99
Crying of Lot 49, 57
CSI: Crime Scene Investigation, 1, 3, 87, 136; Nielsen ratings and, 5; typical audience of, 5
Culler, Jonathan, 21, 23, 51

Daily Show, The, 136
Dallas, 207–8
Danesi, Marcel, 142
Da Vinci Code, The, 36, 136
Democracy in America, 17
Denzin, Norman, 55
Derrida, Jacques, 188
digital: computers and culture, 115–20; contrasted with analog, 113–15; defined, 114–15; virtual communities and, 120–23
Digital Dialectic: New Essays on New Media, 114–15
Dole, Bob, 217
Douglas, Mary, 77
Dr. No, 49–51
Dukakis, Michael, 183
Dun's Review, 71
Durkheim, Emile, 18, 20, 22, 23

Eastwood, Clint, 144
easy-listening light rock radio stations, 7
Eco, Umberto, 41–42, 174
Edwards, Jonathan, 6
Eisenstein, Sergei, 142
Elementary Forms of Religious Life, 19
Elliott, Stuart, 64
Emerson, Ralph Waldo, 129
Emmert, Fredric A., 210
Entertainment Software Association, 124

ethics and media: advertising and ethics, 178–85; artists and ethics, 4; journalism and ethics, 175, 177–78
Exploring Media Culture: A Guide, 36
Eyal, Chaim, 106

fairy tales: *Dr. No* as fairy tale, 49; Propp's functions, 47–49
Ferdinand de Saussure, 21
focal points and mass media, 1–3; America, 3; artists, 3; art work or text, 3; audience, 3; defined, 1–3; medium, 3
Fraim, John, 121
Freud, Sigmund, 22, 166
Freidson, Eliot, 186

Gee, James Paul, 126–27
Gerbner, George, 8, 65, 151–53
Gertner, Jon, 63, 65
Gitlin, Todd, 90–92, 94
Going Live: Getting the News Right in a Real-Time Online World, 161
Google, 117–18
Gowans, Alan, 133, 134
Grand Theft Auto, 136
Greenfield, Patricia Marks, 127

Hamlet, 136
Hayakawa, S. I., 162
hegemonial ideological domination: defined, 21; Marxism and, 21
Herzog-Massing, Herta, 207–8
Heuscher, Julius E., 14
High Noon, 36
Hollywood Reporter, 176
Howard, Niles, 71

Ideology and Utopia, 18
Images of Postmodern Society: Social Theory and Contemporary Cinema, 55

individual and society: Emile Durkheim on, 19–20; Jonathan Culler on, 21–23; Karl Marx on, 20
iPod, 11
Iser, Wolfgang, 77–78
Itow, Laurie, 71

Jakobson, Roman, 28–30, 174
Johnson, Jeffery, 155
Journal of Communication, 213
Journal of Contemporary Ethnology, 54
Joyce, James, 136, 212

Kaiser Family Foundation, 11
Kellner, Douglas, 108
Kennedy, Anthony, 211
Kern, Montague, 182
King Kong, 136, 142
Kurosawa, Akira, 56

Ladd, Alan, 158
Lasswell, Harold, 30
Lazarsfeld, P. F., 186
Lévi-Strauss, Claude, 47, 51, 188
Lost, 135
Lotman, Yuri, 131–32
Lunenfeld, Peter, 114–15
Lyotard, Jean-François, 107, 188

Maltese Falcon, The, 86
Mannheim, Karl, 18
Marx, Karl, 20
Marxism: hegemonial ideological domination, 21; society determines consciousness, 20
Marxism and Literature, 21
mass culture / mass society hypothesis, 187–201; cultural homogenization critique, 192–94; myth or reality, 187–88; popular culture and the destruction of elite culture, 191–92

Mass Culture: The Popular Arts in America, 101–3, 189

mass-mediated texts: convention and invention in, 135–36; critical orientation to arts, 133; functions of arts, 133–34; incidental learning and, 135; M. M. Abrams on what texts do, 132–33; social significance of, 131–49; Yuri Lotman on texts, 132

McChesney, Robert, 203–5

McDonaldization of Society, 191

McDonaldization: The Reader, 191

McGuire, William, 105, 106

McLuhan, Marshall: advertising agencies, 130; hot and cool media, 31–34; *Mechanical Bride*, 130; print media and electronic media, 33–34

McQuail, Denis, 84

Mechanical Bride, 130

media: 9/11 attack, 145–48; aesthetics of, 17; anti-media rage, 101–3; Aristotle on narratives, 140–41; Bakhtin on dialogism, 142–43; consolidation, 203–6; criticism of mass media and texts, 89–101; cultural imperialism hypothesis, 206–8; decoding, 32; defenses of, 103–7; devices owned by young people, 26; ethnicity and, 218–19; genres in, 17; government regulations and, 215–18; hot and cool, 31–34; ideology and, 208–9; impact on texts carried, 35; intertextuality and, 141–44; multitasking, 12; narratives in, 139–40; news on television, 145–46; pornography, 209–12; postmodern approach to, 107–9; social significance of texts, 131–49; in society, 16–17;

spiral of silence, 212–15; UR-texts, 144–45; usage by young people, 25–26; violence and, 151–65; ways of classifying, 31

media aesthetics, 37–57; camera movements as signifiers, 44; camera shots as signifiers, 43; color, 45; decoding mass-mediated texts, 77–79; defined, 37; Lévi-Strauss and paradigmatic analysis, 51–52; lighting, 46; music, 46; Propp on narratives, 47–51; sound effects, 46

Media Literacy, 150, 186

Media, Sex, Violence, and Drugs in the Global Village, 8

Media Unlimited: How the Torrent of Images and Sound Overwhelms Our Lives, 94

Menninger, William, 103

Mind and Media, 127

Mirror and the Lamp: Romantic Theory and the Critical Tradition, 2, 132–33

Mitchell, Arnold, 71

model: defined, 29; Jakobson model, 29–30; Lasswell model, 30

More Than Meets the Eye: An Introduction to Media Studies, 58

Muhammad, 148

Napoleon Dynamite, 136

narratives: importance of, 52–54; paradigmatic analysis, 46, 51–52; syntagmatic analysis, 46–51

Netherby, Jennifer, 119

Newsweek, 149

New York Times, 13, 64

New York Times Magazine, 63

Nielsen, 62–64

Nielsen Peoplemeter, 62–63

Nine American Lifestyles: Who We Are and Where We're Going, 71

Nixon, Richard, 217
Noelle-Neumann, Elisabeth, 213
nonverbal communication, 28
North, Oliver, 36
Npods, 64

Ode to W. H. Channing, 129
Oldenburg, Don, 96

Paik, Nam June, 108
Palance, Jack, 158
Peirce, Charles Sanders, 40
Picture Perfect: The Art and Artifice of Public Image Making, 36
political cultures: as audiences, 76–77; defined, 74–75; grid/group theory and, 77; kinds of, 74–75
popular culture, 4
"popular culture and the American child" website, 24
Portable People Meter, 63
Poster, Mark, 110, 111
Postmodern Condition: A Report on Knowledge, 107
postmodernism: defined, 54–55; Google search on, 118; impact on media, 56; relation to modernism, 54–55
Potter, W. James, 150, 186
Practice of Everyday Life, 139–40
Pride and Prejudice, 136
Propp, Vladimir, 46–51
Provocateur: Images of Women and Minorities in Advertising, 179–80
Psychiatric Study of Myths and Fairy Tales, 14–15
Public Perspective, 197
Pulp Politics, 143–44
Pynchon, Thomas, 57, 108

Radway, Janice, 83
Rashomon: as postmodern film, 56; problem of what is reality and, 56
Rashomon Case, 173
ratings: contrasted with shares, 62; defined, 62; problem of accuracy, 62–63
Reading the Romance, 83
Real, Michael, 36
Real World, The, 91
responsive chord theory, 17
Rheingold, Howard, 112, 122, 196
Richardson, Glen W., Jr., 143
Richardson, Laurel, 52–53
Ritzer, George, 191
Rosenberg, Bernard, 101, 103, 189

San Francisco Chronicle, 104, 154
San Francisco Sunday Examiner and Chronicle, 71
Saussure, Ferdinand de, 22, 38–40
Scheuer, Jeffrey, 184–85, 202, 215, 217
Schiller, Gail, 176
Seib, Philip, 161
Selected Writings in Sociology and Social Philosophy, 20
semiotics: defined, 38; editing techniques and, 44–45; icons, 40; indexes, 40; lying with signs, 41–42; Peirce's trichotomy, 40–41; Saussure on concepts and relationships, 9, 39–40; Saussure on signs, 38–40; symbols, 40; used instead of semiology, 39
Shakespeare, William, 157
shares: contrasted with ratings, 62; defined, 62
Sherman, Barry, 61–62
Signiorelli, Nancy, 151–53

Sims, The, 136

Six-Gun Mystique, 136

Sound Bite Society: Television and the American Mind, The, 184–85, 202, 215–18

speech acts: elements in, 29; Roman Jakobson on, 28–29

Spengler, Marie, 72

Spielberg, Steven, 36

SportsCenter, 136

Star Trek, 135

Star Wars, 52

Stewart, Jon, 10

Structuralist Poetics, 51

Super Bowl, 3

Survivor: genres used in, 57; as post-modern text, 57; reality programs, 91

Tam, Pui-Wing, 218

Taming of the Shrew, 103

Target the U.S. Asian Market, 67

Teenage Research Unlimited, 13

Telecommunications Management: Broadcasting/Cable and the New Technologies, 61–63

television: and 9/11 tragedy, 146–48; amount watched by young people, 13, 25; commercials, 137–39; news and violence, 158–61; vicious cycles and, 14–16. *See also* media; violence

Terminal Papers, 173

Terminator, 55, 129

texts: convention and invention in, 135–36; conventional use in academic discourse, 1; defined, 1; fairy tales and genres, 144–45; importance of commercials in television, 137–39; incidental learning from,

135; intertextuality, 141–44; Lotman on, 132; narratives, 139–41; political cultures and, 76–77; social significance of, 131–49; UR-text question, 144–45

Thatcher, Margaret, 18, 23

Theall, Donald, 24

Theory, Culture and Society, 108

Tillich, Paul, 103

TNS Media Intelligence, 137

Tocqueville, Alexis de, 17–18

Ulysses, 136

Unchanging Arts, 133–34

Understanding Media, 32, 33–34

Understanding Media Semiotics, 142

VALS (Values and Lifestyles) typology: categories of consumers, 72–74; psychographics and audiences, 70–71; values defined, 71

Video Business, 119

video games: bio-psycho-social analysis of, 123–28; criticisms of, 125–26; Game Cube, 123; *Pac-Man* analyzed, 128; PlayStation 2, 123; PlayStation 3 (PS3), 123; positive aspects of, 126, 127–28; Xbox 360, 123

violence: causality and correlation, 151; children and, 161, 162–63; defined, 152–53; impact on audiences, 153; kinds of violence, 156–57; news broadcasts and, 158–61; quality versus quantity, 157–58; television viewing and, 154–56; visceral impact, 164–65

Violence and Terror in the Mass Media: An Annotated Bibliography, 151–52

Virtual Marshall McLuhan, 24

Virtual Reality, 122

Wall Street, 56

Wall Street Journal, 218

Warhol, Andy, 108

Welles, Orson, 103, 142

West Wing, The, 52

What Video Games Have to Teach Us about Learning and Literacy, 127

White, David Manning, 101, 103–4, 106, 189

Wildavsky, Aaron, 74–75

Williams, Raymond, 21

Wise Up to Teens: Insights into Marketing and Advertising to Teenagers, 66

Witherspoon, Elizabeth M., 114

Wong, Angi Ma, 67

X-Files, The, 135

Zollo, Peter, 66

ABOUT THE AUTHOR

Arthur Asa Berger is professor emeritus of Broadcast and Electronic Communication Arts at San Francisco State University, where he taught from 1965 until 2003. He was a Fulbright scholar at the University of Milan in 1963 and a visiting professor at the Annenberg School for Communication at the University of Southern California in 1984. He taught a short course on advertising and American culture at Heinrich Heine University in Düsseldorf in 2002 as a Fulbright Senior Specialist, and has lectured at more than a dozen universities in countries such as Brazil, China, England, Finland, France, Thailand, Turkey, and Vietnam. His books have been translated into Arabic, Chinese, German, Indonesian, Italian, Korean, Russian, Swedish, and Turkish.

Berger has been writing about media and popular culture for almost fifty years. His MA thesis in 1956 was on the reception of historian Arnold Toynbee in the American magazine press, and his doctoral dissertation in 1965 was on Al Capp's comic strip *Li'l Abner*. His dissertation was published as *Li'l Abner: A Study in American Satire*. He has written sixty books and numerous articles and book reviews over the course of his career. He was in the Army from 1956 to 1958, and covered high-school sports for the *Washington Post* during this period.

In recent years, Berger has written a number of comic academic novels that also function as textbooks: *Postmortem for a Postmodernist* (1997), *The Mass Comm Murders: Five Media Theorists Self-Destruct*

(2002), *Durkheim Is Dead! Sherlock Holmes Is Introduced to Social Theory* (2003), and *The Hamlet Case* (2000). His books are available on the Internet at sites such as www.amazon.com and www.barnesandno ble.com.

Berger is married to Phyllis Wolfson Berger and has two children and three grandchildren. He lives in Mill Valley, California. He can be reached at arthurasaberger@gmail.com or arthurasaberger@ yahoo.com.